Best wishes
to Bob and Irene
from Jerome and Joyce
August 1998

Frontispiece drawing by C.Galle from 'R.P.Petri Writi Mors', published Antwerp, 1651.

Reproduced by permission of the Rector, Stonyhurst College, Lancashire.

BLESSED PETER WRIGHT, S.J.

(1603/04-1651)

HIS LIFE AND TIMES

*'THE LAST NORTHAMPTONSHIRE MARTYR'**

by

J.R.Betts

(*) Quotation from G. Anstruther, Vaux of Harrowden

ISBN 1 897589 20 4

Printed in Great Britain for Becket Press, Northampton
by Printek Ltd. Rushden, Northamptonshire

Title Page

'Blessed' is a title accorded by the Roman Catholic Church to anyone whose life and death has been recognised as showing heroic and exemplary virtue. Such a person is said to be 'beatified' after due legal and ceremonial procedures. They may, in the course of time, be 'canonized' and known as a 'Saint' if sufficient information about their life is forthcoming.

‘Ad Majorem Dei Gloriam’ *

(*) To the greater glory of God (Motto of the Society of Jesus)

CONTENTS

List of Illustrations

Cover design and illustrations 4, 5, 7, 10, 11, 12, 13, 14, 17, 18, 20, 21 and 22 were executed by Mr.Peter Koenig. Photographs 2, 3, 9, 23, 26, and 27 were taken by Miss Karen Cooper. The Frontispiece and illustrations 15, 16 and 19 are the work of Pye and Co., Clitheroe.

FOREWORD

It was in 1990 that I first visited St. Paul's Church, Thrapston, and was delighted to discover a shrine to an English Martyr, the only such shrine in a parish church of the Northampton Diocese. So I particularly welcome this study of the life of Blessed Peter Wright, properly set in the context of his times. Such a work requires much careful research and energy and I extend my congratulations to the author and to the priests who have helped and encouraged him.

When the 40 martyrs of England and Wales were canonized in October 1970, in Rome, Pope Paul VI spoke of such an event as enhancing an ecumenism worthy of the name. Here are examples of faith that we can all learn from even as they highlight those areas of difference of doctrine that need to be pondered. The Pope added that these martyrs, "will be a true safeguard of those real values in which the genuine peace and prosperity of human society are rooted." In other words, these lives speak also to the world at large.

We very much need the example of such men and women today. As we approach the truly Christian Jubilee of the Year 2000 we can especially take heart from those who have followed Christ with love, even to the shedding of their blood. In the richness of their humanity they show how faith does not destroy but heals and raises up our human nature to its proper stature.

It is always good to be able to read the story of a local man. Here is someone who has walked our streets, grown up in a local family, toiled at his daily work - truly our neighbour. It reminds us that Christ touches the lives of ordinary people. Peter Wright comes across as just such an ordinary human being, with all the ups and downs of early life, until he found his true task and vocation, and grew in virtue before God and man. Long before he returned to England from the Netherlands he had begun his mission by teaching children and then ministering to soldiers as an army chaplain. But this was not to be the end of the story.

He found himself called to that final offering of his life. And at the end, we cannot fail to be impressed, as all his contemporaries were, by his serenity and Christian joy. His was a joy born of faith, hope and charity.

The times in which Blessed Peter lived were very different from our own, but his prayers continue to help and his example provides inspiration for everyone. May this study of a devout Catholic and Northamptonshire man, encourage us all to follow the way where true joy is to be found.

Leo, Bishop of Northampton

Preface

The history of English Catholics in the Civil War remains to be studied in depth by recusant scholars. When Charles I raised his Standard at Nottingham on 22nd August 1642 he gave the Catholic gentry together with their retainers a first and long-awaited opportunity to demonstrate to fellow-countrymen their unquestioning loyalty to the Crown: it was nearly forty years since the mischievous manipulation ot the Gunpowder Plot by Robert Cecil had left an almost indelible slur on their good name.

From the first indecisive engagement at Edge Hill to the defeat of the royalist army at Naseby in Peter Wright's native Northamptonshire they formed a large proportion of the King's forces. From abroad many Catholics fighting against the Dutch in the interminable wars of the Netherlands crossed back to England along with the senior boys in the English school at St Omer.

The central chapters of this book open up a subject of intense interest to the historian. Basing House was only one of the great Catholic houses that became a royalist fortress. To the west stand today the sad and haunting ruins of Wardour Castle, so stoutly defended by Lady Blanche Arundell while her man was out in the field with the King.

It was a twofold cause for which the Catholics fought alongside the emerging Anglicans: their common enemy were the Puritans so easily roused to fanaticism, men with no time for music, the theatre , medieval statuary, stained glass, the ancient faith or its monuments. It was at the hands of these men that Peter Wright suffered. Perhaps his story will bring others to work this rich seam of Catholic history.

Philip Caraman, S.J.

Author’s Preface and Acknowledgements

First, I would like to thank the Bishop of Northampton, the Right Reverend Patrick Leo McCartie, for his encouragement and for agreeing to write a Foreword to this book. In an earlier letter he wrote that, compared to other dioceses, we do not have many martyrs associated with our own. This fact has made the task of sifting the evidence, and recording the story of Blessed Peter Wright doubly rewarding, since both the Catholic Diocese of Northampton and the civil County of Northamptonshire can bask in the reflected glory of a man of God who was born, and lived his early life, in the quiet village of Slipton, albeit almost four hundred years ago.

It is difficult to be precise about the date when the idea for this book was first mooted. Certainly the setting up of a shrine to the Jesuit martyr at St. Paul’s Catholic Church, Thrapston, in 1979, was an important stimulus towards further research. The aforementioned village of Slipton is today within the boundaries of the Catholic parish of Thrapston and Raunds (See below).

At this point, I must pay tribute to Fr.Charles Crawford, who was parish priest of the combined parish of St. Paul the Apostle, Thrapston, with St.Thomas More, Raunds, from 1977 to 1980, because he was instrumental in obtaining a relic of the martyr, and a copy of his portrait, which together with a carefully constructed prayer constitute the structure of the present shrine. The notes and correspondence which Fr.Charles left to the parish, when he moved, formed the basis from which this volume has evolved.

I have to thank the two most recent parish priests of St. Paul’s, Fr. Stephen McGuinness and Fr Kenneth Bowen for their continuing interest and also for permission to take and use photographs of the church and shrine, which appear in the Appendices. Overleaf is a map of part of East Northamptonshire, which shows the boundaries of the Catholic parish of Thrapston and Raunds, with the position of Slipton clearly marked, although it is now absorbed by Lowick for civil purposes.

In 1977, Mrs.June Brassington, who now lives in Slipton, had an article published in Strapetona’, the Journal of the Thrapston District Historical Society, entitled ‘A Slipton Martyr’, which was a resumé of the few known facts relating to Blessed Peter Wright. She, in turn, had been stimulated by a newspaper article of July, 1957, printed in the Northamptonshire Advertiser (a subsidiary of the Kettering Evening Telegraph). In such small ways are local historians motivated and we must be grateful to Mrs.Brassington for her initial research and helpful knowledge of present day Slipton.

My most heartfelt thanks must be given to Fr.John Koenig, parish priest of Thrapston and Raunds from 1986 to 1994. He is the real instigator of this work and without his painstaking research, correspondence and visits to archives, in many different locations, the project could never have been completed. Not only has he provided working notes but also acted as proof reader and typist. Throughout the writing process his collaborative advice has contributed enormously to the finished book. I am pleased that he has agreed to write the Epilogue.

The following historians, archivists and librarians have been specially helpful over the last ten years during which time material has been accumulated:- Fr.Godfrey Anstruther, O.P.,

Map of East Northamptonshire showing boundaries of the Catholic parish of Thrapston and Raunds

(R.I.P.), historian, for a card index of Northamptonshire Recusants deposited at the Northamptonshire Record Office and also copies of several of Blessed Peter's sermons given to the parish of Thrapston; Fr.Philip Caraman,S.J., historian, for advice and encouragement and for agreeing to write the Preface; Fr.Ian Dickie, archivist, for help in locating the 'positio', concerning Blessed Peter, deposited in the Westminster Diocesan Archives c.1929; Fr.Francis Edwards, S.J., Fr.T.G.Holt, S.J., and more recently Fr.Thomas McCoog,S.J., archivist/historian, for making available all relevant documents in the archives of the English Province of the Society of Jesus; Mr. Michael Hodgetts, historian and General Editor of the Catholic Record Society, for advice on publishing matters and for providing information on priests associated with Drayton House, Slipton and Lowick during the early seventeenth century; Mrs.Jacqueline Minchinton, archivist, for particular research into Peterborough Diocesan Records of the early seventeenth century; Mrs Margaret Osborne, archivist/librarian, for assistance in unearthing material at Bishop's House, Northampton; Fr.F.J.Turner,S.J., archivist/librarian, of Stonyhurst College, for sorting out and explaining the various important biographical items held there. A particular thanks go to Fr. Roger Edmunds, priest of Northampton Diocese, for his translation of the Latin inscription from the Oxford tomb of Colonel Sir Henry Gage.

The Northamptonshire Record Office at Wootton Hall Park has already been mentioned and it is important to register thanks to the county archivist, Miss Rachel Watson, and her team of assistants for their unfailing courtesy in dealing with obscure requests. Similarly the staff of the Catholic Central Library, Westminster, must be thanked for their assistance and prompt service particularly when dealing with orders by post.

Permission to quote from the many published works of the late Fr.Godfrey Anstruther, O.P., has been freely given by the archivist of the English Province of the Order of Preachers (Dominicans), Fr.Bede Bailey, O.P., and I am most grateful for his good wishes, Fr.Thomas M.McCoog, S.J., archivist of the English Province of the Society of Jesus and Fr.M.Bossy, S.J., Rector of Stonyhurst College, Lancashire have both given their blessing to the work and their kindness is herewith acknowledged. I am likewise indebted to Dom Aidan Bellenger, O.S.B., of Downside Abbey School, Bath, who has been most generous in permitting me to quote from his book on English and Welsh priests.

I must also rccord my gratitude to the following copyright holders and literary agents who have, without exception given permission to make use of short quotations from their publications listed in the Bibliography, and identified individually by footnotes:- Alan Sutton Publishing Limited, Stroud, Gloucestershire; Anthony Clarke, Wheathampstead, Hertfordshire; Basil Blackwell, Oxford; Burns and Oates, Tunbridge Wells, Kent; Cambridge University Press; Catholic Truth Society, London; Constable and Company Limited, London; Darton, Longman and Todd Limited, London; Harper Collins, London; Jonathan Cape (Random House U.K. Limited), London; Longman Group Limited, Harlow, Essex; Manchester University Press; Northamptonshire Record Society, Northampton; Oxford University Press; Peters, Fraser and Dunlop Limited, Literary Agents for estate of E.Waugh, London; Phillimore and Company Limited, Chichester, West Sussex; Rogers, Coleridge and White

Limited, Literary Agents for [*] P.Caraman, London; The Historical Association, London; Veritas Publications, Dublin, Ireland; Weidenfeld and Nicolson (Orion Publishing Group), London; Yale University Press, London.

Additionally, I am very much obliged to the following who have allowed pictures and maps to be included or photographs to be taken as shown in the list of illustrations:- Gerald Duckworth and Co.Ltd., London; Rev.D.H.P.Foot, Cranford, Northants.; Rev.Ron. Howe, Brigstock, Northants.; Phillimore and Company Limited, Chichester, West Sussex; The Provincial, English Province of the Society of Jesus; The Rector of Stonyhurst College, Lancashire; The Rev.Mother, Lanherne Carmelite Convent, Cornwall; Mr.L.G.Stopford Sackville, Drayton House, Lowick, Northants.

Special thanks are due to Mr.Peter Koenig for his fine illustrations and the cover design. Miss Karen Cooper is to be congratulated for the photographs which are attributed to her. I am also indebted to Pye's of Clitheroe for their prompt service when photographing items only available at Stonyhurst College.

The Rev.Mr. Robin Cooper, and his staff at the Becket Press, have been particularly helpful in smoothing the path from manuscript to printed word. Robin's calmness was always very reassuring even when panic reigned elsewhere.

Many other friends and family members have made material contributions towards the production of this book and I would like to record my best thanks to them by inscribing their names:- Fr.David Barrett, The Becket Press, Mrs.Joyce Betts, Mrs. June Brassington, Mr.John and Mrs. Pat. Carroll, Mrs.Anne Collings, Mr.Brian Davies, Mrs.Marcelle Grant, Mr.George Grynowski, Mr.Tony Ireson, Fr.John Koenig, Mrs.Hildegard Koenig, Mrs.Anne Lepine, Fr.Robert McCormick, Mr.Derek and Mrs.Catherine Mott, Mr.Graham and Mrs. RoseSmith and Mrs.Anne Wardle.

Finally, I must thank my wife for her support and patience over many months. She has acted as first proof reader and been ready to correct grammatical errors. Any mistakes which remain, either of fact or syntax, are mine alone. If I have forgotten anyone who has contributed to this work, I offer my sincere apologies and belated thanks.

J.R.Betts

Raunds
1997

[*] *Refers to "Priest of the Plague - Henry Morse S.J." published by Longman, Green*

Introduction

A Joyful Death. [1]

On Whit-Monday morning, the nineteenth of May [2] 1651, a procession slowly approached the Tyburn gallows from the direction of London's Newgate prison, a distance of about two miles. The first vehicle, in this parade, was a kind of hurdle, made of osier and straw, resembling a low cart and linked to this sledge were five or six horses decked out with plumes and little bells. Watching, with great interest and sympathy, was an immense crowd of spectators who thronged the streets and observed that the sole occupant of the unusual mode of conveyance was Peter Wright, a Jesuit priest, who had become well-known to the Londoners as a result of a much discussed trial.

Normally the method of conducting anyone, convicted of treason, to the place of execution was to tie the prisoner firmly in a prone position and allow the bumps of the road to exact some extra punishment. However, this hurdle had been so packed with straw that the condemned man was able to sit almost upright. He was not bound tightly, merely secured with loose bonds, which caused him to smile and ask if they did not expect him to run away.

Peter's appearance might have been sad and melancholy but instead his aspect was joyful, almost triumphal, as he looked about him with every sign of happiness and contentment, blessing those who pressed forward to touch him. On his head he wore a cap or hat with forehead exposed and a violet coloured mantle had been thrown over his body. Passing the Marquis of Winchester's house he noticed, on the balcony, the whole family saluting him. Though horsemen, pikemen and musketeers marched on either side, ostensibly to keep the crowds at bay, some men, seeking a blessing, were able to kiss his hands and some women sat on the very hurdle.

The contrast with the three carts of condemned common criminals and two coaches of condemned nobles, which brought up the rear of the procession, was most marked as all these persons were in great distress.

Eventually the cortège reached its destination and a hodman, dressed in a hempen smock, came to assist Peter from his hurdle. With some astonishment he recognised, in this apparent minion of the law, Edward Latham, a fellow Jesuit priest, who had been with him as a camp missioner in the Spanish

[1] *Information given by two eyewitnesses; (a) a letter sent to Rome, on the twenty-ninth of May 1651, by Fr.Francis Foster S.J., the Provincial of the Society of Jesus in England, 1650 to 1653; (b) an account published in Antwerp in 1651 by Fr.Edward Leedes S.J. (alias Courtnay), 'R.P. Petri Writi Mors'. (See Appendix A.)*

[2] *If this date is the 'old style' Julian calendar, it would be the twenty ninth of May by the 'new style' Gregorian calendar established in Catholic Europe in 1582 but not adopted in England until 1752. Discrepancies are unavoidable in recording events of this period.*

Netherlands. Moved round to the other side of the gallows he saw Jesuits everywhere in a huge multitude, of perhaps 20,000 people, with some standing on top of the 200 coaches that had assembled nearby. Daring members of the crowd, in their eagerness to see, had even climbed into the trees of the deer park, which we now call Hyde Park.

Peter was placed on a cart with three men and three women and tried to speak with them, to encourage them, but was prevented by the puritan minister. So he withdrew into private prayer and was left for over an hour with his eyes shut, his hands raised to heaven and the rope around his neck.

Eventually, he was given time to make a long and stirring speech(3) to the waiting crowd before the cart was drawn away. He was not taken down from the gibbet until he had expired and only after life was extinguished were his clothes removed. Then the grisly sequel of the sentence for treason began; first the head cut off and immediately following the body cut into quarters. The heart was removed and thrown into the fire, but without the usual imprecation which accompanied the act. Indeed, the Sheriff of London had acted with compassion throughout and allowed all parts of the body to be taken away by Peter's friends for burial with the words, 'Take the head and members and bury them with all the honour you wish.'

So died a devout and brave Northamptonshire man whose crime had been to practise as a Roman Catholic priest at a time when this was forbidden in England. (4)

(3) *This speech is recorded in full in Chapter VII.*

(4) *Fr.Francis Foster, the Provincial, preserved the following quotation from a newsheet of the time:- 'Today, Whit-Monday, fourteen persons condemned to death were led out from Newgate prison to Tyburn. Of these one was a Jesuit, an excellent man, of firm and undaunted courage, who was hung in defence of his religion and his body, according to custom, quartered.' (As quoted in 'The English Jesuits' by Fr. B Basset, p.218)*

Chapter I

Background - the religious problems of the time (1501-1603).

The modern district of East Northamptonshire is a largely rural area containing many villages including Slipton, the presumed birthplace of Peter Wright. In addition to the lesser settlements half a dozen small towns stretch from Rushden in the west, through Higham Ferrers, Irthlingborough, Raunds, Thrapston to Oundle on the eastern fringe. There are some notable medieval churches in this region and particularly fine spires in Rushden, Higham Ferrers, Raunds and Oundle evocative of an era of religious fervour, piety, devotion and enthusiasm which is all too sadly lacking in our mechanical and materialistic age.

Not far away, but over the county boundary into the ancient shire of Huntingdon, are the villages of Buckden, with its medieval bishop's palace, (now a Catholic mission centre) and Kimbolton, with its part-medieval castle, (now the school). These places have a direct link with the life and times of Peter Wright through events that took place almost seventy years before he was born. For it was in Buckden Towers that Queen Catherine of Aragon, the first wife of King Henry VIII, was kept under house arrest. She eventually died at Kimbolton Castle, in 1536, being buried in Peterborough Abbey[*] (not a Cathedral until 1541). Queen Catherine's husband's break with the Pope in Rome, in 1534, (see below) is truly the first step towards the martyrdom of Blessed Peter Wright.

The year 1501 saw the wedding of Prince Arthur, elder son of King Henry VII of England, and if this seems to be an improbable place to begin a study of the religious changes of the sixteenth century, one has only to visit Arthur's chantry chapel [**] and tomb in Worcester Cathedral to discover that he died less than five months later. This extremely short and fruitless marriage was unconsummated according to the widow, who is better known as Catherine of Aragon, and her testimony would become an important factor in the debate regarding the legality of the union with Arthur's brother, alluded to above and described below. Indeed, the profound changes in the religious constitution of this country, outlined in the following pages, were a direct result of the doubts expressed on the validity of Catherine's second marriage which she contracted in good faith.

Reign of Henry VIII (1509-1547). The break from Rome.

On the eleventh of June 1509, Arthur's brother, by now ascended to the throne as King Henry VIII, married Catherine, who was seven years his senior, following a dispensation granted by the

[*] *Queen Catherine's remains still lie in the north aisle of the presbytery at Peterborough Cathedral marked by banners of England and Spain. Puritan soldiers smashed the original tomb in 1643.*

[**] *Note that this chantry chapel was not destroyed during the reign of King Edward VI (see below).*

Pope, Julius II. It is to be observed here that England was part of, and owed allegiance to, the (Roman) Catholic Church at this time. English kings, as well as their subjects, had been fervent Catholics, acknowledging the Pope in Rome as overlord in all things spiritual since the conversion of the Anglo-Saxon King Ethelbert of Kent in 597.

'Unfortunately it is not known when Henry VIII decided that he had had enough of his wife.' (4) Catherine produced one daughter, Mary, five infants that did not survive, had several miscarriages and was a model wife but by 1525 she was losing her looks and unlikely to provide a male heir.

Henry became infatuated with one of the young ladies of the court, by name Anne Boleyn, whose sister had already been the King's mistress. Early in 1527 he asked his Chancellor, Cardinal Wolsey, to obtain an annulment of his marriage to Catherine on the grounds that, despite the Pope's ruling, it was unlawful to marry a brother's widow. The King's 'Great Matter' was to be bandied about the courts of Europe for the next seven years but the Pope, Clement VII, steadfastly refused to issue a decree of nullity. (A divorce, in modern terms, was never in question.)

In October 1529 Cardinal Wolsey, because of his failure to satisfy the King, was forced to give up the position of Lord Chancellor and was succeeded by a famous layman, Sir Thomas More. However, from this time, Henry began to act more and more as his own chancellor, taking advice from one of Wolsey's diplomats, Thomas Cromwell. The so-called 'Reformation Parliament' had been called in 1529 and more and more pressure was now applied to the Pope by various statutes, such as that by which, in January 1531, every bishop, dean and priest in England was made liable to be imprisoned for life for supporting Wolsey unless they paid a heavy fine and recognised Henry as, 'Supreme Head of the Church of England, as far as the law of God allows.'(5)

On the sixteenth of May 1532, Sir Thomas More resigned as Chancellor. This protest did not deter Henry. Events then moved quickly as Parliament was coerced into passing an Act of Annates which drastically reduced the amount of money payable by the English clergy to the Pope.

Late in 1532 Anne Boleyn was found to be pregnant and Henry resolved that he must wed her with all speed. (6) If the Pope would not set aside the marriage with Catherine, Henry must achieve the same result in some other way.

Old Archbishop Warham of Canterbury had just died and Henry prevailed upon the Pope to appoint Thomas Cranmer to the position in early January 1533. In April, Parliament was persuaded to pass a law forbidding appeals in church cases to be taken to Rome. In May, Cranmer duly declared the marriage with Catherine null and void and recognised the union with Anne Boleyn, who was crowned Queen on the first of June that same year.

(4) *G. R. Elton, 'Reform and Reformation', p. 103.*

(5) *J. Ridley, Henry VIII, p. 196.*

(6) *D.Richards, Britain under Tudors and Stuarts, p. 49.*

The Pope's reply was to excommunicate both King and Archbishop but Henry was not to be stopped and the following year, 1534, promulgated a final Act of Supremacy. This declared Henry to be, 'the only Supreme Head on Earth of the Church of England.'

The consequences were to be far-reaching as the chief men in the kingdom were forced to take an oath denying the Pope's spiritual supremacy and thus severing all ties with the Catholic Church to which most of Europe still adhered. Not everyone complied with the King's outrageous demands and several Carthusian monks together with a Brigittine monk and a secular priest suffered the barbaric sentence of being hung, drawn and quartered for what was called treason. The two most outstanding victims were the holy John Fisher, Bishop of Rochester, and the eminent scholar and statesman, Sir Thomas More, both beheaded on Tower Hill. (These two were canonised by the Church in 1935, exactly 400 years after their martyrdom.) 'In their deaths Fisher and More won the one victory over Henry VIII which could be won, and that victory proved enduring.'[7]

The break with Rome instigated by Henry VIII also coincided with other movements in Europe which had been attacking certain abuses within the Catholic Church such as simony [*] and the sale of indulgences [**]. Martin Luther in Germany, an ex-monk, and Ulrich Zwingli in Switzerland, an ex-priest, began these attacks which soon led to wholesale defections and the break-away of affected states from the unity of Christendom that had been such a feature of the medieval scene. As early as 1521 Luther's writings against the sacraments as taught by the Catholic Church had led to King Henry VIII publishing a book called, 'A Defence of the Seven Sacraments.' In this work he was helped, ironically enough, by John Fisher and Thomas More. The papal reward had been to accord to Henry the title, 'Defender of the Faith'.

Henry's religion was obviously quite orthodox at that time, but once the knot of Church unity was severed in 1534 men of reformist, anti-Catholic views began to have more and more influence. Men like William Tyndale (living in exile) and Robert Barnes advocated a vernacular Bible, while Thomas Cranmer (secretly married) wanted the clergy to be able to take a wife. The most influential voice was that of Thomas Cromwell who persuaded the King to close first the smaller monasteries in 1536, and all the larger religious houses by 1539 with an enrichment of the King's treasury which even today is not fully appreciated. For example, to illustrate the amounts involved, the five abbeys of Bury St. Edmunds, Crowland, Ely, Peterborough, and Ramsey between them yielded two thirds of a ton of silver and Bury also produced 1,553 ounces of gold. [8]

[7] *G. R. Elton, Reform and Reformation, p. 194.*
[*] *'Simony' = buying or selling 'pardons' or 'benefices'.*
[**] *'Indulgence' = remission of temporal punishment in purgatory, still due for sins after absolution.*
[8] *J. J. Scarisbrick, Reformation and English People, p. 87.*

It is significant that the very wealthy shrine of St. Thomas Becket of Canterbury was completely plundered and smashed in September 1538 and the saint's bones burned and scattered. This martyr-saint, of course, once stood up to a previous King, Henry II, and refused to subordinate the Church to the Crown. By royal proclamation, in November 1538, Becket was no longer to be esteemed a saint, his images and pictures being destroyed, his name then erased from all liturgical books and the official prayers for his feast-day said no more. [9]

To those who favoured religious reform, the monasteries were part of an outdated and corrupt system, which depended on such concepts as purgatory, prayers for the dead, pilgrimages and images (religious statues), which they wished to see swept away. Even the copying of manuscripts and the production of books had now been superseded by the printing press.[10] Although monastic establishments maintained fine libraries, founded grammar schools, supported students at the universities, gave aid to the poor and, in their guest houses, ran the only nationwide chain of 'hotels', yet their vast estates of land and property, as well as their links with Rome, made them all too vulnerable.

No responsible historian now accepts, as the whole truth, the damaging reports made by Cromwell's commissioners [11] regarding the laxity of morals in certain religious institutions. These visiting agents of the crown were to provide grounds necessary "to damn the monasteries, not to reform them." [12]

In Northamptonshire, Cromwell's minions were hard-pressed to find many evils and abuses and pleaded for exceptions to be made in the general suppression. Sir William Parr wrote of the Abbey of Pipewell, 'this house being of very small revenue, keeping continual hospitality, relieving the poor, maintaining divine service in a virtuous and laudable manner ... I beg you have pity on them...' At Delapre, Northampton, the King's commissioner wrote of the abbess, 'She is a good aged woman and her house is in a good state.' At St James', Northampton, the abbot was reported as a godly man and loved by all; 60 to 80 poor people were relieved at the abbey gates and the buildings were in good repair. [13] All this was of no avail.

The abbot of Glastonbury, Somerset, Richard Whiting, is just one example of what happened if heads of religious houses were awkward or did not cooperate. He refused to surrender his abbey, but for this failure he was sentenced to death on a trumped up charge and, after execution, on the fifteenth of November 1539, his quarters were set up at Wells, Bath, Ilchester and Bridgwater while his head

[9] *E. Duffy, Stripping of the Altars, pp. 410-412.*
[10] *J. H. Bettey, Suppression of Masteries in West Country, p. 21.*
[11] *E. E. Reynolds, Roman Catholic Church in England Wales, p. 219.*
[12] *E. Duffy, Stripping of the Altars, p. 383.*
[13] *R. L. Greenall, History of Northamptonshire, p. 44.*
Northamptonshire Past and Present, Vol. II p. 229, Vol. V p. 74.

was displayed over his own abbey gateway. Cromwell's orders to his servants prior to these events ran, 'The abbot of Glaston to be tried at Glaston, and also executed there with his complices.' [14]

Certainly the common people, though cowed by these events, must have regretted the closure of the multitude of religious houses that were centres of pilgrimage such as Bath, Buxton, Bury St Edmunds, Canterbury, Evesham, Glastonbury, Hailes, St Alban's, Walsingham [*], Westminster and many, many more throughout the length and breadth of the land. However, the nobles, wealthy merchants and minor aristocrats were only too willing to lease or buy the lands and property offered for sale at usually below market value.

In Lincolnshire and the north of England a serious, popular and large scale rebellion broke out. This was the famous 'Pilgrimage of Grace', October 1536 to July 1537, which was a genuine revolt not only against the closure of the monasteries but also against the other religious changes as well as social innovations. [15] Unfortunately the rebels made the mistake of trusting the word of Henry VIII and dispersed after being promised pardon. A large number were later executed, including the leader, Robert Aske, who was hanged in chains in York.

At first the attacks on traditional religion, which the northern 'pilgrims' had highlighted, were insidious. As early as 1535 preachers, with licence from the King, were touring the country denouncing not only the Catholic cult of devotion to the saints, but also the fundamental belief in the power of prayers to the Virgin Mary asking her to intercede with God. They also demanded that the 'rood' or image of Christ on the cross be removed from the parish churches. In 1536 the King himself decreed that, from henceforth, all patronal feast-days be abolished together with all the saints' days from the first of July to the twenty-ninth of September (the excuse being that these holy days interfered with the harvest). There was great confusion among the people as some local clergy adopted reformist views while others steadfastly continued to worship as their ancestors had done. [16]

It is not possible to catalogue all the various changes of the last years of Henry's reign. Many historians in the past, and almost all school text-books, have tried to show the King as a conservative in religious belief, citing as evidence the Act of Six Articles of June/July 1539 which ordered married priests to put away their wives and more importantly made the denial of the real presence of Christ in the Eucharist (transubstantiation) punishable by burning. Certainly, during the next few years more executions took place; some Protestants as heretics, some Catholics as traitors and the former Chancellor, Thomas Cromwell, simply for falling out of favour with the King.

[14] *J. H. Bettey, Suppression of Monasteries in West Country, Ch 6.*

[*] *Serjeantson, Longden Wills - In 1531 John Benett of Raunds, Northamptonshire, left money in his Will for a man to go on pilgrimage to Walsingham - evidence of the continuing popularity of pilgrimages - numerous other examples can be found.*

[15] *J. Fines, Pilgrimage of Grace, Chronology and J. Ridley, Henry VIII, pp. 285-297.*

[16] *E. Duffy, Stripping of the Altars, pp. 386-410.*

In part the ebb and flow of Henry's religious beliefs was a reflection of his various matrimonial adventures, but Archbishop Cranmer remained at his post throughout Henry's reign (his wife securely hidden) and he continued to work on an English Liturgy to replace the Latin Mass. An English Bible translated by Miles Coverdale (a former Augustinian monk) and William Tyndale had appeared in 1535. By 1537 this 'Great Bible', so called because of its size, was ordered to be introduced into all the churches in the land.

However, by 1543, by the King's order, no one was to read the Bible in church unless he was appointed by the King or a bishop - ' even at home; women, prentices, serving men and persons of base degree were not to read it at all.' (17)

During the last months of Henry's life it seems that he was playing a game of being simultaneously a Catholic and a Protestant. Perhaps his mind was failing but he actually negotiated with the Pope suggesting that he might return to obedience to the Apostolic See of Peter and, at the same time, announced to Cranmer that he would become a 'sacramentary' (*) (18).

Reign of Edward VI (1547-1553). A Protestant Church.

It must have been a relief to both government officers and churchmen when the crafty tyrant, Henry, died on the twenty-eighth of January 1547. Unfortunately, by his will his heir was Edward, son of the third wife Jane, and Edward had only reached nine years of age. So a Regent, Edward Seymour, the boy's uncle, better known as Protector Somerset and an avowed Protestant, ruled. Later the Duke of Northumberland ousted Somerset. He was much more ruthless and just as reformist in his views. Nevertheless the Supreme Head of the Church of England until his death in 1553, probably from tuberculosis, was the boy King.

By the summer of 1547 the Protestant attack on Catholic practices was in full swing. Orders were given to remove from the churches relics, images, pictures, paintings and even stained glass representations of the saints. The usual parish procession on Sundays was abolished and the ringing of bells forbidden except one to announce the sermon. This was a direct attack on the Catholic doctrine of the Eucharist since bells had commonly been rung to announce the real presence of Christ on the altar at the time of consecration and elevation in the Mass.

Even the use of rosary beads was regarded as superstitious and the clergy were instructed to dissuade the dying from leaving money or goods in their wills for candles and Masses for the repose

(17) *J. D. Mackie, Earlier Tudors, p. 429.*

(*) *'Sacramentary' = Sixteenth century meaning: one who doubted the real presence of Christ in the sacrament of the Eucharist.*

(18) *J. Ridley, Henry VIII, pp. 404-406.*

of their souls. Instead they were to bequeath their money to the poor of the parish. [19]

In December 1547, a Bill was put through parliament to begin to close down chantries, guilds, fraternities and all surviving colleges of secular clergy. At Coventry, Kings Lynn and in London there was such fierce opposition to the closing of the guilds that the government relented and spared craft and mercantile guilds including London livery companies. [20]

The following year saw the implementation of these most sweeping changes as Protector Somerset ordered that all chantries should be dissolved, the chantry priests sent packing and all endowments, altar plate and other items be forfeit to the crown. The excuse for this despoliation and robbery was that saying prayers and Masses for the souls of the dead was of no use since Protestant doctrine denied the existence of Purgatory. Naturally such a long-held traditional belief could not be destroyed without opposition such as at Chipping Norton, in Oxfordshire, where the chantry endowments had provided a living for four priests as well as the vicar, Henry Joyce. [21]

The next year, 1549, on Whit-Sunday, an even more radical change was the introduction of Archbishop Cranmer's First Prayer Book in English to replace the Latin of the Sarum Missal. This was too much for the priests and people of Berkshire, Buckinghamshire, Oxfordshire and parts of Northamptonshire to endure. A serious rebellion against the government broke out but was ruthlessly put down, mainly by local landowners who had profited from the sale of monastery lands and chantries. The leaders were put to death including Henry Joyce who was hung from his own church tower.

In the West Country and Yorkshire there were similar rebellions against the introduction of the Prayer Book and abolition of the Mass. In Devon the affair was very serious, including at least one pitched battle at Clyst St. Mary where the local peasants were slaughtered along with all the prisoners captured by the royal forces. More than 1,000 perished! Exeter was only captured by the government using German and Italian mercenaries after a six weeks siege. [22]

None of this stopped the reformers who, in 1550, demanded the destruction of all Catholic prayer books, missals, primers, manuals, processionals and the like as well as all images of stone, timber, alabaster or earth carved or painted; on pain of imprisonment at the King's pleasure.

This was followed by the pulling down of altars and the substituting of tables. In some dioceses the reverencing of the Sacrament of the Eucharist was strictly forbidden. The Catholic Mass was apparently to be banished for ever.

[19] *E. Duffy, Stripping of the Altars, pp. 449-453.*

[20] *J. J. Scarisbrick, Reformation and English People, p. 66.*

[21] *R. Jeans & M. G. Meades, Church of St Mary Virgin, Chipping Norton, pp. 7-8.*

[22] *J. D. Mackie, Earlier Tudors, p. 489 & H. R. Williamson, Cardinal in Exile, pp. 142-150.*

It is worth noting here that according to foreign observers the English in the early sixteenth century were exceptional for their attendance at Mass - and not only on Sundays - while their devotion to Our Lady (Virgin Mary) was shown in the public recitation of her Office. They understood the faith they practised, and the circulation of devotional and instructional books among a population of only three million may be gauged by the fact that in the holocaust of Catholic piety, which Cranmer initiated, a quarter of a million liturgical books were destroyed. (23)

In November 1552, a second Book of Common Prayer brought into use even more Protestant doctrine than the first, particularly in regard to funeral rites. Commissioners were then sent round the country to make sure that each parish only possessed the bare essentials for worship as defined in the new prayer book - "a surplice, a couple of tablecloths, a cup for the communion and a bell." (24)

The surprising thing was that so many parishes had still retained the trappings of Catholicism. In many places it seems images had not been smashed but either sold or hidden - to be bought back and brought out again when the religious climate changed, as it was soon to do, with the accession of a Catholic Queen in Mary Tudor, daughter of Henry VIII and Catherine of Aragon.

Reign of Mary I (1553-1558). Return to the Catholic Faith.

Mary was 37 at the time she became Queen after the death of her half-brother on the sixth of July 1553. She was not, however, present at Edward's demise, having been warned of a plot to arrest her and proclaim Lady Jane Grey, a second cousin, as monarch. This treachery was the work of the Duke of Northumberland and Lady Jane, his daughter-in-law, was really an innocent victim. On the tenth of July the usurper was proclaimed Queen in London but, by this time, Mary was already in East Anglia where she took refuge in Framlingham castle.

Northumberland soon found that he had miscalculated the extent of support for his 'coup' and met with no encouragement as he advanced to give battle with Mary's forces. Indeed there was no military engagement as news came that Mary was proclaimed in Buckinghamshire, Berkshire, Middlesex, Northamptonshire, Oxfordshire and elsewhere, and that ships sent to intercept Mary if she attempted to flee abroad had declared in her favour at Yarmouth. (25)

In Northamptonshire Mary was proclaimed Queen by Sir Thomas Tresham of Rushton. So we read:-

'And out of Northamptonshire came Sir Thomas Tresham and a great number of Gentlemen out of divers parts, whose names were too long to reherse.... These captaines with their companies being

(23) *E. Duffy, Stripping of the Altars, p. 480-499.*

(24) *Ibid. p. 477.*

(25) *J. D. Mackie, Earlier Tudors, pp. 527-528.*

thus assembled in warlike manner, marched forward towards Norfolk to the aid of ye Lady Mary and the further they went ye more their power encreased.' [26] [*]

In 1556, for the help received from the Borough of Higham Ferrers, Mary and her husband Philip (see below) bestowed a new charter allowing the small town to return its own member to parliament. The first M.P., Ralph Lane, was a nephew of Tresham. [27]

By the twentieth of July Northumberland had conceded, and within a few days was held fast in the Tower of London with a few chief supporters including the Protestant Bishop Ridley. From the dark and dismal dungeons of the ancient fortress there emerged the Duke of Norfolk and the Catholic Bishop of Winchester, Stephen Gardiner - the latter to become Chancellor of England.

Mary entered London on the third of August to a tumultuous welcome of bells ringing and crowds cheering. With her came her half-sister Elizabeth and Anne of Cleves (Henry VIII's 'divorced' fourth wife) together with a splendid train of ladies and gentlemen. Coming to the city by Aldgate she received the mace from the mayor while music played, gunfire sounded and decorations fluttered in the breeze. All very different from the greeting accorded poor, duped Jane who, with her husband, was also in the Tower.

England had declared for a Queen whose right seemed good but who was bound to face difficulties.

One of Mary's biggest problems was that, until Parliament revoked the legislation, she was by law 'Supreme Head of the Church of England', a Protestant church. Her cousin Cardinal Pole, whose mother, the Countess of Salisbury, had been beheaded by Henry VIII in 1541,was despatched from Rome in early August 1553 with a commission from the Pope to reconcile England to the universal Church and to absolve its people from the sin of schism, but for various reasons [**] Pole did not arrive in England until November 1554. [28]

One reason for the delay was a short-lived revolt in Kent, led by Sir Thomas Wyatt, with the avowed intention of removing Mary and substituting her half-sister Elizabeth as Queen. Then the question of Mary's marriage had to be resolved and unhappily (as it turned out) the choice fell on her cousin Philip of Spain who was eleven years younger. The marriage took place on the twenty fifth of July 1554, at Winchester Cathedral.

[26] *M. E. Finch, Five Northamptonshire Families, p. 68 and Souvenir of 700th Anniversary of Borough of Higham Ferrers. As quoted.*

[*] *This proclamation was made at Northampton on 18th July 1553. In 1557 Sir Thomas became the last Prior of the restored Order of St John in England. Dying in 1559, his property was inherited by his grandson, also Thomas, only 15 at the time, but who is remembered for his staunch Catholic faith, and many notable buildings which still stand as a lasting memorial (see later references).*

[27] *Charters and Insignia of Higham Ferrers.*

[**] *For reasons see P. Hughes, Rome and Counter-Reformation, Ch. III.*

[28] *G. R. Elton, Reform and Reformation, pp. 378-379.*

It has been estimated that almost 800 Protestants fled abroad at this time to Frankfurt, Geneva and Zurich [29], setting a pattern perhaps for the many more Catholics who were to flee to Europe during the next reign of Elizabeth. However, it seems that the majority of the population rejoiced at the return of the Mass, and in some places the people ordered their clergy to return to the Catholic rite immediately Queen Mary was proclaimed. At Melton Mowbray the altar stones were put back very quickly in order to sing Mass and 'Dirige' (prayers for the soul) of the young King who had put an end to Masses for the dead. [30]

To rebuild all of the monasteries and return their lands was impossible for the new owners of these properties would not allow this to happen. Nevertheless, by the end of the reign, a few religious houses had been refounded. A significant change in emphasis was that Cardinal Pole, the new Archbishop of Canterbury, in 1555 required the clergy to preach every holy day, and before every sermon plainly to recite 'and diligently teach' the Lord's Prayer, the Hail Mary, the Creed and the Ten Commandments in English, 'exhorting their parishioners to teach the same likewise to their children at home.' [31]

This was not the only way that Pole anticipated the Council of Trent which, from 1545 to 1563, worked for the reform of the Catholic Church. He instituted seminaries for the training of priests, saw to it that a Catholic Primer, or instruction book, was printed and ordered to be used instead of the previous manuals. These 'Wayland' Primers ran to ten editions. [32]

Sadly the reign ended unhappily as Mary's husband was forced to return home when his father died and he is better known as Philip II, King of Spain. Mary did not conceive a child and died in some agony in November 1558, possibly from cancer of the womb. She had done her best to rebuild the Church of her ancestors. Unfortunately she is not remembered for her undoubted strong faith and moral virtue but for the persecution of Protestants.

The 'Book of Martyrs' by John Foxe, printed in 1563, was a catalogue of Protestant men and women put to death as heretics and included 273 burned during Mary's reign, including the former Archbishop Thomas Cranmer. The lurid accounts of the various deaths should not let us forget that burning was the accepted punishment for heresy throughout Europe at this time, [*] or that some 12,000 would have been put to death for petty offences, such as sheep stealing, during the same period. Foxe's book would eventually be placed in all the churches in England, alongside the Bible, and do incalculable harm to the Catholic cause in future years.

(29) *Ibid. p. 382.*

30) *J. J. Scarisbrick, Reformation and English People, p. 104.*

(31) *E. Duffy, Stripping of the Altars, p. 534.*

(32) *Ibid., p. 539.*

(*) *Anabaptists were burned in England during Edward VI's reign. John Calvin had Michael Servetus, a fellow Protestant, burned in Geneva in 1553. Cf. P. Hughes, Rome and Counter-Reformation, p. 128 & p. 97.*

Reign of Elizabeth I (1558-1603). Protestant ascendancy.

Elizabeth was Anne Boleyn's daughter and had been imprisoned in the Tower, at one time, suspected of treason against her half-sister. She was not as devout as either of the two previous rulers and might, if allowed, have been tolerant in religious matters, although her sympathies were with the reformers.

However, by June 1559, two new Acts of Parliament had been foisted on an unsuspecting English public; the Act of Supremacy, making Elizabeth 'Supreme Governor of the Church of England' and the Act of Uniformity which abolished the Mass and re-introduced a modified version of Cranmer's prayer book. [*] The second act passed one of its readings by only three votes and many spoke against it. [33]

It cannot be doubted that, at this time, the number of Catholics in England exceeded Protestants but the exact proportions are unknown. Contemporary estimates of the number of Protestants vary from as low as one per cent to a high of thirty three per cent. [34] In spite of this imbalance, the failure to swear to the new Oath of Supremacy was punishable, in the last resort, by death, and clergy who refused to use the Protestant prayer book were liable to imprisonment for life. Only one of the Marian bishops took the Oath. The others were deprived, kept in prison, or placed under house-arrest. The last Catholic Bishop of Peterborough, David Poole, deprived November 1559, died in the Fleet Prison, May 1568. [34A] The laity were to be fined twelve pence for every absence from church. By the end of the reign such fines were increased to £20 per month with additional confiscation of goods and imprisonment for failure to pay. Many Catholics attended the Church of England services through fear and became known as 'Church Papists'.

The bench of bishops under Matthew Parker, the new Protestant Archbishop of Canterbury, (Cardinal Pole having conveniently died on the same day as Queen Mary) began to draw up a code of religious practice and belief. There were to be Thirty-nine Articles of doctrine adopted by the Anglican Church in convocation in 1563. It was not until 1571 that the Queen, exercising her royal prerogative in all things spiritual, allowed these Articles to be approved by Parliament.

The Articles confirmed the strongly Protestant position of the Church of England. In particular Article 31 condemned Masses for the dead as 'blasphemous fables and dangerous deceits.' In 1883

[*] *The Elizabethan Reformation was master-minded by Sir William Cecil, aided by the Marquis of Northampton, the Earl of Bedford, the Earl of Pembroke and Sir John Grey. Cf. P. Hughes, Rome and Counter-Reformation, p.133.*

[33] *E. Duffy, Stripping of the Altars, p. 566.*

[34] *J. B. Black, Reign of Elizabeth, p.12.*

[34A] *Northampton Diocesan Souvenir, 1950, p. 30.*

Cardinal John Henry Newman wrote, 'What the 31st Article repudiates is undeniably the central and most sacred doctrine of the Catholic religion'. [35]

In the Northamptonshire villages the practice of the Roman Catholic rites of religion in the ostensibly Protestant parish churches continued well into the 1580s. At Irthlingborough in 1570 there were two altars standing and not pulled down. Other complaints of openly defiant Popery came from Astwell, Barton Seagrave, Cransley, Crick, Culworth, Guilsborough, Grafton Regis, Harringworth, Passenham, Pattishall, Roade, Rockingham, Scaldwell [*], Sibbertoft and West Haddon.[36] How many more parishes refused to conform to the Elizabethan church laws we shall probably never know, or how many Marian priests, turned out of their livings, disguised themselves as serving men and moved about the country sustaining the officially proscribed creed. We do know however about the 'Hermitage', a building between Desborough and Market Harborough, which still stands, where Catholic priests were hidden. [37]

In 1569 a Catholic rising occurred in the north of England and Mass was once again said in Durham cathedral and other churches in the region. Protestant prayer books were burned and altars and holy-water stoups unearthed from middens and quarries. [38] Again the rebellion did not spread to the south and was ruthlessly put down with some hundreds of Catholics, mostly of the labouring class, being hanged. Thomas Percy, Earl of Northumberland, was eventually beheaded at York. [39]

The Pope, St. Pius VI, perhaps influenced by reports of the northern rising, issued a Bull (declaration) on the twenty fifth of February 1570, which stated that Queen Elizabeth was a heretic and that her subjects were freed from the oaths taken and 'from every obligation to allegiance and obedience.'

The majority of the people knew nothing of this development although a copy of the Bull had been nailed to the gate of the Bishop of London's palace. Inevitably the laws against Catholics were made more stringent and an Act of 1571 made it treason to introduce or implement any papal Bulls, or to reconcile anyone to that Church, or to give absolution as a priest. Those who brought in from

35) *M. Ffinch, Cardinal Newman, p. 81.*

(*) *R. M. Serjeantson & H. I. Longden, Northants Wills, p. 187, footnote: 'Fifth of Oct., 1581 in ... Scaldwell were founde sartayne images and other manuments of poperye - ye pycture of Chryst callyd ye roode, ye picture of Saynt Peter, both of wood undefaced, the pycture of ye Trinitye & ye pycture of Saynt Mudwyn wt hyr cowe - undefaced - a tabernacle of wood whych in ye time of poperye dyd stande uppon ye aulter wt a great number of images - all of alabaster undefaced.'*

(36) *G. Anstruther, Vaux of Harrowden, pp. 75-79 & Northants, Notes & Queries Vol. I p. 57 & p. 158.*

(37) *Ibid. p. 87.*

(38) *E.Duffy, Stripping of the Altars, pp. 583-584.*

(39) *E. E. Reynolds, Roman Catholic Church, p. 228 & E. Mackie, Reign of Elizabeth, pp.131-142.*

abroad, 'tokens, crosses, pictures, beads (rosaries) or such like superstitious things' would be subject to the statutes. [40]

A few years earlier, in 1564, a document known as 'The Creed of Pope Pius IV' had been published in Rome. This was a restatement of Catholic doctrine resulting from the Council of Trent which had deliberated, in three sessions, from 1545 to 1563. In its vigorous condemnation of Protestantism and firm definition of Catholic faith it was the inspiration of a movement often known as the Counter-Reformation. [41]

One fruit of this new movement was the founding of many seminaries or training colleges for Catholic priests. Obviously, after 1558, it was impossible to set up such a college in England but in 1568 one was set up at Douai in Flanders (then in the Spanish Netherlands, but northern France today) by William Allen (later Cardinal). Until the French Revolution this college was to be the main source of priests for the English mission. [42] The word mission was used because, in the eyes of Rome, England had now lapsed into heresy.

Before the death of Elizabeth almost 450 priests were sent back to England from Douai. Other colleges for English Catholics were set up at Rome (1579), Valladolid (1589), Seville (1592) and eventually in Madrid (1611) and in Lisbon (1627). The colleges at Rome and Valladolid still flourish. These colleges provided an education for the sons of Catholic families persecuted for their religious beliefs in England. Not all were suitable or desired to be ordained but some 800 secular priests are known by name and place of origin from this period up to 1603. [43]

The Northamptonshire contribution ran into double figures including the Hanse brothers, Everard and William, Henry Holland, Matthew Kellison, Richard Newport (see Chapter III), Edward Osborne, John Paine and John Roberts, [44] names which could be found in a twentieth century telephone directory. These 'missionaries' were known as 'seminary priests' to the English government after 1571. When they returned to preach in England they were liable to imprisonment and execution and so had to use aliases and travel in disguise. (The spies of Sir Francis Walsingham, Secretary of State to Elizabeth, infiltrated even the mission colleges and reported on priests being ordained even before they were sent back to work in this country.) [44a]

Other men and women went abroad at this time to join religious orders that had been suppressed in England such as the Benedictines, Dominicans and Franciscans. Many of these also came back as

[40] *E. E. Reynolds, Roman Catholic Church, p. 229.*
[41] *V. H. H. Green, Renaissance and Reformation, pp. 192-196.*
[42] *E. E. Reynolds, Roman Catholic Church, pp. 227-228.*
[43] *G. Anstruther, Seminary Priests, Volume I, Introduction.*
[44] *D. A. Bellenger, English and Welsh Priests, 1558-1800, p. 179 & Appendix II.*
[44a] *S. Foster, Cardinal William Allen, p. 7.*

priests to minister to the faithful in chapels concealed in the private houses of wealthy Catholic patrons. (The influence of the Society of Jesus and the priests sent by this relatively new religious organisation will be dealt with in a subsequent chapter.)

Apart from religious issues the long reign of Elizabeth was full of political intrigues, and plots to overthrow her government were being formulated almost from the beginning. King Philip II of Spain considered that he had as good a claim to rule England as Elizabeth because of his marriage to Mary. (It is often forgotten that, from 1554 to 1558, the coinage and official documents were headed, 'Reign of Philip and Mary'.) Another possible claimant was the recently widowed Catholic Queen of France, better known as Mary, Queen of Scots, who had returned to Scotland in 1561 and was also Elizabeth's second cousin and next in line of succession to the Queen if she died suddenly. In 1568, Mary took refuge in England after escaping from imprisonment in Scotland by the Protestant Lords of Convocation. (Elizabeth's own claim was only valid if her father's marriage to Anne Boleyn was valid and Catholics could legitimately argue that it was not.)

After the Pope's excommunication of Elizabeth in 1570, Mary became the centre of a series of plots to oust or even assassinate Elizabeth. Some of these plots were bizarre; one involved marriage (it would have been her fourth) [*] to the Duke of Norfolk. Gradually the many houses placed at Mary's disposal became prisons until on the twenty fifth of September 1586, she was incarcerated at Fotheringhay Castle in Northamptonshire. By this time, Sir William Cecil, Elizabeth's chief minister together with Sir Francis Walsingham, secretary and chief spy-master, had planned a trap to incriminate Mary. So successful was this ploy that the unfortunate Queen of Scotland was found guilty of treasonous plotting against the Queen of England and sentenced to death by beheading. The sentence was carried out on the eighth of February 1587.

The night before her death Mary had remarked to her servant, Jane Kennedy, 'I knew they would never allow me to live, I was too great an obstacle to their religion.' [45] Strangely Elizabeth bitterly regretted the execution and had the man who had delivered the warrant to Fotheringhay imprisoned and fined.

The full truth of the tragic life and death of Mary, Queen of Scots, will never be known although a very large number of books have been published on the subject. What is certain is that, in the manner of her death, she was the victim of religious persecution being refused the offices of her priest (who was in the house) or Catholic burial. She was not allowed to be buried in France, as she had requested, but was eventually interred, using Protestant rites, in Peterborough Cathedral. (In 1612, during the reign of Mary's son, James I, the coffin containing the remains was removed to Westminster Abbey.) [46]

[*] *Although her third marriage to James Hepburn, Earl of Bothwell was probably invalid.*

[45] *A. Fraser, Mary, Queen of Scots, p. 578.*

[46] *Ibid. pp. 568-603.*

With the death of Mary, King Philip of Spain's claim became more urgent and an invasion of England, already planned, using troops from the Spanish Netherlands, was set in motion. The problem of conveyance could not be overcome, although a motley collection of 130 vessels, mostly unseaworthy, was assembled at Cadiz and eventually sailed towards the English Channel in May 1588. The story of the defeat of this 'Armada' partly by English seamanship but more by a mixture of Spanish incompetence and bad weather, is well known. However, this was not the end of the war which dragged on for the rest of Elizabeth's reign with the main battlegrounds the Netherlands, France, Ireland and at sea.

During these troubled times there can be little doubt that the majority of English Catholics remained loyal to Queen Elizabeth. [*] They were, however, faced with a dilemma of which the government took full advantage. [47] In Northamptonshire Sir Richard Knightley (a noted Puritan) and Sir Edward Montague, Deputy Lord Lieutenants, were charged in a letter from Sir Christopher Hatton dated the sixth of February 1587/88 with rounding up recusants (Papists) but were apparently very dilatory in the matter. In common with most Englishmen they had no serious doubts about the loyalty of their Catholic neighbours. [47a]

The laws against Catholics had been made more stringent and increased after the first seminary priests trained in Douai landed in England in 1574. Two years later Cuthbert Mayne, a priest trained at Douai and a convert to Catholicism whilst a student at Oxford, began his mission in Cornwall and Devon. He was captured by Richard Grenville and tried for possessing an 'Agnus Dei' [**], for adhering to 'the Bishop of Rome' and for saying Mass. It was unfortunate that Richard Grenville had a grudge against Cuthbert Mayne's patron, Francis Tregian, because, although there was no proof of his priesthood, his execution was ordered by the Council at Westminster, as a warning to other Popish priests, on the application of Grenville who was rewarded with a knighthood.

Cuthbert Mayne was the first of this new breed of priests to be executed. He was hanged at Launceston on the thirtieth of November 1577, cut down while still alive, disembowelled and quartered. His skull is preserved at Lanherne convent, Cornwall, where a portrait of Peter Wright (the subject of this study) can also be found. In 1970 Cuthbert Mayne was canonised (declared to be a saint) by the Catholic Church.

Between 1570 and 1581 other priests and laymen were put to death for adhering to the Catholic faith. In 1581, a further Act of Parliament made it High Treason to reconcile or to be reconciled to

[*] *In 1596 English students for the priesthood in Rome rejoiced at Spanish defeats, Cf. P. Hughes, Rome and Counter-Reformation, p. 231.*

[47] *E. E. Reynolds, Roman Catholic Church, p. 229.*

[47a] *Ed. J. Goring & J. Wake, Northants Lieutenancy Papers, (1580 -1614) p. xvii and pp. 46-48.*

[**] *Agnus Dei: A wax medallion stamped with the figure of the Lamb and blessed by the Pope.*

the Romish Religion. From this date until 1603 more than 180 men and women suffered martyrdom. The women, Margaret Clitherow at York, 1586, Margaret Ward at Tyburn, 1588 and Anne Lyne at Tyburn, 1601, were put to death for harbouring (giving shelter to) priests.

A Northamptonshire born priest martyred at this time was the previously mentioned Everard Hanse (alias Duckett) who was hung, drawn and quartered at Tyburn on the thirty first of July 1581. He was educated at Cambridge and trained as a priest at Rheims where the seminary from Douai had moved. We do not know his exact birthplace, though possibly it was Harrowden, but he was arrested when he ventured to visit the Catholics in the Marshalsea prison, from whence, at once acknowledging his priesthood, he was sent to Newgate prison. [48] He was beatified in 1886. In 1582, on the second of April, another locally-born priest, John Paine, was martyred at Chelmsford after working at Ingatestone, Essex. He was canonised in 1970.

Here it must be stated that not all the priests who returned to England after training abroad were captured. As mentioned earlier, many moved around the country in disguise using aliases and were hidden in specially constructed hides built into the houses of Catholic gentry such as the one that still exists at Drayton House, Northamptonshire. [49] This is very near to the village of Slipton which was the birthplace of Peter Wright. (See subsequent chapters for further references to Drayton.) Other priest holes are known to have existed at Rushton Hall, Harrowden Hall and Kirby Hall in central Northamptonshire, with many others known in the surrounding counties. Most of these were designed and contrived by 'Little John', an alias for Nicholas Owen who was a Jesuit brother.

One way in which the Catholic gentry maintained their religion, at this time, was to inter-marry with other Catholic families. So in 1563 William Vaux of Harrowden married Mary Tresham of Rushton. [50] Similarly Lewis 3rd Lord Mordaunt of Drayton married Elizabeth Darcy (of Addington?) c. 1558. In 1605 Thomas Brudenell of Deene married a later Mary Tresham. These Catholic aristocrats were rich enough to employ learned men to teach their younger offspring at home and it is not surprising to learn that these school masters were often priests in disguise. At Harrowden Elizabeth Vaux organised a school c. 1590 to educate her sons and other Catholic boys until they were old enough to be smuggled out of the country to Douai. [51] (The English mission College returned to Douai from Rheims in 1593.) [51a]

Three boys are known to us by name; John Mulsho of Finedon, who later became a Jesuit priest, John Swetnam, who also became a Jesuit and was the son of Elizabeth Vaux's baker, and Henry

[48] *G. Anstruther, Seminary Priests, Volume I., pp. 145-147.*

[49] *M Hodgetts, Secret Hiding Places, p. 144.*

[50] *G. Anstruther, Vaux of Harrowden, p. 94.*

[51] *Ibid pp. 244-245*

[51a] *S. Foster, Cardinal William Allen, p.7.*

DRAYTON HOUSE - NORTH WING
SHOWS POSITION OF HIDE

Photograph reproduced by permission of Mr. L.G.Stopford Sackville

"Under a floor of a closet in the north wing which (was) added in 1584 (by Lewis 3rd Lord Mordaunt - 1538-1601) is a hiding-place 10ft. by 9ft. 4ins., entered by a trapdoor 3ft. by 2ft. 6ins. The trapdoor is modern, but part of the joist below has been cut away for the baulk of wood on the underside of the original trapdoor. In the hide is a seventeenth-century chest with the letters POB marked on the lid in nails; it was perhaps for keeping vestments clean and dry. The floor is of lime-ash.

An unusual, though not unique, feature of this hide is that it has a two-light mullioned window. This appears to have been part of the original construction for the sake of symmetry, and is not necessarily as dangerous as it sounds since glass appears black from outside unless backed by something which will reflect light. The window would certainly make that outside wall much less suspicious."

Quoted from "Secret Hiding Places" by Michael Hodgetts and reproduced by permission of Veritas Publications, Dublin, Ireland.

Killinghall, who had been born in York jail where his mother was imprisoned for her faith. Some of the tutors were not Catholics, such as one Tutfield who was afterwards reported as instructing Lord Mordaunt's children at Drayton (Chapter III) where he was then described as a dangerous papist. Much of this information is obtained from the writing of John Gerard, a Jesuit priest,who had once escaped from the Tower of London in 1597, and spent a long time riding around Northamptonshire staying at Vaux houses at Irthlingborough and Harrowden, among other refuges. (See Chapter II, III and IV.)

An abortive Spanish invasion of Ireland in 1579 had made Elizabeth's government pass the Act of Persuasions, previously mentioned, and the arrival of the first Jesuit priests, although known to William Cecil's spies, was used to tighten up the laws and apply them more severely. As a result many leading Catholic laymen were not only regularly fined but arrested and confined to prisons in London and also in country castles such as Ely, Kimbolton, (where Catherine of Aragon had died) and Wisbech.

No reckoning could be made of the total number to suffer in this way, but some hundreds of notable country gentlemen were deprived of their liberty including Lord Vaux of Harrowden and Sir Thomas Tresham of Rushton. Some of the more unfortunates were hanged for helping priests and others were put to death for being reconciled to the Catholic religion. A few indeed died of starvation, disease or torture; although this last horror was usually reserved for priests and inflicted by Richard Young and Richard Topcliffe whose sadism became a byword. (See Chapters II, III and IV.)

In 1593 Parliament passed the severest statute, of Elizabeth's reign, against those who professed the Roman faith. By this act Catholics were placed under a system of restrictions which prohibited them from approaching within five miles of any corporate town and Catholic parents were in certain cases deprived of the right to educate their children. In the eyes of William Cecil, Lord Burghley (died 1598); 'loyalty to the state was interpreted as loyalty to the Anglican church and, if loyalty to the Roman church involved acceptance of the papal Bull, there could be no separation between politics and religion.

This confusion of religion and politics made it impossible for impartial justice to be administered. Juries were biased, judges were convinced that every priest was a traitor, and convictions were often obtained on evidence supplied by men of worthless character - renegades, spies and informers. By extracting information with the help of torture, it introduced into England a system of judicial inquiry every bit as bad as that practised by the Spanish Inquisition which it professed to abhor. The majority of priests who suffered death, died not because they were proved guilty of conspiracies - that was the exception rather than the rule - but because they held religious convictions that were considered dangerous.' [52]

[52] *J. B. Black, Reign of Elizabeth, pp. 185-187 & 408.*

The amount of money exacted by Elizabeth's treasury from her Papist subjects is unknown, but Sir Thomas Tresham who, at the start of Elizabeth's reign, had been one of the largest landowners in Northamptonshire, paid out almost £8,000 (a vast sum of money in the sixteenth century) in recusancy penalties between 1582 and his death in 1605. (53) When he could not pay in cash, lands were seized by the crown instead. All this for refusing to attend Church of England services and adhering to the faith of his fathers.

One wonders if the building of Rushton Triangular Lodge and the unfinished Lyveden New Building, both full of Catholic symbolism, were not gestures of defiance at the Protestant ascendancy, as certainly the building expenditure of over £900 could not, once spent, be forfeit to the crown. There is a sense of Catholic frustration and anger in all of this which might well boil over into something more serious in the next reign. (See Chapter II.)

However, before the reign of Elizabeth I was over, one of her courtiers and spoiled favourites, Robert Devereux, Earl of Essex, raised a rebellion against the government. He had failed to subdue an insurrection in Ireland in 1599 and made a truce with the Earl of Tyrone. Recalled to England in some disgrace, Essex suggested to Catholic friends that he would allow them to practice their religion freely and openly if he succeeded in overthrowing the government. The affair took place in London on the eighth of February 1601 and as an attempted 'coup d'etat' it was a dismal failure. Essex was later executed together with four others. Large fines were imposed on the minor characters in this drama including significantly two Northamptonshire men, Robert Catesby of Ashby St. Ledgers who was fined £3,000 and Francis Tresham (son of Sir Thomas) who had to pay £2,000. (54) (See Chapter II.)

Elizabeth died on the twenty fourth of March 1603 and was succeeded by her cousin James VI of Scotland, the only son of Mary, Queen of Scots, who had been judicially murdered at Fotheringhay. James had been taken away from his Catholic mother while still a baby, and brought up as a Protestant Presbyterian in Scotland but he was now to be given the throne of England as well. People wondered if he would favour the Protestant cause or, now removed from the Lords of Convocation, would be more tolerant to the Catholics.

As a postscript to this chapter, it is worth noting that Sir Thomas Tresham proclaimed James I King at Northampton, and in Kettering, just as his grandfather had proclaimed Queen Mary in 1553. (55) Tresham was convinced that James had the rightful claim and would be tolerant to the Catholics. His strong anti-Spanish views were well known and one Jesuit priest described him, in a letter of 1598, as being, 'holden among us as an atheist'. Had the old squire known about it he would have been

(53) *M. E. Finch, Five Northamptonshire Families, Appendix VI.*
(54) *R. Lacy, Robert, Earl of Essex, p. 211 & pp. 268-310.*
(55) *G. Anstruther, Vaux of Harrowden, pp. 257-259.*

heartbroken since his whole life had been given up to fostering the Catholic religion. (The letter fell into the hands of the government and cannot therefore be regarded as wholly trustworthy evidence.)

In the late 1590s a certain antipathy had grown up between the Catholic gentry and the Jesuits. This was part of the so-called 'archpriest controversy' (a debate which concerned the organisation, discipline and management of the various groups of Catholic clergy working in England). This lamentable conflict between most of the Jesuits on one side and some of the secular priests on the other was deliberately encouraged by the government hoping to split the Papist ranks, which it nearly did. [56] The very existence of these disputes, which even spread to the Wisbech recusant prison, is an indication of the very large numbers of Catholic clerics at work in supposedly Protestant England. Many of the Catholic noblemen hoped to achieve a complete relaxation of the penal laws and petitioned the new King on no less than three occasions between April and July 1603. (See Chapters II and IV.)

This then was the England into which Peter Wright was to make his appearance and in the next chapter we need to portray the religious and political climate which existed during his lifetime.

[56] *J. Bossy, English Catholic Community, p. 33.*
J. Scarisbrick, Reformation and English People, p. 159.
P. Caraman, Translation - J Gerard, Autobiography of a Hunted Priest, p. 273 (Notes).

Chapter II

The political and religious situation in England, with particular reference to events in Northamptonshire, leading to the Civil Wars (1603-1651).

Peter Wright was probably born at Slipton, a village between Kettering and Thrapston, sometime late in 1603 or early 1604, remembering that at the time the year ended on the twenty fourth of March, not the thirty first of December. The parish records for this period have been lost or stolen and the family were also well known as 'Recusants' [*] [1] so that no closer date can be ascertained.

The situation for 'Recusants' was very difficult. They were debarred from holding responsible public positions, from military service, from the practice of professions such as lawyer or schoolmaster and their movements from place to place restricted. Baptisms, marriages and funerals were often carried out in secret and no records kept. Those who could afford it smuggled their children abroad to be educated and sometimes stayed there for years. It was safer not to keep family papers and conveyances of property sometimes used fictitious names. Aliases and pseudonyms abound (Peter Wright was later to use the alias Beale or Bele) and records of fines for not attending the state church, although plentiful, are not always reliable evidence. [2] (Further discussion in Ch. III.)

Reign of James I (1603-1625). Division, plots and counter-plots.

The England that James inherited was a divided nation and not just between Catholics and Lutheran Protestants. Since the accession of Elizabeth a Puritan element had been establishing itself. The members of this faction were followers of the doctrines of John Calvin who had set up an extreme Protestant church in Geneva, Switzerland, in the period 1541 to 1564, which fostered a Presbyterian form of church government. The system included the election of ministers by the various congregations (hence Congregationalism) and abolished the office of bishop. In Scotland during the second half of the sixteenth century a form of Presbyterian worship was adopted in the lowland towns and cities under the influence of the preacher John Knox. Although King James VI (I) had managed to modify the effects of Calvinism and continued to appoint Anglican-style bishops, the (Roman) Catholic church was effectively destroyed, except in the highlands, by the end of the century. [3]

[*] *Latin: Recusare, to refuse.*

[1] *G. Anstruther, Vaux of Harrowden, Preface:- 'A Recusant is one who refuses. Early in Elizabeth's reign it meant one who refused the Oath of Supremacy. It was later used to designate a papist who refused to attend services in Protestant churches'.*

[2] *Ibid.*

[3] *W. E. Brown, Reformation in Scotland, p. 72.*

The Calvinistic Puritans were particularly strong in the English Parliament and were to prove a stumbling block to James in his attempts at personal rule. Other Protestant creeds were also beginning to emerge such as the Anabaptists and some Independents. Perhaps, not understanding the true situation, and being all things to all men, James made a statement to Parliament in these words, "I acknowledge the Roman church to be our mother church although defiled with some infirmities and corruptions. My mind was ever so free from persecution." [4] Certainly the penal laws against Catholics were relaxed as evidenced by the fact that Sir Thomas Tresham (See Ch.I) paid no fines for recusancy in 1603 and was exonerated from paying by royal warrant in July 1604.

During the first nine months of James's reign no fewer than 140 priests entered England, the chapels of the Catholic embassies were thrown open and Catholic sermons preached in the open air. James's Queen, Anne of Denmark, had secretly become a Catholic some years earlier. [5] At Catholic houses such as White Webbs in Middlesex, where Anne Vaux acted as housekeeper, Mass was not merely said but sung to glorious settings recently composed by William Byrd who often played the organ himself. [6]

Unfortunately, in 1603/04 an unstable priest named William Watson devised a plot to kidnap the King and capture the Tower of London. This Bye Plot was in some way connected with a Main Plot which, with Spanish help, was supposed to put Lady Arabella Stuart on the throne. It was Henry Garnet the Jesuit superior and George Blackwell the secular arch-priest who warned the government of the danger but Parliament, and in particular the Secretary of State, Robert Cecil, Earl of Salisbury, had been waiting for just such an opportunity. Immediately an Act of Parliament was passed to reimpose and reinforce all the statutes against Catholics. All priests were ordered to leave the country and any persons receiving a Catholic education abroad would be prohibited from inheriting property.

'Back in Northamptonshire Sir Thomas Tresham was soon in trouble with the authorities for, as witnesses agreed, speaking at Brigstock and Thrapston with very great reverence towards the late Queen Mary and with as small reverence either towards the late Queen Elizabeth or the now King's Majesty as could be.'[7] The Lord Chief Justice was involved and Tresham was obliged to resign his position as commissioner for royal forests, an office he had only just taken up again after so long being excluded.

This happened during the summer of 1605 and some time earlier than this the government had received news of a much more serious plot being hatched by a few disaffected and desperate Catholics. The traditional story of the Gunpowder Plot is so bristling with difficulties that some

[4] *E. E. Reynolds, Roman Catholic Church, p. 261.*
[5] *W. E. Brown, Reformation in Scotland, p. 71.*
[6] *M. Hodgetts, Secret Hiding Places, p. 157 .*
[7] *G. Anstruther, Vaux of Harrowden, p. 266.*

writers have maintained that it was a government fabrication from the start, cleverly foisted on the Catholics. There are, however, grave objections to this theory; in particular the account in the Brudenell collection of the death of Francis Tresham (son and heir of Sir Thomas) in the Tower of London, written by William Vavisor his servant. This document has never been in the hands of the government, who might have altered the evidence, and it is above suspicion. Tresham told Vavisor how, on the fourteenth of October 1605, Robert Catesby and Thomas Winter came to him at Lord Stourton's house in Clerkenwell and, after having extracted a promise of secrecy, 'entered presently into matters of treason, and said they intended to blow up the Parliament House with gunpowder.'[8] Tresham declared that he counselled against the project.

The usual account of Guy Fawkes et al is so well known as not needing to be retold here. What is of interest, in the context of this narrative, is the number of conspirators who had connections with Northamptonshire, particularly Robert Catesby of Ashby St Ledgers, the reputed leader.

Most of the other plotters had family connections with Catesby or with one another, were participants in the abortive rebellion of the Earl of Essex in 1601 and had been placed under arrest at the time of the death of Queen Elizabeth. Thomas Percy, who rented the cellars where Fawkes was found, was brother in law to John and Christopher Wright of Plowland Hall, Yorkshire and these were cousins of Thomas Winter. John Grant had married Winter's sister. [9]

There is absolutely no reason to suppose that Bl. Peter Wright's family were in any way connected with the Wrights of Plowland Hall; Wright is, of course, a common enough name. However, another conspirator, Ambrose Rookwood, a cousin of Catesby was also related to Robert Keyes who, with his wife (a Pickering of Titchmarsh), was a close dependant of the Catholic peer Lord Mordaunt at Drayton House only a mile away from Slipton where Peter Wright's family dwelt. Keyes was, in fact, the keeper of the Mordaunt's other house at Turvey in Bedfordshire. [9A]

Guy Fawkes was tortured, for several days, to reveal what he knew and gave a number of names to the Lord Chief Justice, Sir John Popham. These included Sir Everard Digby, who had extensive estates in Rutland, Francis Tresham and the Robert Keyes mentioned above. Indeed King James encouraged his ministers to use torture, 'starting with the gentler tortures and working up, if that was what it took to make him talk.' [10]

Several of the plotters including Catesby and Percy were killed at Holbeach House in Staffordshire on the eighth of November 1605. This did not prevent their severed heads being exhibited in London. The rest including those revealed by Fawkes were soon rounded up and placed in the

[8] *Ibid. pp. 260-286.*

[9] *M. Nicholls, Investigating Gunpowder Plot, pp. 11-12.*

[9A] *N. V. Stopford-Sackville, Drayton House, p. 8.*

[10] *M Nicholls, Investigating Gunpowder Plot, pp. 11-13.*

Drayton House, Northamptonshire - North Wing
(and part of West aspect)

Drayton House, Northamptonshire - East aspect

Tower of London, if they were of gentle birth. More than ninety other Catholics were also imprisoned and thoroughly questioned, to try and implicate them, simply because of their religion.

On the twenty seventh of January 1606 Digby, Grant, Fawkes, Keyes,Rookwood, Robert and Thomas Winter together with Bates, a mere serving man, were brought to trial and soon condemned. Four were hung, drawn and quartered in St. Paul's churchyard on the thirtieth of January while on the following day Guido Fawkes, Thomas Winter, Ambrose Rookwood and Robert Keyes received the same ghastly punishment in the Old Palace Yard at Westminster.

Robert Keyes, the man from Drayton and Turvey, 'went stoutly up the ladder, where, not staying the hangman's turn, he turned himself off with such a leap, that with the swing he brake the halter; but, after his fall, was quickly drawn to the block, and there was quickly divided into four parts. He had been very defiant and ready to die for this cause rather than for another.' [11]

Francis Tresham, although accused of conspiracy with the others, always maintained that Catesby only told him about the plot three weeks before Fawkes was taken. The plotters were short of money and so were forced to reveal all to Tresham but he counselled them against the enterprise. (See Vavisor document mentioned earlier.) Popularly, it has been supposed that, on the twenty sixth of October 1605, it was Tresham who sent the letter warning of the plot, to his brother-in-law, Lord Monteagle, who quickly showed it to the King. Tresham died in prison probably from natural causes although some people believed him to be poisoned.

Several noble lords were also implicated in the affair including the Earl of Northumberland, Lord Mordaunt of Drayton House, Lord Montague and Lord Stourton. Despite the fact that Northumberland would probably have become regent, if the plot had succeeded, he told the court that he had turned Protestant [12] and was then merely imprisoned in the Tower until 1621 having had a suitable fine imposed. The other lords were also fined and imprisoned - Lord Mordaunt's fine was ten thousand marks (£6,666) and he died in prison in 1609, as a result of the confinement. Some of the fines were later mitigated.

In view of the close proximity of Drayton House to Slipton, the supposed birthplace of Peter Wright, it is worth noting here that Henry, Fourth Baron Mordaunt of Turvey, Bedfordshire (as well as Drayton) had succeeded his father Lewis in 1601. He had previously married Margaret, daughter of Lord Compton of Compton Wynyates, Warwickshire whose Catholic faith was very strong. Henry's Will, which is dated the sixth of February 1608 declared; 'for the clearing of my conscience before God and Man, and to give a public satisfaction to the world, concerning such, and those imputations which lately have been laid upon me, and for which I have in a high degree been censured, I mean the late Gunpowder Treason .... I do solemnly protest before God and his Angels, and that

[11] *Ibid. p.55.*
[12] *Ibid., p. 193 .*

without all equivocation or duplicity whatsoever, that I am innocent of that fact, and guiltless of all foreknowledge thereof.' [12A]

The King's chief minister, Lord Salisbury, was determined to incriminate the Jesuits in this matter and named three priests; John Gerard, Henry Garnet and Oswald Tesimond as being guilty even before he had captured or questioned them. Now John Gerard had been imprisoned in the Tower of London once before, from April 1594 to October 1597, but, despite having been tortured, he had managed to escape. (See Ch. IV.) In 1605, he was sheltering with three other Jesuit priests at Harrowden Hall, near Wellingborough, hidden in specially constructed hides and protected by Mrs .Elizabeth Vaux and her seventeen year old son Lord Vaux. Salisbury ordered William Tate of Delapre (the former abbey) to search Harrowden and also the Vaux house at Irthlingborough. Tate had more than 100 men and commandeered all the keys but, search as he might, he could not find Gerard who later escaped to France. However, the pursuivants were allowed to find one hide and there took possession of many Popish books. One priest, Thomas Laithwaite, escaped from Harrowden but then foolishly returned and was captured. Tate sent him to London together with the Vaux family charged with complicity in the Plot. No involvement could be proved and after some years in prison these suspects were eventually released although ruined financially for refusing the new (1606) Oath of Allegiance. This was so heretical that no self-respecting Catholic could swear to it. In 1611 Harrowden was again raided by Sir Gilbert Pickering of Titchmarsh who scaled the walls at midnight, ransacked the chapel, and carried off two more Jesuits. [13]

John Gerard, safe abroad, was able to write his memoirs and an account of the events of the Gunpowder Plot where he explained that he had no prior knowledge. Much of what we know about the involvement of Oswald Tesimond and Henry Garnet is based on two conflicting sources; the Catholic version which Gerard expounded and the government or Protestant version which Lord Salisbury published.

Salisbury was determined to show that the Jesuits, and particularly Henry Garnet their superior, were the real instigators of the Plot. Garnet, however, had taken refuge at Hindlip House, [*] Worcestershire, together with another Jesuit, Edward Oldcorne and two Jesuit lay brothers, Nicholas Owen and Ralph Ashley. Here they were eventually discovered after a long search in late January 1606. [14] Meanwhile Oswald Tesimond had fled the country.

Oldcorne and his servant Ashley were condemned for alleged complicity in the Plot and received the usual punishment at Worcester on the seventh of April 1606. Garnet and Owen were taken to the

[12A] *G. Collins, Unpublished research deposited at Bishop's House, Northampton..*

[13] *G. Anstruther, Vaux of Harrowden, pp. 310-396.*

[*] *Hindlip House had eleven hiding places. For vivid description see Hodgetts' book (cited below).*

[14] *M Hodgetts, Secret Hiding Places, pp. 171-177.*

Tower of London where Owen, the designer of most of the hiding places in England, including those at Harrowden, died following torture on the rack on the ninth of March 1606 - a previous hernia having burst open.

Henry Garnet was kept for a long time in the Tower while government agents tried various means to get him to 'confess'. First, they gave him good food and allowed him to write and receive letters which were, of course, all read by the guards. Next he was placed in a room which was adjacent to the cell occupied by Edward Oldcorne, the priest captured with him, and with a hole in the wall allowing them to converse, while hidden agents took notes. (15) These ruses having failed Garnet was then told falsely that Oswald Tesimond had been captured and given evidence against him. The Jesuit superior was also examined (questioned) on twenty-three occasions with at least one of these under torture. On the eighth of March 1606, he wrote some sort of 'confession' to the effect that he only knew of the Plot from Oswald Tesimond under the seal of confession and that Tesimond himself had also learned about it from Robert Catesby under the same seal. The whole sorry business reads more like a story of Gestapo proceedings in the twentieth century. Garnet's deposition, still extant, contains more than a hint of forgery about it but since the English government did not recognise the seal of confession, it was enough to condemn him and he suffered the same barbaric sentence as the others on the third of May 1606, in front of St. Paul's Cathedral.

The main outcome of the affair of the Plot was that all Catholics continued to be persecuted for their religion and Jesuits, in particular, received an unjustified bad name for plotting and equivocation. (See Chapter IV.)

Lord Salisbury, who was mainly responsible for the home and foreign policy of James I, died in 1612. Previously the King's daughter, Elizabeth, had married the extreme Protestant Elector Palatine, Frederick. This occurred in 1609 and thereafter, for a short time, James was almost the leader of a Protestant alliance against the Catholic powers of Europe.

However, sometime after his elder son Henry died, in 1612, James became attracted to the idea of a Spanish bride for his second son Charles. Apparently he thought that such an alliance would prevent England being drawn into the serious wars of religion which were brewing on the continent. (16)

One of the first consequences of this new policy of friendship towards Spain was that Sir Walter Raleigh, who had been imprisoned for treason in 1603, released in 1616 to lead an expedition to find gold in South America, was executed for fighting the Spaniards (although another reason was given). The same year that saw Raleigh's execution also saw the release of a hundred Catholic priests from prison and their safe conduct overseas. (17)

(15) *G Anstruther, Vaux of Harrowden, pp. 340-369.*

(16) *G Davies, Early Stuarts, pp. 54-55.*

(17) *Ibid., pp. 56-59 .*

Unfortunately this apparent magnanimity of James towards Catholics was merely to appease the Spanish throne in order to obtain the £600,000 dowry which the Spanish infanta was expected to bring. As Parliament in England was against the match, and Spain demanded that three years absence from persecution of English Catholics must ensue before any marriage could be sanctioned, the whole project was doomed. Nevertheless Prince Charles and the Duke of Buckingham went to Spain to try to woo the princess personally, hoping also for Spanish help in Germany.

The Thirty Years War, which had begun in Europe in 1618, did not make matters any easier for the English suitors for the war was partly religious and partly dynastic. Charles's Protestant brother-in-law, Frederick, was soon to be driven out of his territory by the Catholic Holy Roman Emperor (based on Austria) and the Spaniards would certainly not fight against the Emperor. The result was that Prince Charles turned his back on the Spanish match, returned to London and found the ultra-Protestant Parliament rejoicing as King James made ready to go to war against Spain on behalf of the Protestant alliance.

A war with Spain must inevitably mean a new treaty with the Dutch who were still fighting to secure their independence from Spanish rule. An official English army of 12,000 men landed at Flushing late in 1624 or early 1625 but was so poorly equipped and led that it was soon reduced to barely 3,000 fit men. Protestant volunteer regiments had been serving in Holland, with rather more success, for many years before this under commanders of the stature of the Earls of Oxford, Southampton and Essex.

A surprising anomaly is to be found in the fact that from the Summer of 1622 a Scottish Catholic regiment, under the command of the Earl of Argyll, together with an English Catholic regiment, having Lord Vaux (he of Harrowden) as Colonel, had been sent out to fight on the Spanish side. Both these regiments totalling in all some 8,000[*] troops were licensed by King James. The sergeant-major of the English force was Sir Edward Parham who was married to Sir Thomas Tresham's daughter. Other captains included well known Recusants such as Sir Valentine Brown, Sir James Creighton, Roger Tirwhitt, John Timperly, Sir William Tresham and most significantly Henry Gage. (See subsequent chapters for the connection with Peter Wright.) These soldiers were active in the siege and attack on Bergen during 1622 and 1623 but were not very successful and soon in need of reinforcements. Letters still survive from the Protestant English volunteers defending Bergen complaining about having to fight against the Catholic English troops licensed by an English government. [18]

[*] *The number seems too high but is quoted by Anstruther.*

[18] *G. Anstruther, Vaux of Harrowden, pp. 432-436.*

The farcical nature of these proceedings is emphasised by the further information that on the twenty fourth of March 1624 [*], a royal proclamation announced the termination of the treaties with Spain. Yet by a permit dated the fifth of June 1624, Lord Vaux was again allowed to 'depart the kingdom with such officers and soldiers as shall be willing to serve the King of Spain and to continue there till the King's pleasure signified to the contrary; with license to him to travel to or from England on his private affairs. [19]

In the event the permission was revoked and Vaux resigned his commission. The English Catholic regiment, however, continued to serve the King of Spain for many more years with at least one other member of the Vaux family acting as a captain and other Northamptonshire families represented by names such as Brudenell of Deene and Bentley of Little Oakley. (More of this anon.)

Reign of Charles I (1625-1649). Wars, Puritans, the Great Rebellion.

When James died in March 1625, he bequeathed to his son a Spanish war, Dutch and Danish alliances and the need to support the ill-fated army still struggling in the Netherlands. The new King, within three months of his accession, proceeded to form a French alliance which included marriage to princess Henrietta Maria, sister of the King of France. As part of the bargain it was demanded that the Queen's household should be of the Catholic religion and that the penal laws against Papists should be suspended. [20]

The Puritan element in Parliament were furious at this giving in to French Catholic demands and Charles found it almost impossible to get them to grant money to pay and equip either sailors or soldiers. The war against Spain was an unmitigated disaster and to make matters worse by 1627 England was at war with France as well. Parliament continued to condemn the war and in particular the handling of it by Charles's favourite, the Duke of Buckingham. In 1628 the Puritans rejoiced when Buckingham was assassinated by an unpaid officer.

The alienation of King from Parliament had begun in the previous reign but was now to be intensified as the Puritans began an attack on the newly appointed Bishop of London, William Laud. First installed in 1629, this formidable churchman was transferred to the See of Canterbury four years later. Calvinistic, Puritan Parliamentarians were angered by Laud's insistence on church ceremonial and elaborate ritual. The particular cause of their wrath was the new order that the communion table should be moved out of the body of the church and erected at the east end as an altar, railed off from the congregation - reverting to the old position before the Protestant Reformation. To the Puritans

[*] *This might refer to 1625 by the reformed calendar, in which case there is no anomaly.*

[19] *Ibid p.434.*

[20] *G.Davies, Early Stuarts, p.60.*

Laud was bringing back Roman Catholic practices - which was not the case - and, since Charles supported Laud he too was attacked by the method of refusing grants of money.

Charles was so exasperated by this behaviour that from 1629 to 1640 he ruled without Parliament, imprisoning Puritan Parliamentarians who refused to pay the taxes he imposed. Relying more and more on advice from the Queen and Archbishop, the King was perceived as being a crypto-Catholic which was not true. It is true that the persecution of Papists was generally in abeyance at this time, and no priests or laymen were put to death between 1628 and 1641, but recusant fines were still collected as this was a tax that the Crown could not afford to relinquish.

In fact shortage of money needed to promote a war in Scotland was to lead to Charles's eventual downfall. By 1638 an attempt to force an English style Episcopalian church on the mainly Presbyterian lowland Scots led to the so-called 'Bishops' War.' The King's untrained militia were defeated by the Scots and in order to raise a stronger force, he first appointed Sir Thomas Wentworth, Lord Deputy of Ireland, as his chief adviser and then, acting on his advice, recalled Parliament.

The first Parliament of 1640 was only to last three weeks, as the grievances of the past eleven years were raised, and instead of helping the King to fight his war petitioned against it. Northumberland and Durham were occupied by the Scots who demanded money before they would return home. At his wits end, Charles reluctantly recalled Parliament again. This assembly would not be dissolved until after the King was dead.

Inspired by Puritans like John Pym and John Hampden a triumphal Parliament began a sustained attack on the King by impeaching both Thomas Laud, Archbishop of Canterbury and Sir Thomas Wentworth, Earl of Strafford. Both were condemned for treason with Strafford being executed in a few days and Laud three years later. Charles signed Strafford's death warrant for fear of danger to his Catholic Queen and on the advice of his Council, but in this act he had probably also signed his own death certificate.

That Charles had reason to fear the Puritan hatred of Catholics is shown by the fact that, on the third of November 1640, he had been forced to sign a proclamation which banished all Jesuits, priests and seminarists under penalty of death. Between 1641 and 1646 this renewed persecution resulted in the execution or death in prison of not less than 21 priests. One of these, Henry Heath, had been born in Peterborough and trained as an Anglican clergyman but after converting to Catholicism in 1622/23 he had joined the Franciscan order. He was a studious and very devout man who was not cut out to be a missioner and was soon captured and executed when he returned to England in 1643. [121] On the day this martyr arrived in London, all the French Capuchin Friars who had ministered to Queen Henrietta had been arrested.

[21] *P. Waszak, Henry Heath, Various articles and notes.*

By 1642 Charles was forced to leave London by the intransigence of the majority of Parliament who were supported by the City of London Trained Bands (militia). Going to York the King found some support but did not officially declare war until the twenty second of August when he raised his standard at Nottingham. The English Civil Wars had begun, (known in Europe as the English Revolution).

In the ensuing struggle the country was roughly divided by geographical regions. The prosperous south and east mainly supported Parliament while the wild and rugged north and west supported the King. Most of the sea ports took the side of Parliament to the great disadvantage of Charles who was extremely short of money and supplies. To some extent the war was a religious one with the adherents of the Anglican church, as it existed, being mainly Royalists while those who wanted to reform the church still further (the Puritans) sided with Parliament. The Catholics, who looked to Charles's French Queen for protection, mainly supported the King. One point of local interest was that the heir to Drayton House and First Earl of Peterborough [*], son of the Lord Mordaunt who died in prison in 1609, was general of ordnance in the first Parliamentary army but he died in 1642. [22]

Although the great men of the country took part in this conflict, 80 peers and 175 commons on the King's side and 30 peers and 300 commons opposing, [23] most of the population were not actively engaged. The poorest classes took little part except when forcibly enlisted by one side or the other.

The King failed in an attempt to capture London although helped by his German Protestant nephew Prince Rupert, who led the cavalry gallantly but recklessly, in the first major engagement of the war at Edgehill on the borders of Oxfordshire, Northamptonshire and Warwickshire. This indecisive battle was fought on the twenty third of October 1642, and subsequently the Parliamentary army under Essex withdrew towards London and Charles moved into Oxford which continued to be his headquarters for the rest of the war.

The religious nature of the war is portrayed in an incident during September 1642 which occurred at Coughton in Warwickshire, occupied by units of the Parliamentary army. The following is an extract from one soldier's report:-

'... and there lived a great Papist, one Frogmorton (Sir Robert Throckmorton) [**], who hearing of our coming fled away from his house, and his whole family, which the Soldiers did plunder, and found abundance of Images and Pictures, which they broke and committed to the fire. They likewise

[*] *He had been brought up under the guidance of George Abbot, Puritan Archbishop of Canterbury, and married a strong Puritan. His son the Second Earl was to become a very devout Catholic.*

[22] *D.N.B.*

[23] *D. Richards, Britain under Tudors and Stuarts, p. 239.*

[**] *Sir Robert Throckmorton's other house was Weston Underwood, Bucks.*

Playing at soldiers

burnt many popish Bookes, some of them being - printed in parchment, and others were throwne into a great moate. The Soldiers dranke up his Perry, Sider and Beere almost all.' [24]

Without any doubt the Papists were the real enemy in the minds of those who supported the Parliament most strongly. With monotonous reiteration, nearly every declaration and proclamation of Parliament held up the Papists as the true authors of the war. For example:- 'The Lords and Commons now in Parliament assembled being certainly informed that Papists and other wicked and ill-affected persons have traitorously combined together - ' and so on. [25]

The King at first forbade Recusants to serve in his armies (probably to stop Parliament accusing him of siding with the Catholics) but as early as the twenty seventh of September 1642, Charles wrote to the Lancashire Recusants and commanded them to arm themselves in his service. The Earl of Newcastle's army of 8,000 men was reputed to contain 6,000 Catholics and in areas controlled by the King the Catholic religion was openly practised. According to Lord Fairfax, the Parliamentary commander, as early as June 1642 Mass was being said in every street in the city of York and very few people were attending the Protestant churches. [26].

That the King was well supported by his Catholic subjects is borne out by the statistic that two fifths of the Royalist officers killed came from Recusant families. [27] Many of these aristocratic Catholics were to suffer dearly for their adherence to the Royalist cause as their homes were looted and, at the end of the war, their lands and possessions were confiscated.

1643 was a year of skirmishes and small engagements but an important development was that Parliament approached the Scots for help. The Calvinist party in Scotland would only agree to send an army if Parliament agreed to sign a 'Solemn League and Covenant' promising to put down 'popery' (Roman Catholicism) and 'prelacy' (Church government through bishops). As this was in accord with most Puritan M.P.'s own thinking, the Summer of 1644 saw a Scottish army in the field assisting the 'Roundheads' in the north of England. ('Roundheads' was a nickname given to the Parliamentary soldiers by the Royalists.)

By the beginning of the month of July 1644, an allied army commanded by the Scottish Earl of Leven was besieging the city of York which was defended for the King by the Earl of Newcastle. To relieve the situation Prince Rupert brought his cavalry from the south and with infantry from Lancashire sought to confront the Parliamentarians (on the second of July) at Marston Moor. This battle proved to be the turning point of the war as both Royalist cavalry and infantry were defeated by Parliamentary soldiers commanded by Lord Fairfax, Sir Thomas Fairfax and the Earl of

[24] *P. Tennant, Edgehill and beyond, p. 51.*
[25] *B. Magee, English Recusants, p. 163.*
[26] *Ibid. pp. 163-165.*
[27] *Ibid. p. 123.*

Manchester. The better discipline and training of the Eastern Association army was a significant factor and in particular the new corps of cavalry trained by the M.P. for Cambridge, Lt. General Oliver Cromwell.

Later in the year the King's forces rallied and the two most senior Parliamentary commanders, the Earl of Essex and Earl of Manchester, were blamed for mismanagement. Sir Thomas Fairfax was appointed as the Lord General of a New Model Army with cavalry trained by Cromwell.

The most serious and complete military defeat for Charles, in what has become known as the first Civil War, was fought out in Northamptonshire. Following the Royalist's brutal capture of Leicester on the thirtieth of May 1645 [(28)], the combined armies of Charles and Rupert encamped first at Daventry and later in the neighbourhood of Market Harborough, awaiting reinforcements, when news was received of the approach of the New Model Army.

Fairfax and Cromwell joined forces at Kislingbury on the thirteenth of June and immediately pursued the King's armies, meeting up near the village of Naseby on the fourteenth. The resulting battle was to bring a complete and overwhelming victory to the Parliamentary army. Charles and Rupert escaped with a few cavalry but all the Royalist artillery and arms together with the King's personal correspondence were captured. The letters showed that attempts were being made to bring over Irish soldiers to help the Royalist cause and that the Catholics were being promised better treatment.

Charles continued to ride up and down the country for several months after this disaster, eventually returning to Oxford on the fifth of November, having ridden 1,200 miles since Naseby. [(29)] During this time, Fairfax and Cromwell had been systematically mopping up the King's supporters in the south and west so that further continuation of the struggle was pointless.

After escaping from Oxford in disguise, Charles surrendered to the Scots' army encamped at Newark. This occurred on the fifth of May 1646 and Oxford itself capitulated on the twenty fourth of June. The King's forces in the university town had conducted a heroic defence for many months under a succession of governors. One of the most noteworthy being Sir Henry Gage who was knighted for his exploits in 1644. The Jesuit priest who acted as chaplain to this brave soldier was none other than Peter Wright, the subject of this narrative. (See Chapters V and VI.)

The King's attempt to parley with the Scots was thwarted by his refusal to give in to their demand that Presbyterianism be imposed on England. In consequence of his failure to agree to their terms by January 1647, the royal person was sold to the English Parliamentarians for £400,000 and was back in Northamptonshire, a prisoner at Holmby (Holdenby House).

[(28)] *M. Ashley, English Civil War, p. 126.*

[(29)] *Ibid. p. 138 .*

This house is very close to the county town of Northampton, which had been a stronghold for the Parliamentarians since the outbreak of hostilities. Indeed, one of the chief supply routes for the 'Roundhead' forces was London to Coventry via Northampton. By the winter of 1642/43 Northampton was well established as one of Parliament's most important garrison towns and it is an accepted fact that the town and county's boot and shoe industry became firmly established as a result of supplying footwear to the Parliamentary soldiers. (30)

Not all county men were for Parliament. The Earl of Northampton of Castle Ashby was one of the King's commanders in the Midlands, while Lord Spencer took £10,000 to help the Royalist cause.

Members of the Catholic Brudenell family of Deene were also prominent Cavaliers despite persecution by Parliament. For example, on the sixteenth of January 1643, Thomas Lord Brudenell and family, with 12 servants, were given permission by Parliament to travel to France, but first his house was ransacked and later his coach and money stolen by Parliamentary soldiers. (31) Lord Brudenell had tried not to become involved in the Civil War but was hounded and made fugitive over many counties because he was a 'Recusant'. He was eventually captured at Hereford with 120 others on the sixteenth of December 1645. A letter from Colonel John Birch, to Parliament, after his Puritan soldiers had plundered the town contained the phrase, 'by this, the Pope's nest in Hereford is spoiled'; (32) a clear indication of the continuing religious nature of the war.

Northamptonshire, being crossed by so many routes north to south and east to west, probably suffered more than most counties by the passage of rival armies. In 1643 Prince Rupert and the Earl of Northampton with their Royalist cavalry plundered Brackley, Towcester, Daventry and the villages around. Carts, wagons, beds, food and 1,200 horses were taken from the long suffering country dwellers. (33)

Later Rockingham Castle was captured and the village with its church virtually destroyed by Parliamentary forces under Lord Grey of Groby. (34) Other incidents occurred at Grafton Regis and Weedon Lois. Puritans pursued a course of church damage as official policy following the ordinance of the twenty sixth of August 1643 for the: 'utter demolishing, removing and taking away of all Monuments of superstition and Idolatry'. (35) There is no doubt of the terrible impact of the 'Puritan revolution' on the fabric and furnishing of the parish churches and cathedrals. Peterborough Cathedral was wantonly desecrated by Colonel Oliver Cromwell's soldiers where they not only destroyed all the medieval stained glass windows but Catherine of Aragon's tomb as well. The chief

(30) *P. Tennant, Edgehill and beyond, p. 156 & R L Greenhall, Northamptonshire, p. 60..*

(31) *J Wake, Brudenells of Deene, pp. 131-135.*

(32) *Ibid. p. 136.*

(33) *P. Tennant, Edgehill and beyond, pp. 81-82.*

(34) *J. Wake, Brudenells of Deene, p. 129.*

(35) *P. Tennant, Edgehill and beyond, p. 231 .*

Civil War

iconoclast, of this period, was William Dowsing who, working mainly in Cambridgeshire and Suffolk, defaced and broke down all remnants of medieval piety he could find including the smashing of carvings on baptismal fonts and even going so far as to fire bullets into the carved angels in the roof, as at Blythburgh, Suffolk. Village crosses were not immune to the depredations of Puritans, as witnessed at Isham near Kettering, where the attack and destruction, in June 1642, caused a riot. (36)

Some churches in Northamptonshire were deliberately set on fire for harbouring enemy soldiers. This happened at Kilsby, Weedon and Kings Sutton. At Canons Ashby, Parliamentarian tax collectors, supported by soldiers, were driven into taking refuge in the church tower by Royalist cavalry, who then ignited the building so as to force the Puritans to surrender.

The confused nature and uncertainties of this period are well illustrated by what befell Lord Montague of Boughton House, near Kettering. In 1642 he had been created Lord Lieutenant of Northamptonshire and although a strong Puritan proceeded to call out the militia (citizen soldiers) to fight for Charles. For this, and in spite of his 80 years, he was imprisoned in London by Parliament. Montague's cousin was the Earl of Manchester of Kimbolton, the Parliamentary commander, who himself had a brother, Walter, who had become a Catholic in 1635 and was imprisoned in the Tower from 1643 to 1647. Walter was exiled in 1649, and became the Abbot of the monastery of St Martin near Pontoise in France. (37)

Towns and villages, as well as families, could be divided by the politics of the time as instanced at Wellingborough. (38) A Clerk of the Peace, by name Francis Gray, was accused of molesting those who were well-affected to the Parliament in 1640, and of having caused, 'his servants to make a great store of bullets to be employed against the well-affected to the Parliament whom he called round-headed rogues.' His house was attacked by the Parliamentary forces in 1642, who brought a warrant for his arrest. The inhabitants flocked to his assistance, but he was taken prisoner and in the riot which ensued, from him, 'being Clerk of the Peace, they take away the commissions of peace, the session rolls, together with his own evidences and leases, all his household stuff, even to his very bed-cords, leaving but one sheet for his wife and five children.' Gray was taken to London and examined before a Parliamentary Committee. He was released after nine months detention, but not fully discharged until 1645.

The fact that Wellingborough people had very differant attitudes from the inhabitants of Northampton is also borne out by an incident which occurred in 1650. A Parliamentary General, Zouch Tate, sent 300 men to harass the town because of its Royalist and Laudian church sympathies. These soldiers arrested the Vicar, the Rev. Thomas Jones and dragged him off as a prisoner. Despite

(36) *Northants. Past and Present, Vol. I, No. 3 p. 17.*

(37) *J. Wake, Brudenells of Deene, p. 139 & D. N. B.*

(38) *Northants Record Society, Vol. I, p.246.*

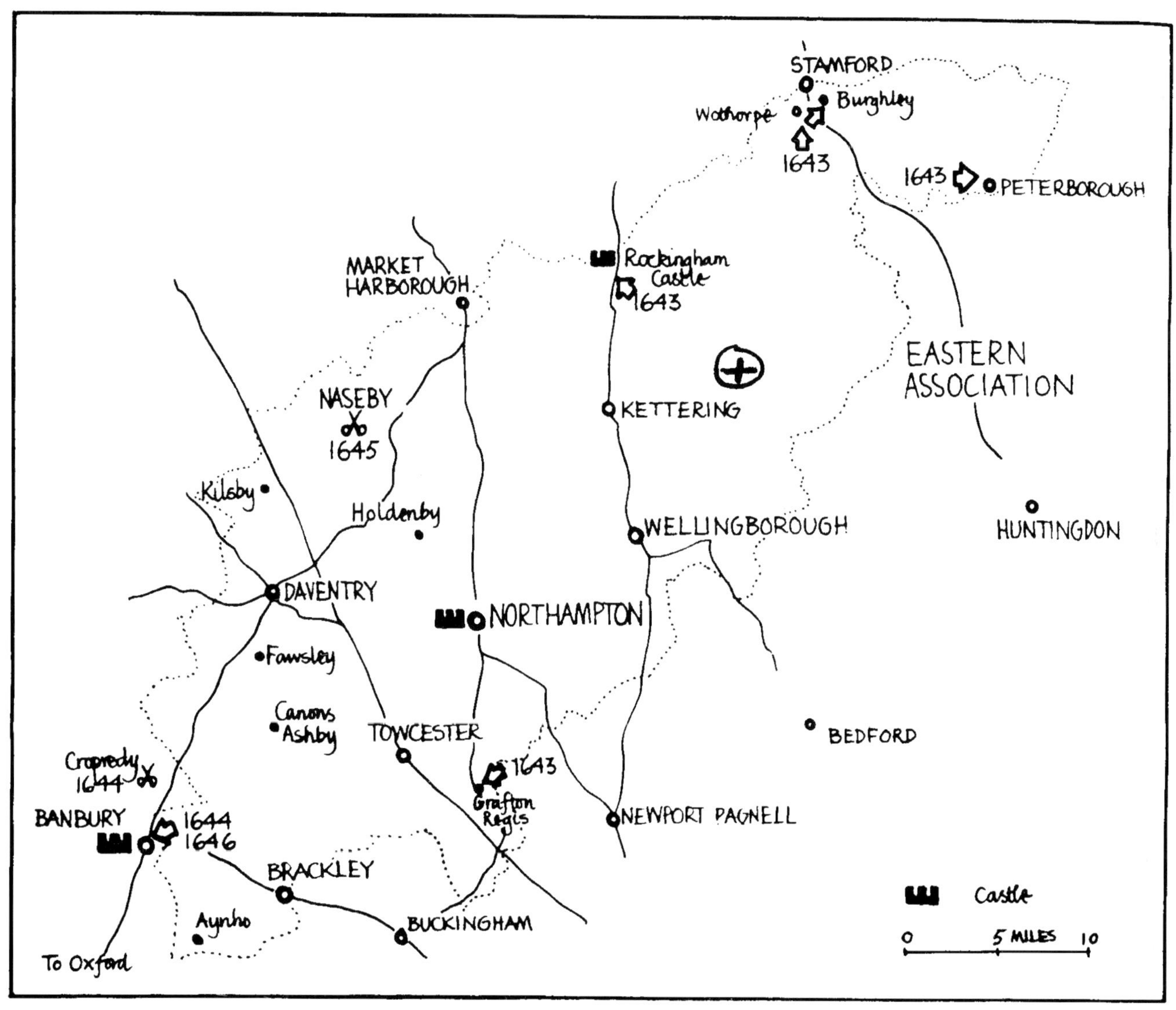

= SLIPTON

The Civil War in Northamptonshire

Reproduced by permission from A HISTORY OF NORTHAMPTONSHIRE by Ron. Greenall, published in 1979 by Phillimore & Company Ltd., Chichester, W.Sussex.

his age and his office he was forced to ride on the back of a performing bear which had been stolen from a barber. Imprisoned for a time at Northampton, he was released eventually but being a man of principles continued to preach and instruct his parishioners as before. The consequence was that he was re-arrested and died in jail at Northampton.

Jones was only one of many deprived Anglican clergymen. In 96 Northamptonshire parishes Vicars and Rectors were ejected and replacedby Presbyterian intruders. From 1643 a Calvinistic regime was nominally established in the Church of England, though the Parliamentary army forced it to tolerate Baptists and Independents; Quakers, Unitarians and Catholics were not treated so kindly. [39]

From January to June 1647 the King's enforced stay in Northamptonshire as a 'guest' of Parliament was not particularly unpleasant. Some days he spent reading, playing chess and walking in the garden with one of the Commissioners (his guardians) but he was also allowed to play bowls at Althorpe, the home of Lord Spencer, and at Boughton, near Northampton, at a house belonging to Lord Vaux - he may also have played at Harrowden. The visits to Boughton are attested by none other than Peter Wright, the Jesuit, who is the subject of this history. In a letter dated from London, 'this is the twenty third of April 1647' he writes: [40]

'The Scottish Commissioners .... are at length come to town to join our Commissioners to try if they can persuade his Majesty to take the Covenant and pass the resolutions, and 'tis said they will give him ten days to consider, at the end of which, if he refuses, then let him look to himself. He, on the contrary side, remains the same and seems resolved to condescend unto them in nothing. He hath leave now to go some days in the week to the Lord Vaux's house at Boughton to bowls.' (Appendix B.)

Charles's attempts to procrastinate were brought to a sudden end on the fourth of June when he was carried off by Cornet Joyce and 500 troopers to the Parliamentary army headquarters at Newmarket. This action was forced on the army by the refusal of the 'Rump' of the Long Parliament to pay them their arrears in wages.

Eventually, on the twenty fourth of August, the King was taken to Hampton Court while the army occupied London. Soldiers and politicians continued squabbling over money matters and both parties tried negotiating with Charles about a new constitution. Amid the confusion, on the sixteenth of November, his Majesty escaped and made his way to the Isle of Wight. It is unclear as to his motive for this manoeuvre, but being apprehended he was kept in custody in Carisbrooke Castle by Colonel Hammond. He refused his assent to fresh proposals from Parliament and in December 1647 made a secret treaty with the Scots by which he accepted Presbyterianism and obtained the promise of a Scottish army. Debate continues to this day over the exact terms of the agreement and whether Charles had any real intention to keep to them.

[39] *R. L. Greenall, Northamptonshire, p. 63.*

[40] *G. Anstruther, Vaux of Harrowden, p. 468 (quoting from Foley, II, p. 561).*

Rev. Thomas Jones forced to ride a bear

A second Civil War followed but Royalist risings in Kent, Essex, Wales and a few other areas were soon suppressed by Fairfax and Cromwell. A Scottish army was also routed at Preston before September 1648.

By November of that year certain elements in the army were demanding the death of the King and on the twenty third of December he was first transferred to Windsor and three weeks later moved to St James's Palace. A court, constituted by the remnants of the House of Commons, in which Cromwell was active as a prosecutor, was convened in St. Stephen's Hall, Westminster, on the twentieth of January. (The same venue had been used for the trial of St. Thomas More - See Chapter I.)

Charles refused to acknowledge the jurisdiction of the court but was nevertheless condemned on a charge of 'treason against his subjects' on the twenty seventh of January 1649. The execution, by beheading, took place in Whitehall (near to the site of the present Cenotaph), on the thirtieth of January. The great groan which emanated from the crowd should have warned the Puritan authorities that the act was not condoned by the majority of the nation. Many rushed to soak their handkerchiefs in the martyr's blood.

The Interregnum - Third Civil War (1649 - 1651).

When the news of Charles I's execution reached Scotland, there was an immediate outcry and on the fifth of February 1649, the King's son was proclaimed in Edinburgh, as Charles II. A similar action was taken in Ireland. It would be eleven years before such a proclamation could be made in England.

In fact, the establishment of a republic (later designated Commonwealth) began twenty six days before the death of Charles I. The 'Rump' of the House of Commons voted: 'that the people, under God, the original of all just power.... that the commons of England, in parliament assembled, being chosen by, and representing, the people, have the supreme power in this nation...' [41]

The office of king was abolished together with the House of Lords on the seventeenth and nineteenth of March but only about one tenth of the Commons elected in 1640 remained to pass this legislation. Eventually these few were to be ejected by Cromwell and the army in April 1653.

It was at this time that Fairfax stood down as commander of the army (privately he was unhappy about the King's execution) and Cromwell took over. His first task was to reconquer Ireland, landing near Dublin in August 1649, with 12,000 men. What followed was a fierce military campaign designed more to terrorise than conquer; with the slaughter of the garrisons at Drogheda and Wexford,

[41] *G. Davies, Early Stuarts, p. 160.*

when they refused to surrender, being remembered for generations afterwards. In a letter justifying his cruelty Cromwell wrote that the Catholic Irish were: 'made with their bloods to answer the cruelties which they had exercised upon the lives of divers poor protestants'. [42] (The seeds of hate had been sown.)

Charles (II) meanwhile had retreated to Paris and from there to Breda in Holland. Meeting the Scottish Presbyterians he found that he would not be allowed back for his coronation unless he agreed to sign the Covenant which his father had found impossible to accept. Nevertheless by June 1650, after conceding the Scottish commissioners' terms, Charles was in residence at Falkland Palace, Fife.

On the third of September 1650, a Scottish army supporting Charles was defeated at Dunbar by an English army led by Cromwell. This should have ended the third Civil War but, before any peace settlement could be concluded, Charles was crowned King of Scotland, with ancient ceremonial, at Scone, on the first of January 1651. Later that year collecting another army and evading Cromwell, who was still in the lowlands near Perth, Charles and the Royalist Scots marched south into England as far as Worcester. Here very few English supporters joined the invading force and the final defeat, in the conflict which had begun nine years before, took place on the third of September 1651. The seemingly invincible Cromwell described his success as 'a crowning mercy' since his victory was achieved in three hours; forgetting to mention that he had command of 23,000 men to oppose a mere 13,000 on the side of Charles. [43]

The uncrowned King of England escaped to France, after many adventures; being helped by several Catholic families on the way. A republican form of government existed until 1660, by which time the Lord Protector (the title taken by Oliver Cromwell as ruler of the Commonwealth) was dead.

Previously, in May 1651, our martyr, Peter Wright, had also departed this life and in the next chapter it will be necessary to try to establish the pattern of his early years.

[42] *Ibid., p. 163.*

[43] *M. Ashley, English Civil War, pp. 185-186.*

Chapter III

Recusants in Northamptonshire during the early years of the seventeenth century - Drayton House - the Wright family - Peter's early life and formative years. In the Netherlands as a soldier - becoming a Jesuit.

The Northamptonshire Record Office at Wootton Hall Park is the repository for most of the county's Anglican church registers of Baptisms and Marriages as well as some Roman Catholic records. Unfortunately the records for the parish of Slipton do not begin until 1671 too late for the purpose of trying to identify members of the Wright family believed to be living there during earlier years. The 'Montagu Musters Book' of 1602-1623 [1], however, contains the information that Slipton was not an independent parish at the beginning of the seventeenth century, at that time being joined to Twywell. (Today Slipton is part of Lowick parish for civil administrative purposes.)

A perusal of the Twywell registers, which begin in 1586, is not very revealing as the first pages are badly torn and defaced. Before 1630 the name Wright is not discernible in the list of Baptisms but a Thomas C ... married Sibbell Wright in 1607 and a William Right (sic) married Margery Carrington on the twenty seventh of January 1639. The fact that no Wrights are recorded in the Baptismal list is not necessarily surprising if, as already stated, they were a Recusant family who refused to come to the Anglican church for Sunday services and also had Baptisms and Marriages conducted clandestinely. As we shall discover such secret ceremonies were also made punishable by statute c.1606.

As mentioned earlier (See Chapter II) the penal laws against Catholics were somewhat relaxed during the 1630s and the 1639 entry above may be of significance since Carrington was the surname of a Papist family from Harrowden, later, in the eighteenth and nineteenth centuries, to be found at Kings Cliffe. Possibly of greater importance is the 1638 entry recording: 'Michael sonne of John Wright was baptized the twenty fourth day of Februarie'. A confusing marriage licence in the Peterborough records states that; 'Francis Wright of Lowicke married Florence Lingard, daughter of Robert Lingard, rector there. At Slipton on the eighteenth of November 1622.' (But see Appendix E for notes about Wright family of Lowick.)

Our knowledge of the Wright family, based on local sources, is therefore extremely sketchy, but on consulting the extracts from the Peterborough Diocesan Recusant Rolls, deposited in the N.R.O.

[1] *J.Wake ed.. N.R.S., Vol.VII, p.1O.*

in 1967, and backed up by recent research [2], a hazy picture begins to emerge. Illumination of this faded image can only be achieved with patience, some historical insight and a lot of luck.

The Recusant returns for a single year, taken on their own, are not always reliable for a variety of reasons. Sometimes the information was gathered by the churchwardens and clergymen though later records were made by parish constables. One gets the impression that, more often than not, the officers responsible were reluctant to report on their neighbours. Only the most blatant cases were 'presented' [*] and even one attendance at the Anglican church in twelve months might be sufficient to avoid the censure and fines. The thousands of ‘church Papists’ do not get registered and are seldom mentioned.

At this juncture it might be helpful to try to establish how many Catholics there were in England, and particularly in Northamptonshire, circa 1603. Here we have some difficulty as the first official census was not taken until 1801 and the first, and only, religious census not until 1851. Various estimates of the population, in 1600, by social historians, give a total figure for England and Wales at between three and a half million and four million rising to five and a half million by 1700. Obviously there are great problems in attempting to count the number of Catholics at this time because, as already stated, their religion was officially proscribed and they were subject to restrictions and penalties. This means that it is impossible to know what proportion of the population was 'well-affected' (to use a seventeenth century term) towards the old faith because this was not something that would be shouted from the house tops.

We are forced to rely on estimates made at the time by officials and envoys. For example, in 1613 the Papal Nuncio at Brussels stated that there were about 600 priests working in England, and that each missioner served fully 30 families. [3] He suggested a total of 90,000 Catholics but, he noted, these were ones who were bold enough to practise their religion. In 1618 the Spanish ambassador to England, Sarmiento, (later Count of Gondomar) estimated the number of Recusants at 300,000 and the number of Catholics attending Protestant worship as 600,000 out of a total population of 3,600,000. [4] In other words, he thought that one quarter of the people were Catholic at heart but only one twelfth were brave enough to ignore completely the penalties exacted for non-attendance at Protestant, Anglican services and worship regularly using the Roman rites; by attending Mass and receiving the sacraments secretly in private houses, barns and attics.

It is only fair to add that another author, whose work was published in 1975, revised the number of regularly practising Papists downwards to a figure of 40,000 [5] in 1603 rising to 60,000 by 1641.

[2] *Research by Fr.G.Anstruther, O.P. in 1967 and Mrs.J. Minchinton, Archivist in, 1989/90.*

[*] *'presented' = legal term meaning indicted or accused.*

[3] *B. Magee, English Recusants, p. 104 (Quoting from Meyer, England and Catholic Church under Queen Elizabeth, p. 63).*

[4] *Ibid. pp. 106-107 (Quoting from G.Albion, Charles I and Court of Rome, p.13).*

[5] *J.Bossy, English Catholic Community, (1570-1850), pp. 190-193.*

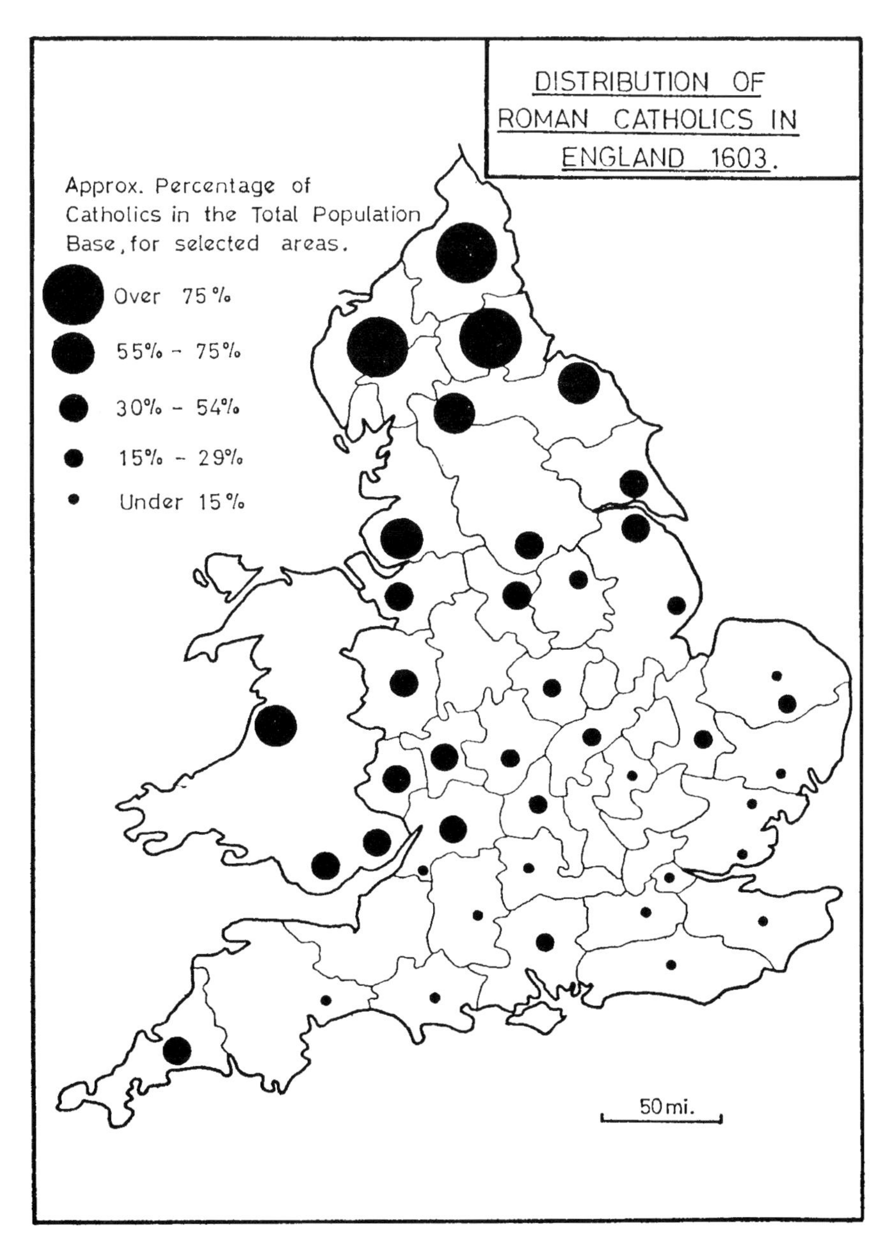

Reproduced by permission from THE GEOGRAPHY OF RELIGION IN ENGLAND by John D. Gay, published in 1971 by Gerald Duckworth & Co. Ltd., London.

These figures are based on the assumption that Protestant persecution during the reign of Elizabeth was more effective than the contemporary authorities believed to be the case. Certainly many villages and towns apparently failed to record any Papists during the early years of the seventeenth century but this is balanced out by those places that registered numbers as high as twenty five per cent of the population, or more. (See below.) It is also necessary to remember that many documents have been lost or destroyed in the almost four-hundred years that have passed. I suspect that the true total of Recusants, men, women and children, is to be found somewhere between the two extremes.[*]

One authority expressed his ideas on the subject like this:- 'It is difficult to account for the perpetual fear (of Papists by Protestants), mounting at times to panic, if the Catholics were an insignificant minority of the nation. Men do not go in fear of an enemy incomparably weaker than themselves; they ignore him. And, whatever else the Protestants of the seventeenth century did, they most certainly did not ignore the Catholics. The atmosphere of the times defies analysis, unless the existence of a very large and vigorous Catholic minority is postulated.'[6]

In the case of Northamptonshire which, at one time, was thought to be a very Puritanical area, we now know that Recusants abounded in the eastern part of the county.[7] There are 650 separate families recorded in the files at Northampton from the period 1577 to 1715. The majority of these are from the period 1600 to 1658 and would indicate a Catholic population of between 2,000 and 3,000 souls.[7a]

The number of gentlemen's houses recognised as Papist, by the High Sheriff, Deputy Lieutenants and Justices of the Peace in 1612/13, from whence they were commanded, by the Privy Council, to seize arms and armour, was over 40.[8] Of these 30 were in the East Division of the county and included the residences of Lord Vaux at Harrowden and Irthlingborough, Lord Mordaunt at Drayton, Sir Thomas Brudenell at Deene and Rushton, Lady Meryall Tresham at Liveden, Messrs, George and John Polton (Poulton) at Desborough, Mr. Arthur Darcy at Great Addington, Mr. Barnard Garter at Brigstock, Mr. Thomas Lawe at Benefield etc., and more particularly in connection with this narrative, the houses of Mr. Edward Preston at Sudborough, Mr. John Stoughton at Lowick and Mr. Alexander Bowker at Slipton.

[*] *Panzani, the papal agent in 1635, suggesed 150,000 open and secret Catholics. (Meyer quoted by G.Davies).*

[6] *B.Magee, English Recusants, p.viii.*

[7] *G. Anstruther, Research deposited at N.R.O., 1967.*

[7a] *J.D.Gay, Geography of Religion in England, p.276, Map 13 Suggests a Catholic population of Northants., in 1603 of between 15 and 29 per cent of total. (See Map).*

[8] *J.Wake, Montague Musters Book, N.R.S. Vol.II. pp.224,226.*

All these homes were centres of Catholic activity and especially the larger ones such as Harrowden Hall, Deene Hall and Drayton House. Drayton was very large, having 60 hearths (= rooms), recorded in 1662, and in respect of this establishment there is a paper, still existing, from Lord Salisbury's collection relating to 1605, at the time of Lord Mordaunt's committal to the Tower of London. (See Chapter II.) The paper contains observations about priests and other Catholics associated with this stately home which, perhaps surprisingly, had entertained King James I and his court on the third of August of the same year:- 'Staughton, Bowker and Halle are known recusants and have sons at seminaries abroad. His (Mordaunt's) house appears to be a receptacle of most dangerous persons, and there is a continual concourse between it and foreign seminaries.' [9]

A spy by the name of William Allen rendered a very full report to the government of the activities in and around this corner of Northamptonshire, 1605/06, which is still extant. [10]
The following is a verbatim account:-

'The priests after named, as seems, have made their common resort to and much abode at the Lord Mordaunt's and at his servants' houses: viz. at Staughton's his steward's and at Bowker's his horse-rider's, where they have often said Mass, as is supposed.

Imprimis, one priest commonly apparelled like a plain countryman called Mr.Baylye;

another called Mr.Androwes, carrying himself in port (bearing) apparel and attendance very gallantly;

two other priests and brothers calling themselves Newports;'

(These were Charles and Richard Newport, sons of John Newport of Ecton, Northamptonshire. Richard, alias Smith, was a secular priest, not a member of a religious order, who had been educated at Rheims and was ordained in Rome in 1599. After a period at Douai he was sent to the English mission during 1602, banished in 1606, returned in 1607 and was again banished. Despite the risks, he came back a third time and was arrested once more towards the end of 1611. On the eighteenth of May 1612 being brought to trial he acknowledged that he was a priest and had been twice banished but said he was guilty of no treason. He also said, "They might condemn Christ himself if he were upon earth." Being found guilty with William Scott O.S.B., another priest, he protested that they could not justly be condemned for neither one nor the other could possibly be a criminal. On Whitsun Eve the two priests were hung drawn and quartered at Tyburn, it being the thirtieth of May 1612. [11] Richard Newport was beatified in Rome on the fifteenth of December 1929.)

[9] *Ibid., Introduction, p.xliii.*

[10] *M.Hodgetts, Gen.Ed. Catholic Record Society, 'Hatfield Calendar' XVII p.626.*

[11] *R.Challoner, Memoirs of Missionary Priests, p.326; Menology of England and Wales, p.245; C.R.S. 34, 74 - Summary from papers at Bishop's House, Northampton.*

The spy's report continues:-

'another priest whose name is not remembered, who is brother to one Francis the aforesaid Staughton's man;

two other priests, the one called Mr. Fynch the other Mr.Lankaster alias Willowbye, both came out of France and had been in Spain in Lent last, shortly after making their repair to the Lady Mordant - marginal note: Finch is commonly at Mr.Darcye's at Luffwick (Lowick) - , and then Lancaster went to Mr.Pryse's of Washingley and into Lincolnshire to Mr. Thimblebye's . . .

It is likewise advertised that though the Lord Mordant's men most of them be reconciled Papists, yet if any of them were privy to the last said treason, that it is likest to be one Nelltrap who now attends his Lord in the Tower;

next one Tuttfeilde (see Chapter I) bred an Oxford scholar and supposed a priest, now or lately attending the Lord Mordant's son; and one Hill who teaches music.

But the Lady Mordant's confessor and resident priest is an old man called Father ---- ; his name is not now remembered.

There came over with Lankaster and Fynch two young gentlemen, George Nelston and Charles Thymblebye, and two of Mr.Pryse's sons from St.Omer's, (the Jesuit college or school in the Spanish Netherlands), landed by Keene at Gravesend.

The first (sic) - named man, Keene, was made much of by Dr.Webb; and such priests as he landed, he landed secretly at or about Rochester on Palm Sunday.'

This document appears only to be an extract from a fuller account and is undated. Yet since we know that Lord Mordaunt was already in the Tower by Friday, the fifteenth of November 1605, the information contained must refer to the latter part of 1605 and probably to 1606 as well.

The importance of this extraordinarily detailed account is not to be underestimated as it confirms Drayton House as a place where Catholic Mass was celebrated regularly with a resident priest. Additionally it establishes that Mass, and the sacraments, were also freely available in Lowick, at Mr. D'Arcy's, at Staughton the steward's house, and in Slipton, at Bowker the horsekeeper's house.

The Drayton estates, during the early years of the seventeenth century, comprised the manors of Lowick, Drayton, Slipton, Islip, Grafton and Great Addington [12] as well as lands in other parishes including Turvey in Bedfordshire previously mentioned as a Recusant centre. (See Chapter II.) The two nearest manors/parishes to Drayton are Lowick and Slipton and, as most of the inhabitants would have had close association with this most Catholic household, it is not surprising to find a large number of Recusants listed in various records.

In Lowick apart from the steward, Staughton, mentioned in the spy's report, there were, between the years 1607 and 1631 a total of 40 separate men and women presented for being Recusants.

[12] *V.C.H. Northants, Vol.3, p. 231.*

Children under 9 are not listed. Based on the Hearth Tax returns of 1662 [13] (35 houses) the total number of inhabitants in 1620 can be estimated at 150. Therefore the proportion of Catholics could have been as high as 33 per cent - a truly staggering statistic. (Appendix E.)

Slipton at that time, and still today, was the smaller of the two villages as a visit to the two medieval churches will soon reveal. The total area is only 825 acres and the population is well under 100. In 1620 one has to suppose a total of about 90 to 100 inhabitants. [*] This figure is partly arrived at by referring to the Hearth Tax returns for 1674 which gives 25 houses. [14] The number of different Papists dwelling in this place during the period 1606 to 1631 taken from the lists of Recusants, amounted to 20 adults. [15] Allowing for children this means that the surprising proportion of 30 per cent of the people, in this hamlet, stayed away from the Anglican church because of their adherence to the 'faith of their fathers'. The numbers are important because in such a small place everyone would know who was not at church. Secrecy would be impossible. On the other hand the large number of Recusants could support one another.

In more detail, the records show that Alexander Bowker, the horse-keeper of Lord Mordaunt, mentioned above, and his wife Anne were presented as Recusants on the thirteenth of June 1605, on the eighteenth of September 1605 and again in 1606, 1607, 1608, 1609. In November 1610, the Recusants at Slipton are listed as Alexander Bowker and Anna, Robert Wright and Margaret, Alexander Bowker junior, Francis, Elizabeth, Katherine and Anne Bowker, Ann Ibbit and Mary Michill. (See Appendix E.)

The first mention of the Wright family is on the twelfth of September 1606 when Robert Wright and Margaret his wife are presented for not coming to church. This occurs again in October 1606 and twice in July 1608. At Oundle on the fourth of February 1608/09 Alexander Bowker and Anna his wife, Robert Wright and his wife and Mary Mitchell, wife of Edward Mitchell, were all presented, 'for Recusants at the least and having not come to the church these 2 yeres past'. Robert Wright was also presented for having 3 or 4 children and, 'wee know not whether they be christnd or not but he had one child borne since he came to our towne within these 2 yeres and that child was christened in our Church of Slipton.' [16] Here it is to be noted that the government had introduced a penalty for clandestine Baptism in 1606.[17]

[13] *N.R.O., Topographical Index.*

(*) The Compton Census of 1676 gives a population of 112. The present population does not show an increase because of the drift from the land during the late 18th, 19th & 20th centuries.

[14] *N.R.O., Topographical Index.*

[15] *N.R.O., Peterborough Diocesan Records, Recusant Rolls etc. Arch. 17, 19, 24, 55.*

[16] *N.R.O., Peterborough Diocesan Records, Arch. 19.*

[17] *J.Bossy, English Catholic Community (1570-1850), p.133.*

Slipton church of St.John the Baptist

Lowick church of St.Peter

Robert was still being presented for Recusancy in early 1612 but on the sixteenth of September that same year, described as a yeoman, he was separately recorded as having taken the 'oath of allegiance' at Kettering. Many others took the oath at this time. The oath had been first promulgated in 1606 (See Chapter II) and most Catholics had refused it on account of the heretical dogmas inherent in its formula. However by 1612 certain of the Catholic secular clergy argued that it was permissible to swear the oath, while having private reservations, to avoid the persecution of one's family. Indeed the secular arch-priest, George Blackwell, took the oath and was deposed by Pope Paul V as a consequence. [(18)]

By 1613 Robert Wright had died but the family are still being recorded as Papists with Margaret, now depicted as a widow, being supported by her sons; Peter (described as a yeoman) and John. Margaret's name appears again in 1617 and in 1618 with her daughter, also Margaret (described as a spinster). The 1613 report is virtually the only documentary evidence, of the young Peter living in Northamptonshire, to back up the statement found in the first biography, written in Latin and published in 1651, [(19)] that he was born at Slipton in 1603 and that his parents were poor, but rich in faith.

Now the fact of Peter being recorded as a Recusant and Yeoman as early as 1613 does not, of necessity, contradict the statement that he was born in 1603. In 1606 the government of King James had passed a law to the effect that all Recusant children of 9 years of age should be Presented with their parents, (Previously the age had been 16.) The description 'Yeoman' is puzzling, at first sight, in view of his age, but seventeenth century usage of the word could have meant either that he was a servant at Drayton House, or simply that he was a 'young man',[(*)] as well as the more usual meaning of small landowner and farmer.

The early biographical sources also mention Robert Wright, Peter's father, dying prematurely and this, as we have seen, is confirmed. There were, it appears from the same derivation, thirteen children born to Peter's parents but this is not unusual at a time when most babies died in infancy. It seems likely that the Wright family were connected in some way to the Drayton estates but in what capacity we do not know.

There is a strong possibility that Alexander Bowker and Robert Wright paid their Recusancy fines together at Oundle and perhaps, but it is only a surmise, Robert was a groom or assistant horsekeeper. He may equally have been a yeoman farmer, with a small holding of land, but this is unlikely as the records, already quoted, mention that the family had not been living in Slipton for very many years.

[(18)] *G.Davies, Early Stuarts, p.208.*

[(19)] *Edward Leedes, S.J. alias E.Courtenay; 'R.P.Petri Writi Sacerdotis Angli e Societ. Iesu MORS, quam ob fidem passus est Londini 29 May 1651.' (see Appendix A)*

[(*)] *Concise Oxford Dictionary*

Death of Robert Wright

The family were certainly not gentry, that is larger landowners, like William Preston another Slipton Recusant, described as 'gent.' in 1628. This family also produced a priest and member of the Society of Jesus born, probably at Slipton, in 1637, ordained in 1661 and who died 1702. [20]

Not being of the more important landowning class has made the task of tracing the origins of this particular Wright family very difficult, if not impossible. The surname is very common in Northamptonshire and indeed in most parts of England. 450 separate references, to this name, are to be found in the index files at the Northamptonshire Record Office and some of these are also Recusant families such as at Eydon, 1626, Kings Sutton, 1605 and Rothwell, 1626. No links have been established with the Slipton Wrights. As Catholic Wright families can also be found in Lincolnshire, Essex, Devon, Yorkshire and many other areas, there is nothing to be gained by pursuing these lines of enquiry.

Almost by chance a will dated the seventeenth day of August 1624 in the name of Robert Lyon the elder of Drayton in the parish of Luffwick (Lowick) has come to light at the N.R.O. [21]. Lord Mordaunt is made sole executor and the major portion of the estate is left to Robert Lyon the younger of Draiton who is almost certainly the Robert Lyon of Slipton named as a Recusant in 1631. Among several smaller bequests is one to (Margaret White' (sic) 'my granddaughter ten shillings". The question remains: was Peter Wright's mother the daughter of Robert Lyon the elder?

On the other hand many priests, when they adopted aliases, used the maiden names of their mothers. Peter used the alias Beale and there were two Recusant families of that surname living in Slipton during the 1620s and another Beal family at Benefield. Margaret Wright and Margarett Bealle [*] are named together in the Subsidy Rolls for 1628 as; 'not receyving the holie Communion by the space of one whole year past'. They were both fined (viii)^{d}. An Ann Beal is recorded living at Slipton, with a larger than average house in 1670. It is doubtful whether further research would reveal much more than this regarding the family name of Peter's mother. (See Appendix E.)

There is another riddle, which may never be solved, and that is to discover where Peter received his early education. From the age of perhaps thirteen, and for a period of about ten years, he worked as a clerk in a solicitor's office in Thrapston, three miles from his birthplace. This in itself was an achievement for a boy from the servant class or possibly yeoman stock. He was certainly very intelligent, with a capacity for hard work and considerable strength of character, as is made evident by his subsequent career. His sermons (See Appendix B) portray a man grounded in the Classics as well as the Scriptures. Where did he obtain his basic knowledge of Latin and Greek?

[20] *Dom. A,Bellenger, English & Welsh Priests (1558-1800), p. 179.*
[21] *Peterborough Will Volume. Ref.C.107a (Original in Latin).*
[*] *Subsidy Rolls = Lists of tax payers and fines and penalties imposed for a variety of offences during reigns of James I and Charles I,*
Record in Isham/Longden MSS. Vol. XXXVIII. N.R.O.

The Nine Arches Bridge, Thrapston

Peter Wright as a lawyer's clerk

One can only assume that his obvious willingness to learn and talent for absorbing knowledge had been spotted by one or another of the many priests that he must have encountered during his childhood. The probability is that the schoolroom at Drayton House, which was inferred in the spy's report as catering for the children of Lord Mordaunt, also accommodated a number of the more promising of the villagers' offspring.

Such a school would have mirrored the one set up at Harrowden Hall in the 1590s by Lady Vaux, and one of the teachers, Tuttfielde, filled the same role in both locations. It is tempting to imagine the child Peter learning his Latin verbs at Drayton but a room in the Bowker residence might have served the same purpose.

The small town of Thrapston, towards which the future martyr wended his way at about the age of 13, was situated close to the River Nene where a medieval bridge enabled travellers, on the rutted highways, leading from Kettering to Huntingdon and Northampton to Peterborough, to cross the frequently flooded meadows dry-shod. A weekly livestock market was held every Tuesday, in the main street, with annual fairs around Michaelmas and the feast of St. James. [22] Although the market had been granted to Baldwin de Vere, Lord of the Manor, as early as 1205, the town had not prospered and the population in the seventeenth century, computed from the Hearth Tax returns of 1669 (122 houses) would only amount to about 500 (the 1801 census gives 675 inhabitants). By the early seventeenth century the Mordaunt family of Drayton, appear to have become Lords of the Manor. Perhaps this connection explains how Peter obtained his employment.

Peter's basic knowledge of classical grammar rules and vocabulary would have been extended by his sojourn in the lawyer's office, as, at the time, all legal documents were still written out in the Latin language. As was usual, in those days, for an apprentice clerk, he lodged on the premises with the solicitor's family and the household being, as is supposed, Protestant, he was forced to attend the Anglican services at the parish church of St. James. It is possible that he temporarily gave up the practice of his faith but more likely that he became a 'church Papist' or 'schismatic'. [*]

There was also in the house a young lady, a relative or perhaps ward of the solicitor, whose charms seem to have captivated the young scribe and there may have been thoughts of matrimony. The attorney eventually became aware of the infatuation and sent his relative away, no doubt to the chagrin of both parties. It is not clear whether this was the occasion for Peter's leaving his employment as a legal clerk but shortly afterwards, as many a young man has done in similar circumstances, he left England and joined one of the various regiments fighting in the war in the Netherlands.

[22] *V.C.H.*

[*] *'schismatic'; seventeenth century word - meaning person who was Catholic at heart but who outwardly conformed to the state religion. (Used this way by John Gerard, S.J. in his auto- biography).*

This would be, we suppose, 1626 or 1627 and at about this time, perhaps earlier, perhaps a little later, he was reconciled to the Catholic faith by the good offices of his sister, who later became a Benedictine nun in Flanders. Some writers refer to Peter being converted to Catholicism but this does not, of necessity, mean that he had ever been a convinced Protestant because, in the sixteenth and seventeenth centuries, the term 'convert' was used to describe one who had returned to the practice of the faith after a period of lapsation as well as for one who had become convinced of the truth of the Catholic religion after being reared in Protestant error.

Now the war, in the territories known as the Lowlands and Flanders, which today comprise Holland, Belgium and north western France, had been started as early as 1565 and was part of the wars of religion sweeping through northern Europe from 1562. In the Low Countries, religious strife also took an a nationalist dimension, since the Calvinist cause, espoused by many in this region, became indistinguishable from the struggle for independence from the rule of Catholic Spain. The whole history of this religious war, as well as the nationalist fight, of the Dutch people of the northernmost provinces under their great leader, William the Silent, is however extremely complicated. At times the struggle was punctuated by acts of extreme violence; as when the Protestants desecrated the Catholic churches throughout the Netherlands in August 1566 and also when Spanish troops sacked Antwerp in 1574.[23]

King Philip II of Spain (husband of Mary Tudor, Queen of England until her death in 1558 - Chapter I) who ruled a vast empire, in Europe and the Americas, from 1556 to his death in 1598, was determined to root out heresy in his dominions particularly in the Netherlands but also in England where he had briefly ruled. In 1581 the Dutch provinces declared their independence from Spanish rule and, about this time, Philip formed a 'grand design' to put Mary, Queen of Scots, on the throne of England, a Spanish puppet on the French throne and also reconquer the Netherlands.

In 1584 the leader of the Dutch rebellion, William of Orange, was assassinated by a Catholic and in the following year Queen Elizabeth of England sent out an army to help the Protestant Netherlands against the Spanish. Two years later Mary, Queen of Scots, was executed (See Chapter I) and Philip II decided to invade England but could not accomplish this plan because of the failure of his armada of ships to make contact with the Spanish army in the Netherlands, commanded by the Duke of Parma.

This failure of the Spanish plan to invade England did not mean defeat for their forces in the southern part of the Lowlands. The area of modern Belgium, apart from Ostend and Bergen-op-Zoom was now firmly in Spanish hands and was to remain so until 1713. Official recognition of the independence of Holland, or the United Provinces as they preferred to be known, did not occur until 1648 at the end of the so-called 'Thirty Years War'.

[23] *V.H.H.Green, Renaissance and Reformation, p.247 & p.250.*

Fighting therefore continued in this area throughout the remaining years of the sixteenth century and well into the next century as well. A truce between Spain and the United Provinces lasted from 1609 to 1621 but was just a breathing space for the various combatants to take stock before the final phase. As mentioned previously, (Chapter II) English volunteers and mercenaries were to be found on the side of the Protestant Dutch right up to the truce of 1609. Some English, Irish and Scottish Catholic volunteers and mercenaries were also to be found on the Spanish side.

After 1621 the situation became even more complicated because, as previously stated, in 1622 the English government of King James I licensed regiments of Catholic volunteers to go out and fight alongside the Spanish army. Then, just over two years later, England declared war on Spain, resuming a conflict that had been broken off in 1604, and an official English army was sent to the aid of the United Provinces, landing at Flushing at the mouth of the River Scheldt. This would be late in 1624 or early 1625. In spite of the fact that this expedition was a disastrous failure, English soldiers continued to find employment as volunteers and mercenaries, on both sides, in a war which soon became little more than a series of protracted and, at times, bloody sieges.

In 1629 the Calvinist United Provinces had some success with the capture of the town of Bois-le-duc but would not grant freedom of worship to the Catholic inhabitants. This intransigence on the part of the Dutch Protestants ensured that the war would continue for another nineteen years. As a Spanish official wrote at the time; 'If the Prince of Orange and the rebels were not kept by their fanatical intolerance from granting liberty of worship and from guaranteeing of churches and Church property to the priesthood, then a union of the loyal provinces with those of the North could not be prevented.' [24] The implication here is that the Spaniards would have agreed to peace and full unity for the whole of the Netherlands if the Calvinists had not been so bigoted and anti-Catholic.

Sometime between the years 1626 and 1628, (the precise date is unknown) Peter Wright decided to become involved in this messy conflict. Most of the commentaries on the life of our martyr seem to imply that he enlisted in the Protestant English army in Holland (United Provinces). [25] To me, this seems extremely unlikely as he would almost certainly have known not only of the existence of the Catholic volunteer regiment, fighting for the Spaniards, raised largely in Northamptonshire, but would probably have met some of the officers and men. These were known to return to England during lulls in the fighting and for recruiting purposes. (See Chapter II.) [25A] We are told that his departure

[24] *Ibid., p.348.*

[25] *D.N.B. et al: "he enlisted in the English army in Holland."*

[25A] *M.E.Finch, Five Northants Families, p. 187:- 'Sir William Tresham (youngest son of Sir Thomas) returned from Flanders in 1626, obeying Charles I's command to register his name. In 1627, despite being a Catholic, he was nominated a captain in the army to fight against France under the Duke of Buckingham, but, 1628-29, he went back to Flanders and fought for Spain until his death in 1639.'*

was precipitate. What is more natural than that he should have gone to the Netherlands with a returning recruitment officer being lured by tales of adventure and the glamour of fighting, for a righteous cause.There is, of course, the possibility that he either joined the Protestant side by mistake or, in his naivety, was duped into joining the army of the United Provinces while his sympathies lay with the Catholics in the South. Unfortunately we have not enough information about this period of Peter's life to be certain of exactly what did happen.

Many men, in more recent times, have joined, for example, the French Foreign Legion and soon become disillusioned with the life. In the seventeenth century warfare was not the organised, disciplined, and stage-managed affair that twentieth century conflicts have become; it was often difficult to distinguish friend from foe. As uniforms were a rarity different scarves, arm-bands or plumes were worn to identify the separate armies, as in the Civil Wars in England. The war in the Lowlands was a nationalist war, a religious war and also a civil war with all the ingredients for a particularly vicious conflict. Soldiers were seldom paid regularly and, more often than not, expected to live off the country which meant pillaging the local inhabitants for food and other supplies. The sack of Antwerp, mentioned earlier, had been caused by the failure of the Spanish authorities to pay troops their wages on time.

It would not be surprising to find that, after a period of trying to be a good soldier and seeing one's comrades killed, wounded or dying from disease, apparently fruitlessly, a volunteer might wish to have no more of it and desert in the dead of night. Such defections were commonplace in the wars of the seventeenth century.

Peter Wright's earliest biographer [26], however, tells a different story which is that this unlikely soldier could not bear the licentiousness of army life and its depravity and left in broad daylight, rowing or swimming across the River Scheldt, under a hail of bullets. He had only been involved in this conflict for one month when, "he fled to a Catholic region near Santulier, where some Spanish regiments were, in order to fight in the Church's camp."

There is enough detail in this extract for us to believe that the information came from Peter himself but there is also sufficient ambiguity to cause us to be left in some doubt about the exact sequence of events in this whole episode. We have no way of verifying either dates or facts.

Bishop Challoner [27], writing in the eighteenth century, glosses over this unsatisfactory chapter and suggests, somewhat surprisingly, that the future martyr's intention, at this time, was to make a pilgrimage to Rome. More dramatically, it seems, from earlier sources, Peter's journey through the Flanders and Brabant countryside was not at all easy. As he approached Brussels, he was attacked by thieves who stole his money and some of his clothes.

[26] *Edward Leedes alias Courtnay, Petri Writi - MORS, pp. 134-145 (Translation by Fr. J. Koenig, 1990).*
[27] *Richard Challoner, Memoirs of Missionary Priests, (1924 ed.) p.499.*

Peter Wright crossing the
River Scheldt under fire

Peter Wright being robbed

Fortunately, he met an English Catholic gentleman, [*] whose name is not revealed, who helped him and probably directed his footsteps towards the College of the Society of Jesus in Liege. Whether it was by design that he reached this haven or a happy accident is again unknown but, it appears, many of the priests that he met here and elsewhere in Europe knew Northamptonshire and some had even met his parents. He was among friends.

At Liege Peter's Catholic faith was greatly strengthened by the prayerful and efficient instruction of the Jesuit fathers. Quite obviously he had already made up his mind to became a member of this religious society and in a few months he was sent on to Ghent, which housed a Flemish Jesuit College. Eventually, however, it would be necessary to spend two years in the Jesuit novitiate. The nearest college/seminary for this purpose was in the town of Watten in Flanders where it had been established in 1624, remaining there until 1766.

Watten was about five miles from St.Omer and housed a preparatory School for the English college which had been founded in the latter place in 1593. The area was within the Spanish Netherlands during the early part of the seventeenth century but was ceded to France in 1659. The local inhabitants were suspicious of the English schools perhaps fearing they contained spies. In this their fears were partly justified because the English governments of Elizabeth I and James I had indeed infiltrated men into these seminaries whose job was to report on the Catholic boys and men who were receiving an academic and religious training so that, if they became priests, they could be apprehended on their return to England. It was also against English law for families to send their sons abroad, for a specifically Catholic education, yet for two hundred years the tradition was maintained and the present day Catholic schools of St. Edmund's, Ware, Hertfordshire and Stonyhurst, Lancashire are the direct descendants of these academies. Only at the time of the French Revolution was a return to England permitted. [28]

Peter arrived in this hallowed corner sometime in 1629 and threw himself wholeheartedly into his studies. This period of concentrated prayer and learning settled and disciplined his rather turbulent nature. He became a thorough man of God whose chief delight was to go out into the local villages teaching the catechism of the Catholic faith to the children.

The question has to be posed; did our martyr leave England with the intention of joining the Jesuit order but somehow got mixed up with the fighting taking place in the area around the mouth of the River Scheldt? To my mind, the probability is that the idea of becoming a priest, rather than a soldier, was uppermost in Peter's thinking from the very outset of his journey to the Netherlands.

It is particularly unfortunate that none of the early accounts throw any light on the subject of Peter's real objective or goal at the time when he left Northamptonshire. However, my theory of his being determined to become a religious, even before his departure for the Continent, could be substantiated by the short length of time it took to persuade the Jesuit fathers of his worthiness. This is specially remarkable in view of the thoroughness with which the Society of Jesus conducted (and still conducts) its affairs as will become apparent in the next chapter.

[*] *Peter was advised by the unknown "Samaritan" to make a pilgrimage to Rome and supplied with clothes, shoes, cap, pilgrim's staff and a supply of silver money. Cf. Foley Vol.II, p.508.*
[28] *J.Gerard, S.J. "Stonyhurst College", Centenary Record.*

Chapter IV

The Society of Jesus, Jesuits in England and in Northamptonshire.

The Society of Jesus, a religious order of 'regular' [*] clerics, was formally approved by Pope Paul III in his bull, 'Regimini Militantis Ecclesiae' in September 1540; that is twenty years after Martin Luther's initiation of Protestantism, but it would be an error to suppose that the Society was founded merely to counter Protestant ideas and innovations. [1] Many other new religious orders of men and women also began during the sixteenth and seventeenth centuries, such as the Barnabites, Theatines, Oratorians, Vincentians for men and the Ursulines, Sisters of Charity and Mary Ward nuns for women. All these complemented the many orders of contemplative monks and nuns, as well as the mendicant preaching and teaching friars that had been such a feature of late medieval Catholic life; and continued to thrive in Europe despite the catastrophic destruction of English religious orders wrought by Henry VIII and Thomas Cromwell.

A renewal of European Catholicism, now usually referred to as the 'Catholic Reformation' (the phrase, 'Counter Reformation', so beloved by nineteenth century Protestant historians, being outmoded) had already begun before the Protestant revolt took root or made any headway. [2] More importantly, the establishment of the new orders, referred to above, proved the old (Roman) Church to be still vibrant and capable of fresh growth. [3] Movements of spiritual revival in Italy and Spain during the fifteenth century were echoed in England and the fruits are still to be seen in the plethora of churches built and rebuilt in the century up to the Henrician Reformation which began in 1534. (There were almost no new churches built during the next hundred years.) Local evidence is provided by the church of St. Peter, Lowick where a chapel was erected in 1467 and the tower completed with bells c.1500. For further testimony, the book of wills circa 1510 to 1558 compiled by R.M.Serjeantson and H.I.Longden makes quite plain the piety and devotion of the people in the Northamptonshire towns and villages, particularly prior to 1540. (See also 'Stripping of the Altars' by E.Duffy quoted in Chapter I.)

However, if the spiritual state of the majority of Catholics, at the beginning of the sixteenth century, was by no means so degenerate as has been generally maintained by earlier Protestant historians, it is an established fact that the hierarchy and the government of the Church was in a state of grave disorder, and failed to find a remedy for the worst abuses, until the Council of Trent completed its work in 1563.

[*] *regular = living under a rule as opposed to the 'secular' priesthood.*
[1] *K.O.Evennett, New Cambridge Mod. Hist., Vol.II, p.298.*
[2] *C.Dawson, Dividing of Christendom, p.141 (quotes Janelle and Christiani) and N.S.Davidson, The Counter Reformation, p.2 (quotes Evennett, Delumeau and Bossy).*
[3] *G.R.Elton, The Reformation, New Cambridge Mod.Hist.Vol.II,p.3.*

Members of the Society of Jesus, commonly known as Jesuits, were to be closely involved in the deliberations of the Council; but their importance and impact on the Church, and the world in general, was, and remains today, far more significant than as mere theological disputants. The Society was founded by a former Spanish soldier, Don Inigo Lopez de Loyola, who later adopted the name Ignatius. He was born in the Basque region in 1491 and walked with a pronounced limp after being struck by a cannon ball at the siege of Pamplona in May 1521. Surgery was primitive in the sixteenth century and the young soldier's bones had to be broken and reset when he reached his ancestral home. We are told that during the operation, without anaesthetic, as was the custom, he did not utter a single word merely clenching his fist. [4] He was nearly at death's door but submitted to a third operation, to remove a stump of bone, after which his convalescence lasted many months. During this enforced idleness he read books to relieve the boredom, two of which profoundly influenced his attitude to life. The first was a 'Life of Christ' by a German Carthusian monk and the second a work entitled 'Lives of the Saints' by a thirteenth century, Italian Dominican friar.

When his wounds eventually healed, he was a changed man determined to consecrate the rest of his life to the service of God and the Blessed Virgin. In true Catholic style, he first journeyed to the shrine of Our Lady of Montserrat in Catalonia, and after making a full confession of his sins, dedicated himself in an all-night vigil, before the holy statue, to a new life of sorrow for his sins and service to the Church of God. Not content with this, he exchanged his aristocratic clothing with the rags of a beggar and spent the next eight months in the town of Manresa where he submitted to harsh penances, had a series of spiritual experiences and formed the ideas which later developed into his 'Spiritual Exercises'. These Exercises were later published as a manual for devotion and renewal of faith. They could last up to four weeks, being incorporated into Jesuit training and also be used as a retreat course for anyone, male or female.

A woman who met the future Saint Ignatius in 1522, on the road to Manresa described him thus, 'a poor man dressed all in sackcloth as if he were on pilgrimage, not very old, but pale and red-haired. His face was very handsome and serious, and above all he showed great modesty of the eyes, hardly raising his eyes from the ground. His walk was very tired, limping with the right foot'.[5]

A pilgrimage was indeed made to Jerusalem in 1523, crossing Italy alone and bare-footed. He first needed to obtain the Pope's permission and having received the necessary authorisation, finally reached his goal in September. The Franciscan friars, traditional guardians of the Holy Places, would not allow Ignatius to remain with them or join them, for fear of Turkish [*] reprisals and so he returned to Venice after a terrible sea crossing lasting two and a half months.

[4] *P.Caraman, Ignatius Loyola, p.25.*
[5] *Ibid., p.37.*
[*] *Turkey ruled Palestine at this time and until 1917.*

Gradually his ideal of service to God widened, and he felt the desire to give to others his knowledge of the way to God, but first he realised that he needed a more formal education. Arriving back in Barcelona, he discovered friends were prepared to give him accommodation while he took lessons in Latin grammar. Leaving Barcelona he continued his studies at Alcala and then Salamanca but everywhere he went men and women gathered round to be instructed in religion and he tried to direct them according to his 'Spiritual Exercises'. Since he was still a mere layman, not a cleric, the Church authorities, at one time, put him in prison until he could prove that his teaching was orthodox.

In March 1528, this still-limping former soldier, enrolled at the college of Montaigu on the hill of Saint Genevieve in Paris. [6] The University of Paris, which formed a city within a city, was one of the oldest universities of Europe, founded circa 1200, and it was here that Ignatius studied for seven years gathering round himself like-minded disciples who were destined to become the founders of the Society of Jesus.

On the feast of the Assumption of Our Lady in 1534 at Montmartre, Ignatius Loyola with six others including Francis Xavier (later to be canonised), took a famous vow by which they dedicated their lives in poverty and chastity to the service of God, either in the Holy Land or, if this proved to be impossible, by offering their services to the Pope. Meeting up again in 1537 in Venice, they waited for a boat and permission to allow them to journey to Palestine. Unfortunately for them, but happily for the Church, war had broken out between the Turks and the Venetians and no transport was available. After some months debate, these learned men, who had all obtained Master of Arts degrees and were well grounded in theology, [7] were ordained priests by the Bishop of Arbe in the Dalmatian part of Venetia.

The next step was to seek the authority to remain united, add a vow of obedience to the previously taken vows and form a new order which would be specifically employed by the Pope in whatever way he wished. 1539 was not an auspicious time for a new foundation of 'regular' clerics and the group had enemies at the papal court - perhaps they were too religious. The Romans had indeed been astounded by the austere way of life of this band of previous unknowns who wore no religious habit, apart from a black cassock, but preached fearless, inspiring sermons and not just in Advent or Lent, as was the custom.

Their obvious piety and sincerity deeply impressed Pope Paul III together with some influential advisers, and the little band's proposals were accepted with the proviso that the new Society's membership should be limited to 60. Ignatius was elected general of the 'Company' (his favourite description) which was destined to grow, in a surprisingly short time, into the largest of the new orders of the Catholic Reformation.

[6] *Ibid., p.75.*

[7] *Ibid., p.103*

Perhaps this growth was because the Jesuits were devoted clerics and highly organised. They were the most Roman because the 'Company's' headquarters were in Rome where the founder lived until his death in 1556. By this time Pope Paul's original stricture had been rescinded and there were over 1,000 Jesuits (of all grades) distributed among 13 provinces. Sixty years later the Society had over 13,000 members with 32 provinces and by 1679 17,600 men (women were never allowed to join) in 35 provinces [8] worked in all five continents. [*]

How had the Society achieved such success? There were many reasons for this, not least the rejection of monastic-like common recitation of the office and choir singing, which enabled the Jesuits to keep their wills and minds fixed on active tasks. These tasks were preaching, teaching, retreat giving, administration of the sacraments and the corporal works of mercy. Teaching boys the truths of Christianity was not, at first, seen as a primary task, but before many years had passed schools were founded at Watten and St.Omer, previously mentioned. Colleges of higher learning sprang up naturally, Louvain was one. Others were under their direction, as was the case with the Venerable English College in Rome, where they assisted in the long training of clerics who aspired to be accepted into the Order or simply wanted to be ordained as secular priests.

One of the most revolutionary features of this organisation was the thoroughness of the preparation of candidates desiring to become Jesuits. The intending entrant had first to be examined according to the directions given in the written constitution, following which, if character and motivation were deemed satisfactory, there ensued a two year novitiate (probation). This was twice as long as normal religious procedure and included, quite radically, a period of service in a hospital, or other charitable institution, and the making of a pilgrimage, usually barefoot, begging for alms on the way. Between the novitiate, and the final profession of the three vows of chastity, poverty and obedience, an indefinite period of extended education known as the scholasticate was expected. This included studies in humanities, philosophy and theology with perhaps employment in preaching and charitable works.

On being accepted for membership of the Society the aspirant was usually ordained priest and then asked to undergo a second spiritual novitiate known as the 'third probation' or 'tertianship'. Finally on being incorporated into the fellowship, in one of three ways, some were allowed to take the fourth vow of direct personal obedience to the Pope should he wish to send them to work in foreign missions.

In 1556 out of about 1,000 members only 43 had been admitted to the fourth vow. [9] The gradation of members also included lay-brothers (not ordained priests) known as temporal

[8] *J.J.Sacrisbrick, Jesuits and the Catholic Reformation, p.6*

[*] *There were approximately 23,500 Jesuits working for the Church in 1995,*

[9] *H.O.Evennett, New Cambridge Mod.Hist,Vol.II, pp.294-295.*

co-adjutors. Ultimate power and interpretation of the constitutions lay with a general congregation of the fathers professed of the fourth vow but this body did not meet very often or to any regular timetable. Thus the organisation, though based on rigid and exemplary training, was not hidebound by monastic regulations and Jesuits were free to work in ways which accorded with the circumstances in which they found themselves. Because of the nature of their establishment and rigorous training, groups of Fathers were very soon active in the field of education; a college for humanities was set up at Goa (India) as early as 1545 and a boys' college opened at Messina (Sicily) in 1548. Missions to the infidels (Turks and Arabs) and other heathen lands (Asia, Africa and America) were undertaken with some remarkable successes.

For the purposes of this narrative, however, the fight against Protestantism in northern Europe has to be more pertinent. It is not surprising to find the first Jesuit mission to England being organised soon after the execution of the secular priest Cuthbert Mayne in November 1577. (See Chapter I.)

In that same year fifty young Englishmen arrived in Douai, to train for the Catholic priesthood, hoping eventually to be able to return to their homeland and provide help for the Marian clergy [*] as well as the other so-called 'seminary' priests, who were already ministering to their persecuted fellow countrymen. A report from Rheims (where the college at Douai was to move from 1578 to 1593) stated:-

"Many Englishmen this year have been enrolled in various religious orders. About twelve have joined the Society of the most holy name of Jesus with the purpose and hope that, at length, even that Society will visit the afflicted English vineyard and begin cultivating it by its labours, a consummation which all Catholics there desire and many also have asked for by letter." [10]

The word 'even' needs some explanation, but simply means that the English Jesuits, at the time, were over-committed in other parts of the world. For example, Thomas Stevens sailed for Goa in 1579, William Good went to Stockholm in 1577 and William Weston was sent to Spain in 1576. Nevertheless, when, in early 1580, a party of perhaps fourteen men left Rome to join the English mission, two Jesuit priests and one lay-brother were included. The whole enterprise was known to the spies of Elizabeth I's government who termed it a 'Jesuit invasion'. [11] This tells us more about the reputation that the members of the Society had already achieved in Europe than the realities of the situation in England. States already influenced by a Jesuit presence included Bavaria, Bohemia, Hungary, Poland, Lithuania, Moravia, Transylvania, Sweden, Switzerland, the Rhineland at Mainz and Cologne and, of course, in France and Flanders where the arrival of the fathers in a city or province could transform its religious life. [12]

[*] *Marian clergy = priests ordained during Mary's reign who refused to accept the Elizabethan religious regime or enforced Protestantism.*

[10] *B.Basset , The English Jesuits, p.29 (Quoting C.R.S.Vol.2, p.78).*

[11] *E.E.Reynolds, Roman Catholic Church, p.239.*

[12] *J.J.Scarisbrick, Jesuits and Catholic Reformation, p.13.*

Without any doubt the English Jesuits returning to their native land were remarkable men. The leader, Robert Parsons (or Persons), a distinguished scholar, fellow of Balliol College, Oxford, tutor, bursar and dean had been received into the Catholic Church at Louvain in 1574. He started printing presses, during his mission, in order to disseminate carefully worded answers to Protestant Anglican errors. The first press was established at Barking, east of London, but when this became known to the authorities it was moved to Stonor near Henley-on-Thames. Through these means and also by his pastoral endeavours many were brought back to the practice of their religion. A devotional work, 'The Christian Directory' which he had published in Rouen in 1582 was read by Catholics and Protestants alike, with fifteen Protestant editions before his death in 1610. Being forced to leave England, because of the constant harassment by government pursuivants, he founded the Jesuit College at St.Omer in 1593, having previously started a school for the sons of English Catholics at Eu.

The lay-brother, Ralph Emerson, was short in stature but with a very brave heart which was needed to withstand the many years of prison that he was destined to undergo. He arrived back in England on the twenty-fifth of June 1580, disguised as the servant of a supposed diamond merchant, Mr. Edmonds. The latter's jewels, however, were of a different kind because, although accused, when landing at Dover, of being Gabriel Allen, brother of William Allen (founder of Douai) he was, in fact, the foremost rhetorician and Latin scholar of the day, Edmund Campion. Born in 1540, he became the leading orator of his generation, chosen, as a schoolboy to deliver a speech of welcome at Queen Mary's entry into London in 1553, he was again chosen to present a Latin address when Queen Elizabeth visited Oxford in 1566. Not long after this Campion was engaged as tutor to Lord Vaux's nine year old son at Harrowden in Northamptonshire. [13] Perhaps his stay in this most Catholic household was the turning point of his career because in August 1569, he refused to preach no-popery sermons at St.Paul's Cross in Oxford although he was by then an ordained Anglican curate.

By February 1573, he had arrived in Rome via Douai; accepted some months later as a Jesuit novice, his novitiate was spent in Prague, Brunn and again Prague where, after ordination, until 1579 he taught at the university as Professor of Rhetoric. Later, on being summoned to Rome, he travelled south, mainly on foot, and then north again to England where he and his companions were to minister to those souls who remained faithful to the Roman Church. Although these Jesuit fathers would converse with Catholics who had given up the practice of their religion, through fear or ignorance, their first duty was to take the sacraments to those who desired to receive them. They were forbidden, by their Order, to involve themselves in questions of state or send back political reports. [14]

[13] *G.Anstruther, Vaux of Harrowden, p.100.*
[14] *E.Waugh, Edmund Campion, p.80.*

After reaching London the two priests parted company, with Persons making a tour of Northamptonshire, Derbyshire, Worcestershire and Gloucestershire while Campion worked in Berkshire and Oxfordshire; later moving to Lancashire and Yorkshire. Government spies and pursuivants were everywhere and yet for over twelve months these brave men were able to perform their mission tasks successfully, although not without considerable personal danger. Campion's own words, in an excerpt from a letter written to the Father General in Rome, best describe the difficulties [(15)], "I cannot long escape the hands of the heretics; the enemies have so many eyes, so many tongues, so many scouts and crafts, I am in apparel to myself very ridiculous; I often change it and my name also, I read letters some-times myself ... that Campion is taken, ... At the very writing hereof the persecution rages most cruelly. The house where I am is sad, no talk but of death, flight, prison, or spoil of their friends; nevertheless they proceed with courage."

On the seventeenth of July 1581, Campion's prophecy was fulfilled and he was captured while at Lyford Grange in Berkshire. Eliott, the one who betrayed him to the local magistrates, had actually attended the Mass, by pretending to be a Papist, and took notes on the sermon to be used in evidence. The end of July found Campion incarcerated in the dungeon of the Tower of London known as 'Little Ease', where he was examined under torture, by one Norton, the rackmaster, on the orders of the Privy Council. This questioning accompanied by the infliction of severe pain occurred on three, perhaps five, occasions and was so ruthless that even at the time of his execution, on the first of December, it was observed that his finger and toe nails were missing. [(16)]

Why was the government of Queen Elizabeth so determined to break the will of the first Jesuit priest to be apprehended? Perhaps the answer lay in his fame as an Oxford scholar who had become a Jesuit and might influence others, but the more likely reason was the desire to prove the mission to be politically motivated. This could not be achieved but did not prevent all sorts of calumnies being spread about Campion and his alleged 'confessions'. Catholic gentlemen up and down the country were arrested, examined and detained simply because, it was said, Campion had admitted to staying in their houses. In Northamptonshire Lord Vaux, Sir Thomas Tresham, Sir Edward Griffin of Dingley and Sir William Catesby all suffered imprisonment and fines.

Many secular priests were also taken, imprisoned, tortured and put to death about this time; men like Everard Hanse, from Northamptonshire (mentioned in Chapter I), Ralph Sherwin, Alexander Briant (admitted to the Society of Jesus in prison), John Paine (born in Peterborough?), Thomas Ford, John Shert, Robert Johnson, William Filby, Luke Kirby, Laurence Richardson and also another Jesuit, Thomas Cottam. The English government, however, had other and particular causes to denigrate the character of Edmund Campion. Firstly, the affair at Oxford, where 400 copies of his

[(15)] *G.Anstruther, Vaux of Harrowden, p.114 (Quoting from Simpson, p.247).*
[(16)] *Ibid., p.116.*

book, ‘Decem Rationes’ (Ten Reasons) - printed on Person’s press at Stonor had been placed on the benches of St.Mary’s church, as a denial of Lutheran and Calvinist errors, to confound the Protestant divines, and which included the sentence, ‘There will come, Elizabeth, the day that will show thee clearly which have loved thee, the Society of Jesus or the offspring of Luther.’ [17] Secondly, the matter of the future martyr’s statement of faith and intent, including a challenge to debate the religious questions with University Dons and the leaders of English society, which became known as 'Campion’s Brag.’ One passage of the latter needs quoting because it explains how the Jesuits came to be so feared by the Elizabethan Protestant government authorities:

"And touching Our Society, be it known unto you that we have made a league - all the Jesuits of the world - whose succession and multitude must over-reach all the practices of England ... cheerfully to carry the cross you shall lay upon us and never to despair of your recovery while we have a man left to enjoy your Tyburn, to be racked with your torments or to be consumed with your prisons. The expense is reckoned, the enterprise is begun; it is of God; it cannot be withstood. So the faith was planted, so it must be restored." [18]

Debates did take place in the Tower of London with a tortured Campion, on one side, forced to speak from memory, without notes, and as adversaries Protestant clergymen, such as the Deans of St.Paul’s and Windsor accompanied by chaplains, clerks and a table littered with books and papers. There were four such conferences but the government dare not publish the transcripts until two years later and then only with Campion's answers abbreviated. His fame, however, was so widespread that although he and others arrested, at the time, were first indicted on a charge arising from the recently passed Act of Persuasions, which made it High Treason to reconcile or be reconciled to the Romish Religion, this was not deemed enough. In fact, public opinion in England might well have refused to accept any verdict which condemned a man merely on religious grounds. So a fresh and entirely fictitious indictment was drawn up which suggested that, between March and April 1580, the prisoners had formed a conspiracy to murder queen Elizabeth, had exhorted foreigners to invade the country and that the Jesuits came to England to stir up rebellion.

Preposterous though these charges were, it was easy enough for paid informers and spies to put words into the mouths of the defendants which they could only deny. In Campion’s case no evidence was offered about the alleged detailed plot to kill the Queen. This sham trial, nevertheless, ended with the expected guilty verdicts and three of the accused, including Campion, were hung, drawn and quartered at Tyburn on the first of December 1581. Part of the speech which this great Elizabethan made to the court is worth recording here:

[17] *E.Waugh, Edmund Campion, p.139 & A.Butler, Lives of the Saints, Vol.V, p.439.*
[18] *B.Basset, English Jesuits, p.54 & E.Waugh, Edmund Campion, Appendix.*

"The only thing that we have now to say is, that if our religion do make us traitors, we are worthy to be condemned; but otherwise are, and have been, as good subjects as ever the Queen had. In condemning us you condemn all your own ancestors - all ancient priests, bishops and kings - all that was once the glory of England, the island of saints, and the most devoted child of the See of Peter. For what have we taught, however you may qualify it with the odious name of treason, that they did not uniformly teach? To be condemned with these lights not of England only, but of the world - by their degenerate descendants, is both gladness and glory to us." [19]

Among the English martyrs Edmund Campion's bravery and heroic affirmation of his faith has stood out like a beacon to provide inspiration for succeeding generations. It is not surprising to find his name among the list of canonised saints and the details included here are to provide an example of Catholic devotion and Jesuit fortitude occurring just twenty two years before the birth of Peter Wright.

After 1581, with Campion dead and Persons abroad, Jasper Heywood remained for three years as temporary superior of the Jesuit mission which now consisted only of himself. This priest found himself at loggerheads with the Catholics he was ministering to over the question of abstinence from eating meat on certain days of the year. The strict medieval rule had been mitigated on the continent of Europe but English Catholics were very conservative and some demanded that their pastor be withdrawn. Instead of this, he was captured by government agents and confined to the Tower of London. When eventually banished into exile, he complained bitterly and demanded that he should be taken back to England, stand trial and die for his faith.

William Weston arrived back on his native soil in 1584, landing on a remote part of the Norfolk coast. In 1611, at the request of his superior, he wrote an autobiography, which was a remarkable feat for a man who had been imprisoned from 1586 to 1603 and who was rendered almost blind as a result of his privations. He reported the addition, to the English mission, of two more Jesuit Fathers, Henry Garnet (See Chapter II) and Robert Southwell. Also about this time, it appears, the Vaux family (See Chapters I & II) were responsible for setting up a network of private houses, across the country, which could offer shelter as well as Mass centres for Jesuits and secular priests alike. [20] At Hurleyford, near Marlow, Mass was celebrated with elaborate ritual to music composed by William Byrd, the Catholic composer known to the Elizabethan court but protected because of his talents.

Henry Garnet became the Jesuit superior from his landing until his capture and execution in 1606. (See Chapter II.) Gradually the Society increased its numbers in England with men like John Gerard and Edward Oldcorne arriving in 1588 and Richard Holtby and John Currie in 1590. By 1593 eighteen priests were at work although four were in prison. Seventeen years later, and despite the

[19] *E.Waugh, Edmund Campion, pp. 190-191.*
[20] *B.Basset, English Jesuits, pp. 103-106, & G. Anstruther, Vaux of Harrowden.*

banishments following the 'Gunpowder Plot', forty three Fathers were ministering throughout the country. This number increased to one hundred and nine in 1620 with an equal amount training abroad mostly in Flanders. By 1633 the figure of three hundred and sixty four had been reached and this level was maintained for another hundred years despite continuing persecution.

The tremendous popularity which the Society possessed among those training for the priesthood needs some further explanation. It was not that the Jesuits had a monopoly of virtue despite the heroic martyrdom of men like Edmund Campion, Robert Southwell and Henry Walpole. Of 182 men and women executed as Catholics, during the reign of Queen Elizabeth, eleven, at most, could be classed as Jesuits. It was rather that, although the government made them out to be bogey-men, they were orthodox to the core and thoroughly Roman. Their long training did not cease when they arrived in the mission field, because the 'Spiritual exercises' of St.Ignatius were still carried out on an annual basis. Henry Garnet, as superior, was responsible for organising the spiritual development of members of the Society in England as well as arranging their mission centres. He was scrupulous and methodical and most of what we know about individual martyrs, lay people, secular priests, as well as Jesuit fathers, is from his reports to Robert Persons who had overall control over Society affairs in England from his various bases in Europe.

There were, of course, moral dangers for all priests required to lead dangerous, lonely and celibate lives. Some naturally fell by the wayside but, although the Jesuits also had their failures, the general standard among the missioners was particularly high. In order to strengthen them spiritually regular meetings were held which afforded time for confessions and the renewal of vows. At one such gathering, in October 1591, at Baddesley Clinton, Warwickshire, very early in the morning, when the Jesuits were in chapel, the priest-hunters arrived. Disaster was averted by the young Anne Vaux, sister of the lady of the house, still in night attire, arguing with the searchers while all the priests and some others hid in the specially constructed hides which Nicholas Owen (See Chapter II) had devised within the drainage system. [21]

One Jesuit, fortunately not involved in the above affair, Thomas Lister, suffered from claustrophobia and had a very difficult time as a consequence, but because of Henry Garnet's kindness and understanding was able to work happily in the Oxford district for twenty five years. Another, who certainly did not suffer from any kind of fear, was John Gerard whose 'Autobiography of a Hunted Priest', written in 1609, is still a best seller. He was careful to preserve the anonymity of those Catholics who might still be in danger as he described, in an almost racy style, the adventurous life of a mission priest. Much of his time was spent in Northamptonshire (See Chapter 1) after being sent

[21] *B. Basset, English Jesuits,p.124;*
P. Caraman, J.Gerard's autobiography pp.63-69 & Appendix B;
G. Anstruther, Vaux of Harrowden, pp.186-191.

as chaplain to the young, recently widowed, Elizabeth Vaux, and her six small children, at Harrowden. He writes: "When I was domiciled in my new residence, I began by degrees to wean my hostess' mind from excessive grief; showing how that we ought to mourn moderately only over our dead, and not to grieve like those who have no hope.... I thus gradually brought her to change that old style of grief for a more worthy one..." [22]

Gerard, of aristocratic stock from Etwall in Derbyshire, was a born leader, welcome in any part of England, who never had to seek lodgings in an inn. When put into prison, he converted two of the warders as well as many fellow prisoners. So many people came to see him in the 'Clink' that he thought he probably did more good there than when free. [23] Many schismatics, who feared to declare their Catholic faith, were strengthened by encounters with Gerard. Some went on to become priests, like Francis Page who was taken, by his Catholic girl friend, to meet the kind Jesuit in prison.

This courageous member of the Society of Jesus delighted in outwitting magistrates and prison officers using ten aliases in all. He was tortured unmercifully by Topcliffe, being suspended from the roof of the racking chamber, by manacles attached to his wrists, for hours and days on end; yet he betrayed no one and refused to answer all the trick questions put to him. While still suffering from the effects of the rack-master's 'medicine' he, together with a layman, John Arden, escaped from the Tower of London, crossing the moat and curtain wall by sliding down a rope which had been provided by friends on the outside. The break-out occurred on the fifth of October 1597, and could not have taken place without the connivance of a gaoler, who also fled and later became a Catholic.

Gerard was never captured again but he had some very close calls and none more so than when hiding at Harrowden Hall, in one of Nicholas Owen's cleverly constructed secret places, on the twelfth of November 1605. (See Chapter II.) He writes, 'I could sit down all right but there was hardly room to stand. However, I did not go hungry, for every night food was brought to me secretly. At the end of four or five days, when the rigours of the search had relaxed slightly my friends came at night and took me out and warmed me by a fire. It was winter time, just before Christmas. After nine days the search party withdrew. They thought I could not possibly have been there all that time without being discovered." [24] Eluding all pursuit, the excellent and resourceful priest crossed the seas to write his memoirs and died, at peace, in 1637.

Gerard's superior, Henry Garnet, was not so lucky and was executed for alleged complicity in the 'Gunpowder Plot'. (See Chapter II.) These allegations, unfortunately, were not the only ones with which the Jesuits had to contend. Certain secular priests, the deranged William Watson was one,

[22] *P. Caraman, Translation of Autobiography of Hunted Priest, p.176, & G.Anstuther, Vaux of Harrowden, pp. 238-39.*

[23] *B.Basset, English Jesuits, p.129.*

[24] *P. Caraman, Translation of Autobiography of a Hunted priest, pp.288-9*
M.Hodgetts, Secret Hiding Places, p.142 etc.

began, circa the 1590s, through jealousy, to circulate rumours to the detriment of the Society of Jesus. Two main suggestions were made; firstly, that the Jesuit Fathers were against the appointment of a Catholic Bishop for fear of losing influence and secondly, that they only ministered to rich Catholics to obtain money for themselves. To these calumnies the Protestant government of England added the charge of 'equivocation' [*] implying that Jesuits only told the truth when it suited their purposes.

As already related, these imputations, though damaging, and even believed today, by some misguided individuals, did not prevent the continued growth of the Society. Many new English recruits were obtained during the seventeenth century. (See Appendix D for Northamptonshire names.) However, from 1605, a grey anonymity shrouded the English Jesuits and their work as they were forced, more and more, to hide behind their aliases. [25] Due to the increased vigilance of spies and pursuivants, who could earn up to £50 for information, and the corresponding apprehension of Recusants not wishing to be persecuted, from this time, it is much more difficult for a researcher to discover the houses, or the families, that gave succour and provided Mass centres. (See Appendix F.) This was particularly true in the South and the Midlands.

Those priests who were imprisoned, exiled or died as martyrs, are the ones of whom we have the most knowledge. One exception was Richard Holtby, who became superior in England after Garnet's death. He was never captured and did marvellous work in the North East, dying in 1640 at the ripe age of eighty seven. The North, of course, possessed a higher proportion of Catholics than the South. Lay people, like Mrs.Dorothy Lawson on Tyneside, were prepared to build chapels in their houses where the full Catholic ritual was celebrated and the Jesuits could safely make the 'Spiritual Exercises' for eight days every year. [26]

Another famous priest of the Society was John Bennett from North Wales who volunteered, at the age of 75, to nurse plague sufferers in London during an outbreak in 1625. He died a victim of the disease on Christmas Day. A fellow Welshman, Robert Jones became Jesuit superior after Holtby; a brave man who was never afraid to visit fellow priests in prison. In 1617, he was succeeded as leader and organiser by Richard Blount who was so secretive that he, like Holtby, was never apprehended during forty-seven working years. At the time of his return to this country in 1591, after training abroad, his disguise was that of a released naval prisoner of war. In 1619 this brave and competent priest became the first Vice-Provincial of the Society of Jesus in England. At his death, in 1638, Queen Henrietta Maria saw to it that he received a solemn requiem in her private chapel and was buried in Somerset House. [27]

[*] *'equivocation' = using ambiguity to conceal the truth (Concise Oxford Dictionary).*
[25] *B.Basset, English Jesuits, p.139*
[26] *Ibid., pp.148-149.*
[27] *Ibid., pp.155, 159.*

One of the Jesuit Fathers, Henry More, (a relative of St. Thomas More) was made responsible for writing an account of the Society's work. It was he who recorded 109 priests working in England in 1620 with 19 in the London District and the surprising number of 11 working in the environs of Northamptonshire. 40 members met at one of the London foreign embassies in 1622 to elect a delegate to go to Rome and plead for the establishment of an English Province. This request was granted in the following year. [28]

Two disasters struck the Catholic minority about this time. The first, on Sunday the twenty sixth of October 1623 (old style), occurred when a house, in Blackfriars London, being used as a Mass centre, collapsed with the resultant deaths of 80 of the congregation and 2 Jesuit priests. Later, on the nineteenth of March 1628, a house in Clerkenwell, used as an English novitiate college was discovered by government agents.

Earlier, in 1623, the first English Catholic Bishop to be appointed since the reign of Mary took up secret residence here. Unfortunately this good man, by name William Bishop, died during the following year and was succeeded by Dr.Richard Smith. [*] Such a stubborn and tactless prelate was quite the wrong choice for the difficult assignment as he tried dishonourably to discredit the work of the Jesuit priests including the redoubtable John Gerard. The Jesuit Father General refused to allow Richard Blount the Provincial to reply to the false accusations of Bishop Smith to avoid the scandal of open conflict. However, in 1631 Dr. Smith left England and the office of Bishop was in abeyance for some years.[**]

In keeping with Jesuit tradition, the English mission's activities were not confined solely to work at home for, in 1634, an expedition landed in Maryland, North America. The priest leader was Andrew White who had great success converting the Red Indians, but, at the time of the Civil Wars, was captured by English Puritan settlers and sent home as a prisoner. Henry More, who had become Provincial of the English Jesuits in 1635 was responsible for sending out Ferdinand Poulton as superior of the Maryland mission. (Three priests with the same names are known and it is not possible to be certain if this Poulton was from Desborough in Northamptonshire. Cf. Appendix D.)

It is indeed difficult to assemble a complete and coherent picture of the work of all the English members of the Society of Jesus during the first half of the seventeenth century. Although the many who were imprisoned, exiled and vilified may be noted, it is the ones who suffered martyrdom that are best documented. A few of these have already been mentioned in connection with the attempts of James I's government to lay the blame for the Gunpowder Plot on the backs of the Jesuits. (See Ch.II.)

[28] *Ibid., p.165.*

[*] *Dr. Smith spent some of his time at Turvey, Bedfordshire, the home of the dowager Lady Mordaunt.*

[**] *cf.P.Hughes, Rome and Counter-Reformation in England, pp.312-408, for full discussion of a difficult subject.*

After this period of severe repression, and certainly from 1618 to 1628, priests and laymen arrested for practising their Catholic faith were merely fined, gaoled or banished; but in the latter year the Puritan majority in Parliament demanded a more rigorous application of the laws against Papists. Edmund Arrowsmith, a Lancastrian born priest, who had become a Jesuit in 1623, was put to death on the twenty eighth of August 1628, at Lancaster and a layman, Richard Herst, the following day.

For the next thirteen years, and particularly while King Charles I ruled without Parliament, no further executions took place. However, on the third of November 1640, the Long Parliament, as its price for assisting the King in his war against the Scots, demanded the Royal Proclamation to banish Jesuits, priests and seminarists under penalty of death. (Ch.II.) The first to die under the new regime were secular priests, Benedictines and Franciscans. The gentle, Peterborough born Friar, Henry Heath, was one who suffered the usual butchery at Tyburn on the seventeenth of April 1643.

A few months before Heath's martyrdom, the Jesuit priest, Thomas Holland had similarly been hacked to pieces as was Ralph Corby in September 1644. These two Jesuits had something in common with Peter Wright, whose trial and execution will be discussed later. All three had the misfortune to encounter a renegade, apostate, Thomas Gage who, though once a Dominican priest, gave evidence against them. [29]

The family of Ralph Corby originally from Durham had emigrated to Dublin in 1589 to escape persecution. Ardent Catholics, three of the sons became Jesuits, two sisters became nuns and later both parents entered the religious life in Flanders with the father, Gerard, dying at Watten in 1637 as a lay-brother [30] in the novitiate centre.

On the first of February 1643, occurred the execution and quartering of Henry Morse whose colourful and adventurous life, at times, ran parallel to Peter Wright's. Both worked as chaplains or camp missioners to the English regiments fighting on the Spanish side in Flanders. They were certainly together with Colonel Henry Gage (of which more anon) in 1641. Morse, a holy, though somewhat frail priest, was one of nine brothers born to a Protestant family dwelling on the borders of Norfolk and Suffolk. He had legal training before fleeing abroad to become a Catholic and study for the priesthood in Rome. On his return to England in 1624/25, he joined St. Anthony's mission centre (Mrs.Lawson's house) County Durham where he was soon attending plague victims in and around Newcastle.

Attempting to return to Flanders to make his Jesuit novitiate, the boat was stopped and searched and he was flung into the gaol at York. Eventually exiled, he made his way to Watten and commenced the three years of training until, in 1630, he was assigned to the task of ministering to the mercenary soldiers in their winter quarters. Further study at Liege was a prelude to a second return to the English

[29] *Ibid., p.220.*
[30] *Ibid., p.213; & Lives of Saints, Vol.V, p.386; & P.Caraman, Henry Morse, p.62.*

mission. This time London was the venue where 31 Jesuits, and many more secular and other religious, ministered to the still numerous, but heavily persecuted, Catholic minority.

Apart from the foreign embassies, the only Mass centre, not subject to interference, was the Queen's own chapel at Somerset House. Here pursuivants and spies, waiting outside, took note of all who entered or left.

Such hazards were now commonplace and accepted as part of the price for holding on to the Catholic faith. Another problem was the continual mischief-making of a small number of the secular clergy who, in 1633, actually tried to get the Catholic laity to petition King Charles I to banish the Jesuits 'as incendiaries and disturbers of the public peace.' (31)

Such a lack of Christian charity and brotherly love was bound to give rise to further quarrels and dissensions and it is perhaps not surprising to find Henry Morse arguing violently with the secular priest John Southworth. In 1970, both these men were canonised by the Church, and it is salutary to realise that saints are not perfect all the time.

In fact, it was a renewed outbreak of the Plague, during the Autumn of 1635, which eventually brought about some kind of reconciliation as both the aforementioned priests were assigned to minister to plague-stricken Catholics. Their work was mainly in the slum districts of St.Giles and Westminster where the disease spread rapidly in the rat-infested, insanitary areas. The Papists were particularly in need because they were not registered with the authorities and received no relief in money or goods.

At length, the two priests, who had worked unstintingly to bring spiritual and physical comfort to the dying of all religious persuasions, issued a joint appeal to all the 'Catholickes of England' asking for special funds. It is dated the sixth of October 1636 and the principal contributor to the new fund was, as usual, Queen Henrietta, with 500 gold crowns. Poor people afterwards referred to the help given as 'her Majesty's alms'. (32)

Unfortunately Anglican church dignitaries and Puritan preachers became alarmed at the number of converts to the 'old faith' that were being made by these missionaries of mercy (Henry Morse was credited with more than 500). Laud, the Archbishop of Canterbury, acted personally upon receiving a petition from the curate or St.Margaret's, Westminster that, "Mr.Southworth was remarked going into houses on the pretext of delivering alms, but really to seduce the people." (33) Morse was also arrested by the pursuivants John Cook and Francis Newton, tried at the Old Bailey and condemned as a priest. Both missioners, although liable to the death penalty, were reprieved by Charles I almost certainly acting on the intervention of his Queen.

(31) *P.Caraman, Henry Morse, p.75.*

(32) *Ibid., p.92.*

(33) *Lives of the Saints, Vol.V, p.304.*

Morse, as already mentioned, went into exile to Flanders but returned to London in 1644 only to be apprehended again and suffer execution the following year. John Southworth survived until 1654 when he too was hacked to pieces at Tyburn. He thus became only the second Catholic cleric to die under the jurisdiction of the Commonwealth - the other being Peter Wright. St.John Southworth's remains are today venerated at Westminster Cathedral because, although originally interred at Douai, they were accidentally discovered in France in 1926 and transferred to their final resting place in 1930.

The English Catholic priests and laymen who suffered martyrdom became famous in their own day and their deeds are, at least in part, catalogued and remembered. As already outlined, we cannot know or record even the locations of most of the other priest missioners who worked tirelessly, but of necessity secretly, in London and in the depths of the country. The Faith continued to flourish, as a kind of underground movement, reminiscent of the French Resistance during the Second World War.

In such circumstances it is impossible, for instance, to detail with any certainty the bases used by the Jesuit fathers during the seventeenth century in Northamptonshire. What can be gleaned from spies reports (not always reliable), letters to Rome (carefully worded in case they fell into the wrong hands) and various autobiographies like John Gerard's (deliberately obscure with regard to most names and some places), is to be found in Appendix F. The information is sparse, and although avid research, in the archives in Rome, might reveal more, it is just as likely to be fruitless. Harrowden Hall seems to be the centre most frequented by the Jesuits but, even here, after 1612 only one vague reference occurs. At Deene Hall and Rushton Hall where, in 1647, the Brudenell family was known to favour priests from the Society, only one name has been verified after 1620.

The very large number of the Poulton family sons, from Desborough, (Appendix D) who joined the Jesuit order, leads one to suppose that some must have returned to their home district to preach and administer the sacraments but no clues as to when and where have yet come to light. It is the same with Drayton House and nearby Slipton where Peter Wright's parents are stated as being known to the Jesuits at Liege [34] but no names are given. The oblique reference to Robert Beaumont (possible alias of Robert Jenison) as being at Drayton in 1625 disputing with the Anglican Archbishop Ussher (Appendix F) is the sort of snippet one has to rely on.

We shall now try to piece together some further parts of Peter Wright's own story. If the evidence for this, from Northamptonshire, is decidedly thin, happily a few more dates, if not too many details, are available from Jesuit archives to begin to draw a reasonable outline picture although it will not be possible to paint in all the brush strokes.

[34] *Foley Vol.II, p.508*

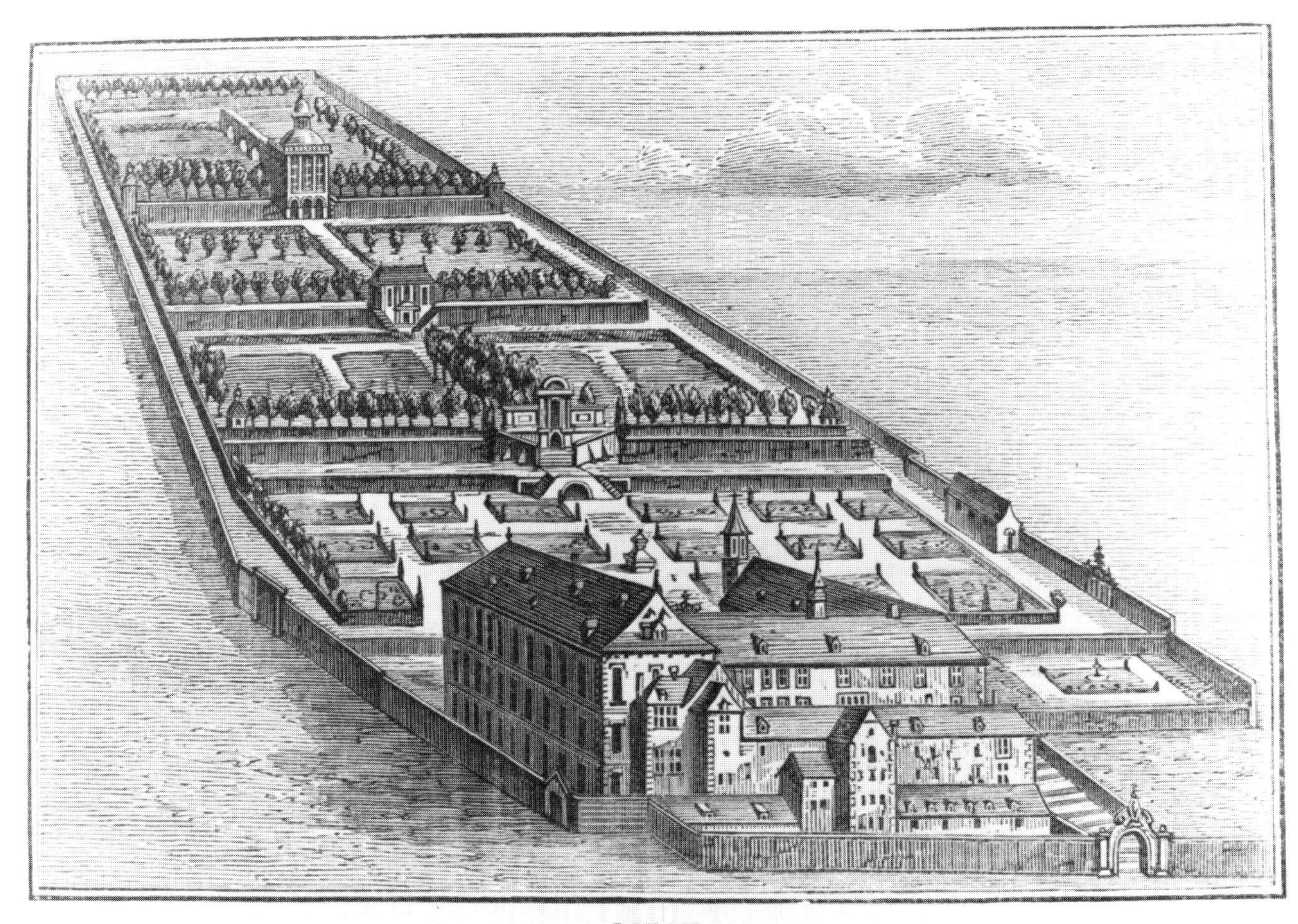

LIEGE

1773--1794

The Anglo-Bavarian College, Liege

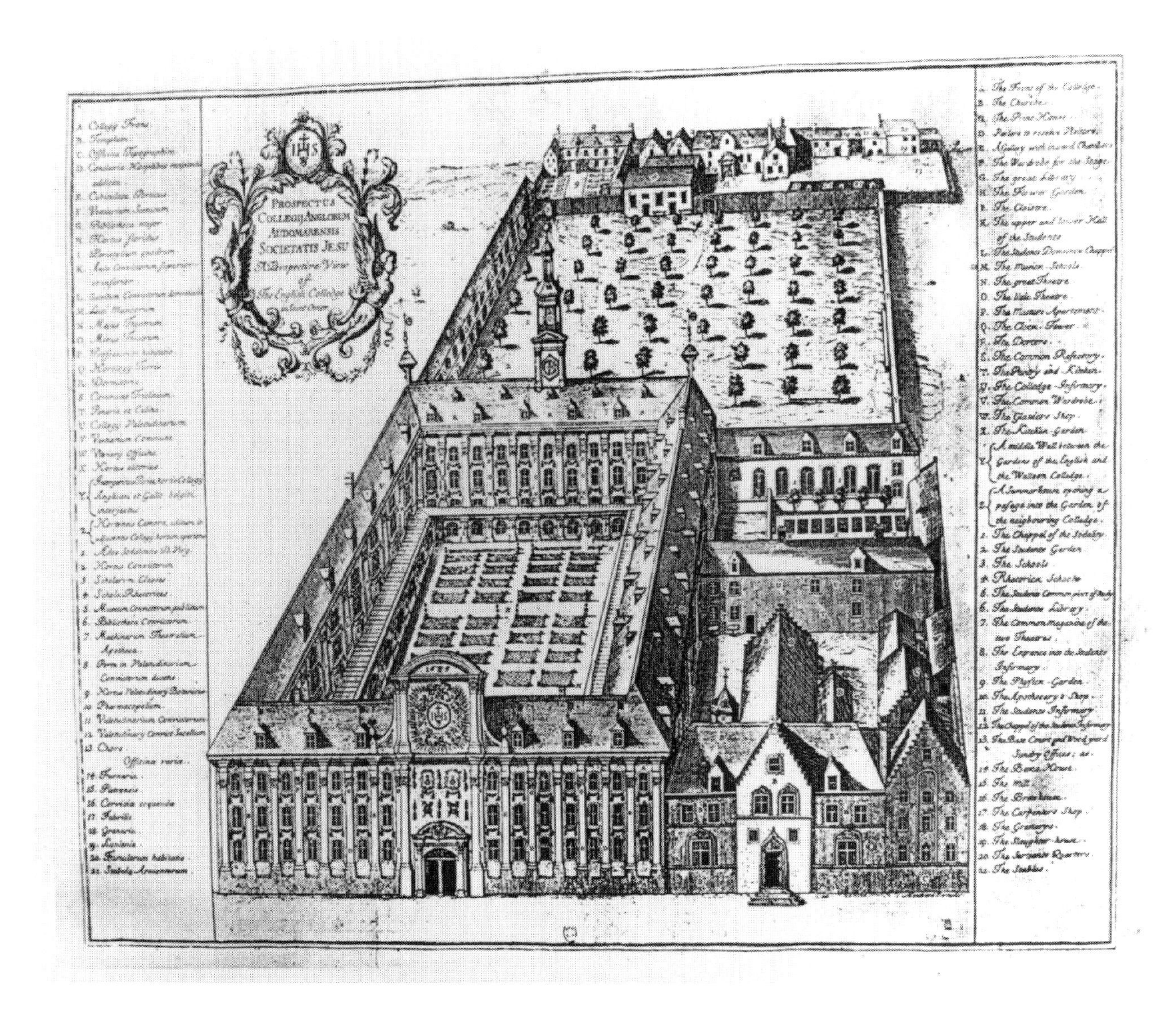

St. Omers College

Chapter V

Peter's Career (1627 - 1643).

As already explained (Ch.III), an element of mystery surrounds Peter's enlistment as a soldier and rapid abandonment of that kind of life circa 1626/27. The fact of there being two English armies operating in the Netherlands, one on the Dutch side and another fighting for the Spanish, makes the statement, 'he enlisted in the English forces in Holland' [1] thoroughly ambiguous. We can only judge his intentions and motivation in the light of subsequent events.

Peter's leaving the scene of military conflict, after only one month, points not only to a loathing for warfare and the military life, but to the probability of a preconceived plan. Perhaps his idea was to make a pilgrimage to Rome and join a religious order in the 'eternal city'. The existence of such a scheme, or half-formed design is, however, nowhere acknowledged by Edward Leedes/Courtnay, the seventeenth century Jesuit biographer, whose Latin essay was translated in the nineteenth century by another Jesuit, Henry Foley. In this last invaluable source, we find the 'good samaritan', who came to Peter's aid, after he had been robbed, depicted as advising a pilgrimage. He also fitted him out with cap, clothes, staff and money for the journey.

The aforementioned, original 'Life' of Peter is more explicit when describing how, having arrived, somewhat fortuitously, at the gates of the English College of the Society of Jesus in Liege, he was welcomed with open arms. We are then told that; - 'The Father Rector, on discovering the talents of the youth, (he was actually about 23 years old) and his parents being: likewise known, was so prepossessed in his favour, - he sent him with letters of commendation from the English residents of Liege, to Ghent (1627). There he spent two years, supported by the pious liberality of the same Catholics, in the Seminary of the Flemish Fathers of the Society.' [2]

There were, of course, many English Catholic exiles in Belgium (or more correctly Spanish Netherlands) during the seventeenth century. The number often exceeded 3,000 and some were wealthy despite having left most of their possessions in England. Examples are to be found in the Leedes family (App.A) and the Wake family (App.D). Which of these wealthy refugee families supported Peter during the succeeding years of study we do not know. It is likewise a puzzle as to why he proceeded to study with the Flemish Jesuits instead of going on to take instruction from the English Fathers at one of their houses. True he was already older, at 23/24, than the majority of scholars being educated at St. Omer, where Robert Persons had founded his college in 1593. The probability is that Peter's command of Latin (perhaps even Greek) was sufficiently advanced for him to progress in Humanities from the teaching supplied by the learned Flemish lecturers in traditional classical style.

[1] *H.Foley, Records of English Province, S.J., Vol,IL, p.507.*

[2] *Ibid., p.508.*

He was a ready and apt pupil which is shown by the fact that, in 1629, he was selected, as an exemplary student, to be sent, together with the best of the young men from St. 0mers [*], to begin a higher course at the Venerable English College in Rome. The most likely outcome of such a progression would have been ordination to the secular priesthood. However, our embryo martyr had already asked to be accepted into the English Province of the Society of Jesus. Thus it was that, instead of journeying to Italy, he enrolled at the Jesuit novitiate house at Watten in Flanders. As the students from St. Omers usually left for Rome, each year, on or about the Feast of the Assumption of Our Lady, the fifteenth of August, we must presume that to be the date when Peter was formally, though not finally, professed of the three vows and became a Jesuit novice. Although from other sources, we learn that the usual day for entry to Watten was the seventh of September.

By the year 1629 the English Jesuits had established several houses of study in the area of modern Belgium and north western France. The college at St. Omer has already been mentioned as being founded by Robert Persons and he it was who purchased, with money provided by a Spanish lady, a house in Louvain in 1604.

A few years later, John Gerard, with funds from rich English relatives bought a site at Liege which eventually became the centre for higher studies. Another house was purchased at Ghent in 1621, with money supplied by the Countess of Arundel, and this was specifically for the third year of probation or tertianship. Yet another training centre for army chaplains existed in Brussels.

The original novitiate for the English Jesuits was at St.John's Louvain but in 1614 it moved to Liege and finally, in 1625, to Watten where it remained until 1765. [3] Here, in this village, (once a more important town) which is situated about five miles from St. Omer, the ruins of an old Augustinian abbey still crown the steep hill which rises abruptly behind the modern settlement beside the river Aa. Between 1621 and 1623 the ancient monastic buildings were obtained and gradually transformed into a Jesuit novitiate centre.

All over the world Jesuit novices followed the same pattern of training for two years. Firstly, for one whole month, they gave their complete attention to the 'Spiritual Exercises' of their founder, St. Ignatius. Menial tasks were regarded as important as study and all entrants, without exception, had to apply themselves to house work, farm labour, tending the orchards or caring for the sick. Among the infirm were Fathers who had been broken in health by service in England like Thomas Stephenson, once a prisoner in the Tower of London (although he died in 1624).

Many of the novices learned Flemish to enable them, once a week, to teach the catechism of Christian doctrine to the local village children. Peter was particularly keen to participate in these instruction sessions with the local inhabitants, travelling several miles from the novitiate house, even

[*] *The English Jesuit College at St. Omer is usually referred to as St. Omers.*
[3] *D.Bellenger, English & Welsh Priests, p.18.*

in the depths of winter. Perhaps he remembered his own young days in Slipton when learning the truths of the Catholic faith was fraught with danger and subject to the risk of fines and imprisonment. As a result of this regular apostolate among the surrounding villages, as many as a thousand people from the district came to worship at the church in Watten to celebrate the greater feasts.[4]

One inspiration for the men doggedly pursuing their vocation to become fully fledged members of the Society, prepared to tackle the rigours of mission life in England, was that, on a clear day, the white cliffs of Dover could be glimpsed from the top of the church tower. The thoughts of home and the difficulties faced by their families and co-religionists helped them survive the pilgrimage which every member had to undergo as a novitiate test. During this examination of fortitude, undertaken even in winter, the postulants had to beg for their food. This departure from the solid, traditional though perhaps boring routine of spiritual reading, was probably welcomed as a break although certainly no holiday. Some novices returned with badly blistered feet needing treatment in the infirmary.

St.Omers' press, started by Robert Persons, provided most of the English reading with titles such as Roper's 'Life of Sir Thomas More' and Persons' own 'Christian Directory'. Other works of theology and humanities were most likely to be found printed in Latin or French. Life was not, however, all work and no play; especially at the time of the great feasts of the Church; Easter, Christmas, Pentecost etc., dramatic and musical items were produced to delight the whole company and visitors who chanced to be there.

Peter is described, during this period, as having a robust constitution, an amenable temperament and an open, frank manner:- 'In the first year of his probation, he had gained so great a mastery over himself and his passions, that whereas he was naturally hot tempered and hasty, he became from that time distinguished for his tranquillity and evenness of temper, his perfect self-control and self-contempt.' [5]

The report at the end of his first year of probation reads: "*Northamptoniensis annum habet aetatis 26, Societatis I^m, vires firmas. Humanista est ingenio valde bone, respondet iudicium et prudentia, experientiam nondum habet, profectus in literis secundum classem bonus, complexio temperata ad pleraque suo tempore futurus est idoneus.*" Translation: "A Northamptonshire man, now aged 26, has been one year in the Society, in good health, (Studying) Humanities, of very high intelligence, shows reasonable judgement and prudence, lacks experience as yet, a good proficiency in letters according to his level, of a temperate nature and when his time comes will be able to set his hand to a variety of tasks." [5A]

[4] *B,Basset, English Jesuits, p.288.*

[5] *H.Foley, Records of English Province, S.J., Vol.II. p.509.*

[5A] *MONUMENTA ANGLIAE : English and Welsh Jesuit Catalogues (1555-1629). Collected and edited by Thomas M.McCoog, S.J. Rome 1992, p.432.*

After thus successfully completing his probationary two years at Watten, under the watchful eye of Fr.Henry Silesden vere Bedingfield, the novice master, the budding Jesuit proceeded to Liege (his first port of call) this time to embark on the scholasticate or extended period of studies in theology, philosophy and humanities. This phase could last for as long as seven years but, after three years of philosophy, Peter asked to be allowed to make a further three year short course in divinity and this request was granted. No doubt he was hoping to be ordained at an early date and be sent to the mission field of England. As we shall see, it would be some years before he was able to return to his native soil. In the meantime, as at Watten, Peter continued, with great fervour, the practice of teaching the Church catechism in the village churches of the local countryside.

At some time or other every English Jesuit, during the first half of the seventeenth century, visited Liege. Here, high on a hill to the north of the city, was to be found the Anglo-Bavarian College; so called because Maximilian I of Bavaria [6] provided an annual pension and was honoured as the founder. In fact most of the money for building had come from the family of the English Lord Montagu and, in particular, through the good offices of a scion of that house, William Browne, who was a Jesuit brother.

The English Jesuits at Liege tried to avoid all possible disagreements with the Walloon Jesuits or clashes with the civil authorities and kept themselves apart. However, their house for higher studies was often frequented by Dutch Recusants, authors, university professors, army chaplains and lay students. The grounds were laid out in terraces comprising gardens, orchards, and a large playing field. Outside the city the English Province owned a farm and also a villa for holidays together with a small chapel built in honour of Our Lady - still standing in the twentieth century.

Many sources refer to the good management of the college at Liege which was, of course, organised like most other European seminaries and universities of the age in a traditional and formal way. All lectures were delivered in Latin and the institution rigidly adhered to the scholastic formula whereby the students, after attending many discourses, given by the professors, prepared long and well rehearsed theses which they defended in public in the college hall.

It would be difficult, if not impossible, to obtain a full list of the professors and other lecturers actively engaged in tutoring at this senior seminary during the years 1631 to 1636 when Peter Wright would be in residence. One eminent man certainly present was Fr.Francis Line, who was professor of Hebrew and Mathematics and also a notable inventor, who had contrived to build a brass sphere which, suspended in water, revealed the time of day and many other 'secrets of geography, astrology and astronomy'. [7] Another lecturer at both Liege college and the university was Fr. Edward Leedes whose subjects included logic, metaphysics and controversy. He left to return to England in 1534 but it seems extremely likely that it was at this period he not only met, but became

[6] Chambers Dict. of World History, Maximilian I (1573-1651) educated by Jesuits. Elector of Bavaria (1623-1651).
[7] B.Basset, English Jesuits, p.293. (Fr. Line later built a similar device in England for King Charles II (1669) and disputed mathematical questions with Sir Isaac Newton.)

friendly with, our future martyr and was thus able to include some biographical details in the 'Mors' account published in 1651 (AppendixA).

Yet another one time professor at Liege was Fr.Emmanuel Lobb, alias Joseph Simons, who also taught at St.Omers (1630-1633) where he was much regarded as an author of several plays. Lobb was a very learned man, though like Peter Wright of humble origins. We know that the two became friends because letters are still preserved at Stonyhurst which were written by Peter in 1647 (Appendix B). In 1656 Fr. Lobb is recorded as Professor of Theology and Sacred Scripture at Liege. [8]

When Peter left the Anglo-Bavarian College, circa late 1636, [*] it was to return to Ghent where he had begun his studies, with the Flemish Jesuits, approximately nine years previously. Now, he entered the English Jesuit Tertian College to undertake the third year of probation which was obligatory on all members of the Society prior to the solemn profession and final acceptance into the Order. This third year, usually lasting only eight to ten months, was dedicated to the renewal of spiritual fervour after the distractions of study and in some instances was followed by ordination to the priesthood.

However, ordination was not automatic once a man had been professed and bound by the three Evangelical vows, Poverty, Chastity and Obedience. Many most distinguished Jesuits, Nicholas Owen, Ralph Emerson, John Lillie, William Browne, Henry Foley among them, never became priests. Others waited for years before receiving Holy Orders; for each man followed the direction of his superiors.

We have no certain date for the ordination of Peter Wright and shortly must make an educated guess. His first assignment, as a fully fledged Jesuit, probably in the Autumn of 1637 was to be one of three Prefects of Studies or Prefect of Morals at St. Omers College. This position would only have been accorded him as a consummate Latin scholar of a serious disposition but it is just possible he was not yet ordained priest. Usually only the First Prefect was given this honour. The earliest time suggested for Peter's ordination is to be found in the 'Positio' [**], prepared in 1925 before his Beatification, which assumes that the sacrament of Holy Orders was conferred immediately after the completion of his higher studies in Liege. This would mean c.1636. Controversially, however, another authority, Dr.John Paul, lecturing in 1966 put forward the year 1639, while Dom.D.A. Bellenger O.S.B. in his thoroughly researched book on English and Welsh priests (1558-1800), published in 1984, reached no conclusion and offered no date at all. On balance of probabilities the most likely period for the future martyr's elevation to priestly rank would have to be c.late 1636, at Liege, before his Tertianship at Ghent as suggested by Fr.T.M.McCoog S.J. in 1995 (See Chronology). Thus we arrive at a probable date of 1636/37 and that is as near as can be ascertained.

[8] *H. Chadwick , St. Omers to Stonyhurst, p.136.*

[*] *T. McCoog, Monumenta Historica Societatis Jesu, Vol. 143 (Chronology of Peter Wright).*

[**] *'Positio' = deposit of material relating to the spiritual life and sanctity of a candidate for beatification or canonization.*

It also appears, from the earliest sources, [9] that the first appointment was not in harmony with his natural inclinations and he found the office very difficult and trying. Perhaps he had set his heart on returning to the mission field of England or maybe his too serious nature was lacking in the sympathy required to oversee adolescent youths. Whatever the reasons for his antipathy towards the post, his character was revealed when, after a time spent in prayer, he went to the Father Rector, Thomas Worsley, or perhaps Thomas Port, [10] and offered to continue as a prefect, if superiors thought proper, during the whole of his life. This showed Peter to be a true Jesuit.

Another factor, not to be disregarded, was that in May 1635 France declared war on Spain and the town of St. Omer was, as part of the Spanish Netherlands, immediately on the front line. [11] The boys of the college worked for a month strengthening the city walls and such disruptions would not have made them so amenable to the discipline of the Prefects. At the same time, 1635, 1636, 1637 bubonic plague had broken out again in Europe and,although the college escaped the worst of the infection,the town was badly affected.

It is quite feasible that the young and vigorous Peter had been sent, c.1637/38, quite deliberately, to St.Omers to assist the elderly Fr.Henry Thunder (b.1575) who had held the title of Prefect for many years, was now First Prefect, but would die of 'sweating sickness' in 1638. Working with the redoubtable Fr.Thunder could not have been easy even at the best of times. This remarkable priest had already held the office for more than thirty years and must have been a very effective discipline master. Unfortunately there are no detailed accounts of his methods except one by James Wadsworth [12], writing in 1630, about his time at St.Omers (1618-1622); "*Father Thunder who appointed Chambers and Studies, make them render account of their studies, keepes hours of study and recreation, and exercises many of his claps upon their breeches*." [13]

During the seventeenth century and most of the eighteenth, including the two years or so of Peter's sojourn, St.Omers was both college and junior seminary. It was also regarded as a grammar school and as such followed the classical humanist approach to learning which had been in vogue throughout Europe since the Renaissance. Pupils were usually 14 years of age on entry and then completed five years of study. Each year was termed a 'school' (class in modern terminology) with a definite objective to be obtained before the student could make further progress.

The three lower classes, known as Grammars, began with Figures and concluded with Grammar and Syntax. The fourth 'school' was Poetry (or Humanities) and finally Rhetoric. About 1632 there

[9] *E.Leedes, (Translation Foley, Vol.ii. p.510.)*
[10] *Ibid. (Fr,Thomas Worsley was later to be present at Fr.Peter's execution and assisted him to die worthily.)*
[11] *H.Chadwick, St. Omers to Stonyhurst, p.148.*
[12] *D.N.B., Wadsworth was an apostate who wrote decrying Jesuit methods.*
[13] *H.Chadwick, St.Omers to Stonyhurst, p.84 (Quotes Wadsworth's 'English Spanish Pilgrime.')*

was added a sixth 'school' but no permanent name was assigned to it. The two lowest classes were sometimes Rudiments and Figures, or Upper and Lower Rudiments, or Great and Little Figures. [14]

When the student reached the climax of his career as a Rhetorician he was expected to be master in fluent, cultivated, classical Latin and hopefully eloquent in classical Greek as well. Latin, in fact, was taken for granted - it was the official language of the College, in the classroom and usually outside it. Only the beginners were allowed some leniency. All this was not a Jesuit innovation, it was common to English Protestant schools of the seventeenth century as well as continental academies. (As an aside, it is worth recalling that a qualification in Latin was still a requirement for entry to Cambridge or Oxford University until some years after the Second World War.)

From the earliest years the boys practised what were known as 'Disputations' and by the end of Syntax were expected to debate extempore and presumably unscripted. When he reached the end of the final year the Rhetorician should have been an expert controversialist. However, apart from the classics the curriculum seems singularly empty, so far as secular studies are concerned. Mathematics, apart from simple Arithmetic, was a matter for higher studies. History and Geography were only alluded to as adjuncts to studies of the classics but Music was particularly favoured. A splendid choir, orchestra and dramatic activities attracted many visitors.

The daily routine was formidable. The hour for rising was 5 a.m. both in Summer and Winter. On Sundays and Feast days a '*long sleep*' until 5.30 was allowed. [15] Within thirty minutes of rising a boy should have washed, dressed, made his bed and spent a quarter of an hour in meditation. Mass followed celebrated in the Study Place where there was an altar. Presumably the domestic chapel was not large enough for the 200 boys on roll in 1635, only 140 in 1638. An hour of Morning Studies ended at 7 a.m. when all went down *silently*, school by school, to the Refectory on the ground floor. At 7.15, and no later, the Prefect (master not pupil) moved them on to their schoolrooms where for fifteen minutes they recited lessons, learned by heart, to the 'decurio' or 'censor', a pupil officially appointed for each group.

At 7.30 the master arrived and the Prefect, patrolling the corridor, departed in peace. 'Schools' lasted until 10 when there was a fifteen minute break during which some talking in Greek or Latin was allowed. All boys then went to the communal Study Place until *dinner at 11 o'clock*. After dinner there was recreation for about an hour but the first half hour of this relaxation time was dedicated to Music in one of the four Music Halls.

Private study began the afternoon session. This lasted for an hour followed by a brief fifteen minute break to allow everyone to attend to necessary bodily functions. Schools (further lessons) then continued from 1.45 to 4.30. Another short break preceded two hours of private study which in most

[14] *Ibid., p,71.*
[15] *Ibid., p.80.*

modern English boarding schools would be called 'Prep'. At 6.30 supper was served followed by a second hour of recreation and finally yet another half hour of study. At the end of supper the Martyrology of the next day was read out and at the mention of any English saint all removed their caps.

Night prayers were at 8.30, when the boys knelt by their desks for fifteen minutes, retiring immediately afterwards, *in silence*, to their dormitories. Even in bed some points for meditation on the following day were read out twice in a clear voice. (16)

To sum up, 5~ hours in the schoolroom and almost as long in private study is a very long day by our modern standards. However, Tuesdays and Thursdays were half-holidays. According to James Wadsworth, Sundays and Holydays were marked by the boys attending Low Mass at 7 a.m. and/or High Mass at 10 when the College choir and orchestra provided the music. On Sunday afternoons the boys were again in church for Vespers and the Litanies of Our Lady. These prayers were always offered up for the conversion of England. On both the church and college doors were written, in large golden letters, the words; 'IESU, IESU, CONVERTE ANGLIAM, FIAT, FIAT'. (17)

Fr.Schondonch , the Flemish Rector of St.Omers (1601-1617) wrote out many of the rules for the conduct of the College. One set, entitled 'Rules of the Prefects', stated that the office is one that demands a man of grave and mature mould who must have a genial disposition. Prefects must also answer to God for any negligence in their duties. Peter Wright seemed to fulfil all the necessary criteria for this important charge and as a man who had obtained perfect self-control should have had no problem with enforcing Fr.Schondonch's rule of silence at the end of each period of recreation; "not only because that is befitting, but in order that these boys, born and destined to distinguished service, may learn in their tender years the lesson of selfcontrol". (18)

So why did Peter find the task so irksome? The answer to this puzzle must lie somewhere between his desire to be professed of his final vows quickly and be sent to work in England and, the fact that, not being schooled at St.Omers himself, he was unable to accept readily the peculiar constraints and apparently petty rules necessary for the smooth running of a boarding establishment. An escape from these unwelcome tasks was, however, already at hand in the escalation of the war in the Netherlands brought about by the entry of France into the conflict and subsequent attacks on St.Omer and other frontier towns.

As mentioned earlier, the France of King Louis XIII had formally declared war on the Spanish Empire of King Philip IV on the twenty first of May 1635, following the Treaty of Compiegne which saw Cardinal Richelieu, the chief minister of Catholic France, recognise Protestant Sweden as an

(16) *H.Chadwick, St.Omers to Stonyhurst, pp.69-97 - gives a very full account of Jesuit school routine.*
(17) *Ibid., p.87.*
(18) *Ibid., p.86.*

equal ally. Thus France was also allied to the Protestant Dutch of the United Provinces. The Thirty Years War which had begun in 1618, as a mainly religious conflict of Protestant north Europe against the Catholic south, now became part of the dynastic and nationalist struggle for supremacy. This would eventually lead to the decline of Spanish influence and see the rise of an equally dominant French imperial successor.

At first the Spanish forces did well partly because the Prince of Orange (Dutch leader) gave no help to the French armies as he did not favour their attacks on Flanders. He was rightly fearful of their ultimate intentions and advised Richelieu and Louis to attack the Spanish mainland. Consequently on the fourteenth of August 1636, the Spanish army, with mercenary help, captured and occupied the French fortress of Corbie, close to Amiens. This was to be the extent of Spanish gains [19] and in the following year Breda fell to the Dutch.

The tide was beginning to turn against Spain and by 1643 their losses were constantly increasing. The most damaging defeat occurred at sea when, in 1639, a fleet of 77 ships was destroyed by the Dutch admiral Tromp in English waters close to Dover. By 1640 Portugal and Catalonia were in revolt against Spanish rule though, in the Netherlands, the Dutch made few gains. A major factor here was the skill and bravery of the English mercenary regiments, fighting for Spain, who were in continual action.

In 1638 St.Omer was again besieged by a French army for six weeks. Some 40 younger boys from the Jesuit school were sent to Ghent for protection but the environs were devastated by marauding soldiers including the town of Watten and St.Omers' holiday house at Blandyke. At times the bombardment was loud enough to disrupt lessons but the buildings escaped significant damage. The town's survival was due, in no small measure, to the military organization and prowess of an 'old boy' of the college, Colonel Henry Gage.

This devout Catholic was commander of one of the English regiments in the service of Spain (Chap.II). His importance in the story of Peter Wright cannot be overestimated because from about the year 1638/39 when it is reasonable to assume that the future martyr was appointed a camp missioner or chaplain to Henry Gage's regiment, the two became firm friends. They were not to be parted until the gallant death of the soldier in January 1645 fighting in England for his sovereign King Charles I (See Chap.VI).

The Gage family's principal house had been Firle in Sussex (App.G) but there were branches in Surrey, Suffolk, Buckinghamshire and Northamptonshire (Rushton and Raunds [20]). Henry was born in 1597. His mother, a sincerely religious woman, had been arrested with St.Anne Line (See Chapter I). At ten years of age the boy was despatched, along with his brother, to be educated by the Jesuits

[19] *C.V.Wedgewood, Thirty Years War, p.406.*

[20] *Heralds Visitation Northamptonshire.*

at St.Omers. After travels and further study in France, Italy, Germany and the Netherlands, he enlisted at Antwerp, c.1620, as a common soldier in the Earl of Argyll's regiment fighting on the side of the Spanish but licensed by the English government of James I (See Chap.II).

In this fighting force he 'trailed a pike' for twelve months until offered a captaincy. [21] During his first major action at Bergen op Zoom he was wounded by a mine, but performed bravely, and again during the following year at the siege of Breda he won renown by his valour and resolution.

The English regiments were reformed when James I turned against Spain and for two or three years Henry Gage was without command. He married at this time and both in England and the Netherlands studied heraldry and the theory of war. By translating many books from Latin into English and from English into French he demonstrated that he was a considerable scholar as well as a fine soldier. When his father lost all his property because of Recusancy, Henry helped out by giving him a property in Croydon.

In the year 1630, Sir Edward Parham raised a new English regiment to fight for Spain and made Sir William Tresham [*] Sergeant Major with Henry Gage Captain-Commandant. When Parham died Tresham became Colonel and Gage Sergeant Major. At the siege of Maastricht the Marquess of Santa Cruz was so pleased with the English regiment that he gave them the guard of his own person. [22]

Some time after this the Marquess gave Gage a commission to raise a regiment of his own in England, licensed, of course, by King Charles I. Within a short while he had command of 900 men but on the death of Sir William Tresham, in 1639, the two English regiments were combined and Gage took over command of the whole force. During this period the English soldiers were continually in action though, it has to be said, campaigns were not usually conducted during very cold weather when all combatants retired to winter quarters. For three summers Colonel Gage's regiment was employed to relieve Gueldres which was being besieged by the Dutch Protestants. Athough the Spaniards eventually lost the town, the area of Guelderland was successfully defended by the English regiment supported by 1400 other horse and foot soldiers. In this important victory Gage was so kind and generous to those of the enemy taken prisoner that the Prince of Orange was persuaded to be equally magnanimous.

When the Civil Wars began in England Gage was naturally sympathetic to King Charles and was soon instrumental in capturing arms meant for Parliament and sending them to help the royalist cause. He allowed any of his soldiers, who wished to fight for the King, to return home and some 200 officers and lower ranks took the opportunity. At last, nothing, not even his wife and family, could prevent him from travelling to England and offering his services to Charles in person. During late 1643 or early 1644 he joined in the defence of Oxford accompanied by Fr.Peter Wright as his personal chaplain.

[21] *E.Walsingham, Alter Britanniae Heros, Life and Death of Sir Henry Gage, pp.2/3.*

[*] *Tresham's relatives lived at Liveden close to Slipton.*

[22] *Ibid., pp.3/4.*

Before considering Fr.Peter Wright's career as an army chaplain in the Netherlands, it is worth making one further point in regard to Colonel Gage's patriotism. It is recorded that when his regiment was ordered into Germany, by the Spanish commander, he refused on the grounds that it was not in his native country's interests. [23]

The exact occasion of Fr.Peter's assignment to a post of camp missioner is not known although some modern Jesuit writers aver that he was with Colonel Gage for seven years or more including service in England. [24] This would suggest circa 1638/39 as the most likely time.

Foley in his notes [25] states that, within an hour of his act of self-sacrifice before the Father Rector of St.Omers, he was warned to prepare himself to become a confessor and chaplain to the English forces in Flanders (Belgium) and "joyfully undertook the appointment". One strange phrase is used to justify the young Jesuit priest's fitness for the task: "having been himself in the army". Surely this expression would not have been used if Peter had ever served in the English army assisting Protestant Holland even for only one month. (See earlier references.)

No exact record of Fr.Wright's work as a camp missioner exists and we can only obtain a brief glimpse of him through two main sources; Henry Foley's notes, based on Fr. Edward Leedes' 'Mors', and Thomas Gage's bitter and spiteful evidence given at the 'Old Bailey' trial (see Chap,VII).

The life of a Catholic priest, appointed to be a regimental chaplain in wartime, has always been both busy and dangerous. As well as looking after the pastoral welfare of the officers and men in camp, supplying their spiritual needs by providing the consolation of the sacraments of the Church, he has also to minister to the wounded and dying - often on the field of battle surrounded by all the attendant perils. Henry Foley, drawing from earlier sources, writes thus: " ... when in active service, whether on the battle field or at sieges,... he (Fr .Wright) refused no labour, and shrank from no danger in the exercise of his functions. So too, when the army was quiet in camp, or resting in winter quarters, he assiduously laboured amongst them, preaching, hearing confessions, comforting the sick, making up quarrels, or relieving the wants of the more needy soldiers." [26]

It would seem that several Jesuit chaplains were occupied in ministering to Colonel Gage's regiment. They may have replaced Dominican priests but the evidence is uncertain. We do know that Frs. Edward Latham and Henry Morse, both members of the Society of Jesus, were actively engaged circa 1640/41/42. [27] The testimony for this was later to be given, at the trial of Peter Wright, by an ex-Dominican priest, Thomas Gage, who, although Henry Gage's brother, had turned Protestant in 1642 and developed a paranoid hatred for his kinsman and all who associated with him (see Chap,VII).

[23] *P.Caraman, Henry Morse, p. 149 and E.Walsingham, Alter Britanniae Heros.*

[24] *J.H.Pollen's revision of Challoner's Memoirs, Foley's Records, Basset's English Jesuits.*

[25] *H.Foley, Records, Vol.II, p.510.*

[26] *Ibid.*

[27] *P.Caraman, Henry Morse, pp.149-155.*

The jaundiced Friar, Thomas Gage, had returned from the New World in 1637, after living for a time among the Indians of Central America, already harbouring thoughts of apostasy.[*] Towards the end of 1639 he obtained permission to visit Rome and confer with the master-general of the Dominican Order. On the way he called on his eldest brother,Colonel Gage,and stayed some days at his winter quarters near Ghent. Here he met Fr.Wright whom he later described as a 'grand Jesuit' and chaplain 'to my brother - and to his regiment in Flanders'. One can almost hear the sneer in his voice. He would eventually report seeing Fr.Peter say Mass on many occasions and also state that he observed him hearing confessions.[28] The slanders uttered by the renegade, in 1651, would be enough to condemn our martyr (Ch.VII.).

According to the vengeful ex-Friar, when the Spanish army was besieging the Flemish town of Salle the chaplains Frs.Morse and Wright had a chapel set up in a tent. They also heard confessions in another tent and Thomas Gage goes on to cite a captain called Vincent Burton, who he (Gage) was sure was trying to murder him, going to confession to Fr.Wright. He also accuses Fr. Wright of being the cause of a Dominican priest, Peter Martyr (alias Craft), being dismissed as a chaplain from his brother's regiment.

Despite this, later revealed animosity, we find Fr. Peter inviting Thomas Gage to the English Jesuits' house at Ghent. All the military chaplains of the Society of Jesus were attached to this community and here during the winter months the missionary aspect of the work was undertaken. The Catholic soldiers were brought together in groups of ten to twenty and given the Spiritual Exercises of St.Ignatius. Assisting in this work were also the Tertians who, after studies at Liege, were spending ten months preparing for the English mission by a second novitiate.[29]

It would appear, however, that not all the soldiers fighting on the Spanish side were, in fact, Catholics. According to the records of the Jesuit house at Ghent, no less than one hundred Protestant mercenaries were received into the Church in the year 1640,[30] perhaps some of these were lapsed Catholics but the record does not make a distinction.

We cannot know any details of the exertions of the camp missioners among the wounded troopers or of the nights spent by the bedsides of dying men. The Jesuit house journal for the winter of 1642 merely records the following: "The labours of the Fathers was principally devoted to the English soldiers in hospitals, though much good was done among the country population. ... The camp mission produced good fruit, fifty nine soldiers becoming Catholics."[31]

[*] *'apostasy' - renunciation of one's religion*

.[28] *G.Anstruther, Hundred Homeless Years, p.168, p.190, quoting from a tract by Thomas Gage justifying his actions, 'A Duel between a Jesuit and a Dominican ... victoriously ended at London on Friday, 16th May, 1651.'*

[29] *P.Caraman, Henry Morse, pp.150/151.*

[30] *Ibid., p.151.*

[31] *Ibid.*

The full horrors of the war in the Spanish Netherlands were certainly witnessed by our priest who was haunted by the scenes at the sack of Tuelmont, a small village in Brabant, for many years afterwards. He described them in one of his sermons preserved at Stonyhurst College (Appendix B) where he writes: "What cruelty soever hath been committed by any tyrant, what rape, what beastliness by any savage or brutish man, what sacrilege soever by Jew, Turk or infidel were there also committed" by the Dutch, the "followers of these new Gospellers". (32) There then continues much more,in graphic and bestial detail, which it is not necessary to specify here, except for the final condemnation that all this was done, "not by the private soldier alone or upon the sudden, or in the height of fury, but in cold blood, after three days consult , by approbation of all their officers."

The question has again to be asked; would anyone have written in such a vein who had ever fought on the side of the Dutch? It is impossible to give the idea any credence. The puzzle of Peter's short career as a soldier, c.1626, remains unsolved but the evidence points away from his enlistment in the forces of the United Provinces. Here we must close this enigmatic chapter.

On the twenty second of August 1642, the Civil Wars in England officially began and, as previously mentioned, the English Catholic regiments in the Netherlands were soon being depleted by reason of men of all ranks asking to be allowed to return home to fight for their King. During the ensuing year Colonel Henry Gage made up his mind to cross the North Sea and offer his services to Charles I at Oxford. The exact dates of the journey are unknown but, by this time, Fr.Peter Wright was regarded as a friend and personal chaplain; so we find the future martyr, accompanying the soldier, also returning to his native land. Neither man would ever cross the waters again.

If Peter had any presentiment of his eventual end, we are not told of it. He was in all probability overjoyed at the prospect of a 'home posting' and like Fr.Henry Morse, (33) fell on his knees and thanked God before telling all his friends the good news.

(32) *Ibid., p.155.*

(33) *Ibid., p.155.*

Chapter VI

Return to England - Oxford in the Civil War - death of Sir Henry Gage - with the Marquis of Winchester's family - London (c.1645 - 1651).

During the first half of the seventeenth century (the span of our martyr's life), every Catholic priest returning to England, after ordination abroad, was in mortal danger the moment he stepped ashore. Instances even occurred of clergy being arrested on the high seas. The Act of Parliament passed in 1585 (27 Elizabeth, c.2) had declared against, "Jesuits, seminary Priests, and other such like disobedient persons". Henceforth it became High Treason for a priest to be within the realm and felony for anyone to receive or give assistance to a Papist ordained in Europe. Most of the martyrs put to death during the next hundred years were condemned under this statute. As we have seen, there were brief periods when the law was not enforced and priests were exiled instead of being executed. Nevertheless the threat was always present and Catholics had to be very circumspect in regard to the protection of their pastors.

Fr.Peter Wright and his patron, Colonel Gage, therefore had to be very careful in making their dispositions for travel. They may well have travelled incognito by assuming completely false identities. We have absolutely no knowledge of their port of embarkation, type of vessel, or where they effected a landing. It is even possible that they sailed separately for better security. Similarly the date of arrival at the King's headquarters in Oxford is uncertain - possibly late 1643 but more likely early 1644.

Catholic writers of the period, such as Edward Walsingham who wrote the only known biography of Colonel Sir Henry Gage, [1] were very careful not to mention priests by name. So it is almost impossible to present an accurate account of the activities of Fr.Wright once he had arrived back home in England. We know that the Jesuit was with the Colonel when he offered his services to King Charles at Oxford and have to presume that the chaplain remained at the soldier's side during the campaigns that followed. Peter was attached to the Jesuit 'Residence of St.Mary' for the years 1644 and 1645, [2] which area included Northamptonshire as well as Oxford, but there is no record of him ever venturing to return to his native county.

When, in August 1642, King Charles I raised his standard at Nottingham and summoned all loyal men to rally to his support against the adherents of the Puritan Parliamentarians, many Catholics, though sympathetic, were loath to declare themselves openly for fear of incurring further financial penalties. As previously noted (Ch.II), the King, at first, declared that Recusants were not required

[1] *D.N.B., Colonel Gage was knighted by King Charles I, on the first of November, 1644, for his services in defending Oxford.*

[2] *T.M.McCoog, English and Welsh Jesuits (1555-1650).*

in his armies but very soon changed his mind and ordered Papist lords and gentry to arm themselves, their servants and retainers, and come to his aid.

By early 1644, when Colonel Henry Gage, with his chaplain, had definitely arrived to offer allegiance, Oxford had been established as the Royalist headquarters for more than a year. (Not that Gage had been idle in the Netherlands, where he had intercepted weapons and supplies bound for Parliament and diverted at least eight thousand arms to help the King's cause.) The governor of the university town from 1643 was Sir Arthur Aston [(3)] although he later met with an accident and was unable to carry out his duties effectively. He was removed from the office on the twenty fifth of December 1644, and Colonel Sir Henry Gage was made governor in his place.

The King had been quick to note the military skill of Fr.Peter's friend and companion and as early as the third of June 1644, when Charles was leaving to campaign in the West country, he appointed Gage one of the council chosen to assist the governor of Oxford. The Colonel's experience at sieges in the Netherlands was invaluable and, despite some opposition from Aston, probably through jealousy, he quickly reorganised the defensive positions around the town. More importantly he infused a new spirit into the troops who were, after eighteen months of fairly ineffective campaigning, beginning to lose heart.

On the eleventh of June, Colonel Gage offered to command a small force from Oxford, with three artillery pieces, to attack Boarstall House, Buckinghamshire, where a Parliamentary garrison was preventing supplies from reaching the Royalist headquarters. Within a day the defenders surrendered and Gage, with his usual generosity allowed them to leave freely. Very few casualties had been sustained and the house afterwards became a Royalist stronghold.

The next task which befell the intrepid Colonel was much more complicated and difficult to achieve. It was thought necessary to send a relieving force to Basing House in Hampshire which had been fortified by the owner, the fifth Marquis of Winchester, one of the richest men in England. From 1642 until October 1645 the great house, more like a reinforced and castellated village than a family residence, was held for Charles I. Winchester's spirited defence was talked about throughout the southern counties of England and earned him the sobriquet of 'Great Loyalist'.

Basing was forty miles from Oxford and in September 1644, had been surrounded by Parliamentary troops, under the command of a Colonel Norton, for three months. The garrison was short of arms and supplies, so besought the King to send aid but he was unable to spare any part of his main army which was still campaigning in the western counties.

A small detachment might have been able to reach the Marquis but would almost certainly be captured, on their return, by the Parliament's forces at Abingdon, Reading and Newbury. Despite

(3) D.N.B., Sir Arthur Aston was a Catholic. In 1649 while governor of Drogheda in Ireland he was killed at the capture of the town by Oliver Cromwell.

these obstacles and perils, Gage volunteered to lead a sortie but insisted that the Royalist lords must provide, from their own servants, sufficient cavalry to comprise two troops of horse to back up the infantry and pack animals. Clarendon writes:- "This being offered with great cheerfulness by a person of whose prudence as well as courage they had full confidence, they all resolved to do the utmost that was in their power to make it effectual." (4)

The adventure began on Monday night, the ninth of September, and the Colonel used an artifice, no doubt learned in the wars in the Netherlands. He instructed all two hundred and fifty troopers as well as the foot soldiers to fix orange-tawny scarves and ribbons to their clothing so that they might be mistaken for Parliament men. Unfortunately an advance party, on reaching the village of Aldermaston, forgot their orders and attacked some horse troopers belonging to the Parliament side. Consequently their progress was no longer secret and they were forced to march on, without rest, arriving within a mile of Basing at four in the morning on Wednesday. (5)

The Marquis's troops had been unable to break out and meet the men from Oxford and Gage was obliged to attack the besiegers in strength. This time the order to all ranks was to wear a white ribbon or handkerchief above the elbow of the right arm. In addition the soldiers were given a password, 'St.George', in case they met the defenders and fought them by mistake. After a grim tussle the besiegers were beaten back and twelve barrels of gunpowder with other arms brought into the garrison. The town of Basingstoke and village of Basing were raided for stores of wheat, malt, oats, salt, bacon, cheese and butter together with fifty head of cattle and above one hundred sheep.

A most successful relieving operation had been effected within the space of two or three days and Basing House would be able to withstand a further two month siege. It is almost certain that Fr. Peter Wright was with the Colonel and so probably met the Marquis of Winchester and family, who were staunch Catholics. It must have been a momentous first acquaintance which would lead to closer affinity in succeeding years.

The problem now for Colonel Gage, his chaplain and weary troops,was to return to Oxford without being challenged by other Parliament forces who were already closing in. On the Thursday night at eleven o'clock with three guides, who knew the country, the little army set out and forded both the rivers Kennet and Thames without meeting the enemy. After refreshment at Wallingford they arrived safely back at Oxford, on Saturday the fourteenth of September, having lost eleven killed and forty or fifty wounded though not dangerously. The other side's losses were not known but over one hundred prisoners had been taken and left at Basing. "It was confessed by enemies as well as friends that it was as soldierly an action as had been performed in the war on either side, and redounded very much to the reputation of the commander." (6)

(4) *Clarendon, Earl of, (Ed.Lockyer), History of the Great Rebellion, p.230.*
(5) *Ibid., p,231.*
(6) *Ibid., p.223.*

On the twenty-fifth of October the Colonel was again in action. This time going to the relief of Banbury town and castle , in Oxfordshire, but on the borders of Northamptonshire. Here the castle defence had been organised by the nineteen year old William Compton, third son of the second Earl of Northampton, but was on the point of surrendering after a prolonged investment by Parliamentary forces. Three crack Royalist cavalry regiments were sent by the King to assist Henry Gage's Oxford based troops and, despite flooded river valleys, quickly reached Crouch Hill to the west of the town causing the enemy besiegers to flee in complete disarray. (7) The Royalist attack had been particularly well conducted and Gage himself entered the town first to relieve the castle. We presume that Fr.Peter Wright was on hand to give spiritual comfort to the wounded and dying, as in the Netherlands, but this cannot be confirmed.

As already noted, Colonel Gage's promotion to knight of the realm quickly followed on these successes. His biographer wrote:- "it is incredible what a general contentment all men took in his promotion and how few repined at his advancement." (8) Within three or four weeks of the success at Banbury, the newly elevated soldier was once again sent to relieve Basing House. This time he had fully one thousand horse troopers, each carrying a sack of provisions, but all expecting a fierce fight because a whole Parliamentary army was known to be at the gates. Yet, when the King's force arrived in sight of the towers of the Marquis of Winchester's fortress, they found all Parliament's foot and horse gone the day before - retired to winter quarters.

The riding accident which was sustained by Sir Arthur Aston, and mentioned previously, was so serious that eventually his leg had to be amputated and this gave the King the opportunity to further promote Sir Henry Gage to the governorship of Oxford. This took place on Christmas Day but the new commandant was not satisfied with merely defending the outskirts of the town. He particularly wanted to secure the road from the south and negate the effectiveness of the Parliamentary garrison at Abingdon.

On Friday the ninth of January, with a force of six hundred men and both Prince Rupert and Prince Maurice (the King's cousins) leading the cavalry, an attempt was made to break down the bridge over the Thames at Culham where it was intended to build a Royalist fort. On the following day a fierce skirmish occurred and as Gage directed operations too close to the action he was shot through the chest with a musket ball. He was carried a little to the rear and prepared himself for death, not forgetting to send a blessing to his wife and children. Fr.Peter Wright was with him at the end and, in a coach, administered the last sacraments to his mortally wounded patron. (9) Some people believed, at the time, that the gallant knight was killed as a result of treachery (10) but this rumour seems to be without

(7) *P.Tennant , Edgehill & Beyond, pp.195,196.*
(8) *E.Walsingham , Alter Britanniae Heros, p.19.*
(9) *B.Basset, English Jesuits, p.219.*
(10) *H.Chadwick, St.Omers to Stonyhurst, p.67.*

The death of Colonel Sir Henry Gage

foundation and no charges were brought. Clarendon later wrote:- "In truth the king sustained a wonderful loss at his (Gage's) death, he being a man of great wisdom and temper, and amongst the very few soldiers who made himself to be universally loved and esteemed."[11]

Fr.Peter had lost his best friend but must have been present, perhaps conducting the Requiem Mass (although there is no mention of it), when Sir Henry was buried, in a prominent position, within Christ Church, Oxford. The brave soldier certainly received full military honours on the thirteenth of January 1645 (O.S.). An epitaph [*] composed in his honour praises his virtue as well as his bravery. His literary gifts were remarkable for a soldier as he had mastered Latin, English, French, Italian and Spanish with sufficient Greek and Dutch to enable him to converse, (all a tribute to the grounding in Classics received at St.Omers).

There is reliable evidence enough to believe that Fr.Peter remained in the Oxford district for a large part of 1645, but no certainty as to his exact whereabouts. The fairly remote possibility exists that he accompanied the Royalists, on the fourteenth of June, at Naseby where they suffered their greatest defeat. If so he would have been within seventeen miles of his birthplace. Is it too fanciful to suggest that he could have sought refuge with family and friends in the aftermath of the disaster? The secrecy of movement necessary for all Catholic priests, seeking to avoid capture, means that there can be no confirmation of such a reunion ever taking place.

All the above is mere conjecture but we are on safer ground in supposing that the Jesuit eventually sought and received sanctuary with the Marquis of Winchester's family. What is less definite is the date of Fr.Peter's arrival to take up an offer of hospitality which seems to have been made in September 1644, at the time of Colonel Gage's first relief expedition to Basing. Foley states:- " ... the Marquis and his wife, who perceiving his (Fr.Wright's) virtue, gave him an affectionate invitation to stay with them, ... as their chaplain."[12]

If, during the late Summer of 1645, Fr.Peter finally decided to accept shelter at Basing, he might well have been present on the sixteenth of October when the defence works were at last breached. The ruthless Oliver Cromwell, himself, concluded the long siege with a large army of several thousand men. The sacking and looting of a castle was the accepted fate for refusing to surrender but the carnage that ensued here was particularly ferocious and brutal. Even Inigo Jones, the King's architect, who had taken refuge with the Winchesters, was stripped of his clothes and forced to flee almost naked. [13] Many of the defenders were slaughtered.

The Marquis was brought before Cromwell, as a prisoner, while his house burned down around him, but reminding the victor that his house was called 'Loyalty' he proclaimed, "that if the king had

[11] *Clarendon, Earl of, (ed. Lockyer), History of Great Rebellion, p.247.*
[*] *See Appendix G.*
[12] *H.Foley , Records, Vol.ii, p.511.*
[13] *R.Ollard , War without an Enemy, p.150.*

no more ground in England but Basing House, he would adventure it as he did, and so maintain it to the uttermost". [14] Cromwell's reply is not recorded but Winchester was sent to the Tower of London charged with High Treason, while his house was levelled to the ground after being pillaged by the Parliamentarians of money, jewels, plate and other household valuables to the extent of £200 000.

Lady Winchester escaped from Basing two days before its final capture and made her way either to the family's town house in Holborn, London, or to some other retreat. Supposing Fr.Peter to have been on the site during this calamity, it seems safe to assume that he most likely helped to escort the lady during her flight and so was not captured. He would, by this time, have been a master of disguises but unfortunately we can only imagine the scene.

Winchester was the premier marquis of England but a large part of his fortune and lands were sequestered by Parliament although, in March 1649, the charge of High Treason was withdrawn. His wife was also detained in the Tower for a shorter period and only paid an allowance for the upkeep of her children with the stipulation that they be brought up Protestants. [15] The Marquis, a broken man, eventually retired to an estate at Englefield, Berkshire, which he had acquired by his second marriage and died there, a Catholic, in 1675, having translated several books of piety and devotion from the French.

Despite the difficulties outlined above, Fr. Peter spent the last years of his life as chaplain to this noble family and most probably resided, as an honoured guest, in the house in Holborn. From 1646 to 1649 he is registered in the Jesuit annals as part of the House of Probation (or College) of St.Ignatius, England. [16] This was not a formal teaching college but merely an administrative device through which Jesuits were organised. C.1623 to 1773 the College of St. Ignatius consisted of members of the Society living in Middlesex, Surrey, Kent, Berkshire and Hertfordshire which, of course, included London.

During the ten years preceding 1651, the year of our martyr's death, the capital city was certainly not a place for a Catholic priest, particularly a Jesuit, to live and move about freely or administer the sacraments in perfect safety.The 'Rump [*] of the 'Long Parliament', which had first met in 1640, had become increasingly puritanical during the war years and more and more determined to root out Papist practices. The unfounded yet fanatical prejudice of this body was echoed among the merchants and citizens because of the constant propaganda of broadsheets spreading scurrilous tales about the now exiled, Catholic Queen, Henrietta Maria and her co-religionists still residing in England.

[14] D.N.B.
[15] D.N.B. The eldest son Charles (first Duke of Bolton and sixth Marquis of Winchester) strongly supported the Whigs during the reign of Charles II and James II and actively supported the Protestant William of Orange in 1688.
[16] T.M.McCoog, English & Welsh Jesuits.
[*] Strictly known as the 'Rump' following Colonel Pride's purge of the Presbyterian members in December 1648.

Every year on or about the fifth of November, the anniversary of the discovery of the Gunpowder Plot, 'no-popery' sermons were preached by rabid Calvinistic clergymen. These anti-Catholic diatribes were delivered using the sort of language, which was calculated to stir up the mob, but if used today against anyone would lead to prosecution for slander. In this climate of hatred and bigotry it is not surprising to discover that, between 1641 and 1646, no less than twelve priests had been apprehended, accused of treason, and executed, at Tyburn gallows (near the modern junction of Oxford Street and Edgware Road), by the barbarous method of being hung, drawn and quartered. Many others were put to death in different parts of the country and still more died in prison.

Recusants were held accountable for each and every mishap or calamity including being responsible for starting the Civil War by giving the King bad counsel. The bitter and unreasoned bias, against all who wished to worship using the ancient rites of the Catholic Faith, continued to be a dominant feature of English political and social life for many years to come. In 1666, the Great Fire of London, despite all evidence to the contrary, was blamed on Papists by many inhabitants of the city. Titus Oates' ridiculous tale, in 1678, about a Popish plot to kill King Charles II, led to a spate of accusations and executions. The whole thing was a fabrication of a disordered mind yet persecution persisted for three years since Catholics were deemed capable of any felony.

The same pre-conceived fear and suspicion, in 1688, played a large part in the ousting of the Catholic King, James II, and the substitution of the Protestant monarchs William and Mary. Subsequent re-enactment of harsh penal laws and the imposition of the Act of Settlement (still in force today), which prohibited any Roman Catholic from ever succeeding to the throne, did not put an end to the harassment of Papist Recusants (Non-Jurors). As late as 1780 an anti-Catholic mob could still be roused to burn houses and chapels in the Gordon riots.

Some of the chapels belonging to foreign embassies, particularly those of France and Spain, had provided refuges as well as Mass centres for the native English Catholics since the reign of Elizabeth I. The existence of these havens of comparative security, as well as the establishment of Queen Henrietta's private chapel in Somerset House, during the 1630s, meant that adherents of the 'Old Faith' were to be found in London in ever increasing numbers until the outbreak of the Civil Wars. After the first phase of the Wars had ended, in 1646, Catholics still formed a significant minority of the population.

The First Civil War saw many acts of vandalism and iconoclasm committed by Puritan hooligans but none more extreme than when the aforementioned Queen's chapel was broken into on Maundy Thursday, 1643. Over the altar was a painting of the crucifixion of Our Lord, painted by Rubens, given to the Queen by the Duke of Buckingham, but a halberd made short work of it. Pictures, statues, candlesticks were battered with fury. Missals, breviaries and all the service books were torn to pieces and then burnt in the private cemetery attached to the house. [17]

[17] G.Anstruther, Hundred Homeless Years, p.181.

Fr. Peter Wright teaching catechism

This sort of treatment was not just reserved for Catholic chapels for the mob also broke into the private houses of known Papists and ransacked them as well. Anglican churches too, particularly those that had installed some of Archbishop Laud's reforms, were not safe from the depredations of these fanatics who even defaced and desecrated the tomb of the saintly King Edward the Confessor in Westminster Abbey.

The fury of the Puritan zealots abated somewhat after the defeat of King Charles I, his later surrender to the Scots, and final imprisonment by Parliament and the army. The energies of those who had fought against the King were now to be expended on other matters. Two of the first considerations were how to pay off the army and how to reorganise the constitution. It must be noted that religious and moral issues were deemed of equal importance to any fiscal or political concerns, and laws were soon passed by the Presbyterian Parliament to curtail swearing, for example, by a system of fines graded according to rank. Church festivals were abolished by this strict regime beginning with an order, in 1644, that Christmas Day was to be kept as a fast and soldiers sent round to check that no one was cooking meat. Three years later, it was forbidden to observe Easter, Whitsuntide and other feasts. (18) These regulations met with much opposition, in many parts of England, but were rigorously enforced for some years, particularly in the capital, until the nation wearied of the rule of the self-styled 'Godly brethren'.

Countless new rules for moral and social conduct were passed by the Puritan Presbyterian remnant of the Long Parliament but this did not please many in General Cromwell's army who were independent in religious thought and action.

The quarrels and political feuds which gradually developed between the two factions were well noted by Fr.Peter Wright during his necessarily secret travels about London during approximately five years of covert ministry.

In the four surviving letters, written to Mr,Joseph Simons (*), during 1647 (App.B), Fr.Peter described, at some length, the attempts to get Charles to sign the Scottish Covenant. On the twenty third of April he gave the names of the Commissioners recently arrived from Scotland and included the sort of detail that could only be obtained by conversations with leading citizens and perhaps even Parliament men. One specific item mentioned was the £200 000 demanded by the army as arrears of pay. An earlier letter alluded to the King's imprisonment at Holdenby House and he remarked that there was almost no news of him. He wrote regarding the treatment of Charles- "Poor man, he is as much afflicted for his conscience as ever poor Papist was, for the Houses will grant him none but Covenanter Ministers, which he refusing is debarred of all." (19)

(18) *G.Davies, Early Stuarts, p.307.*

(*) *Mr.Joseph Simons was an alias for Fr.Emmanuel Lobb, S.J.*

(19) *P.Wright, Letters, Quoted in full in Foley Vol.ii. p.560/561.*

As previously quoted in Chapter Two, Fr.Peter also reported the King as playing games of bowls at Lord Vaux's house at Boughton in Northamptonshire. (One wonders if the information came direct from a member of the Vaux household.) This news was directly followed by an item explaining how Parliament had granted every second Tuesday in the month a play-day to the apprentices of London. (No doubt an ironic remark since it would be common knowledge that the Puritans had already forbidden any form of recreation on Sunday - and Saturday was not a holiday in the seventeenth century.) With more sarcasm the letter concluded- "Exceeding good they (Parliament) are to all sorts of people, for which as some say we shall know what our religion shall be within this month, for from Tuesday next the house hath appointed fourteen days together to consider thereof, and the Assembly of Divines to bring in their places of Scripture." [(20)]

The third and longest letter, from the twelfth of November, had much to say about certain (army) agitators, meeting at Putney, voting to have no King, but that General Cromwell was not, as yet, in favour of abolishing the monarchy. Other disturbances in the army are reported in detail along with some mutinous conduct which went unpunished. Reference was made to the usual 'Gunpowder Day' sermon against Catholics, preached bitterly by a Presbyterian minister before the Lower House of Parliament which; "caused the old inveterate hate to be revived against them, and they to begin to talk in the House to act against them, until Martin, a professed enemy of the King, stood up and in a speech said that treason of the Papistry, nor any treason he could call to mind, were to be paralleled with the King's against the State." [(21)] This letter concluded with a very detailed account of Charles I's escape from Hampton Court although the mystery of his whereabouts or exact means of effecting the break out was not definitely known.

Nothing in any of the preserved letters would have revealed Fr.Peter Wright as a Jesuit priest and all are good examples of how careful Catholics, especially clerics, had to be to avoid betraying themselves to the authorities. The one written on the fifth of December 1647 is printed in full (Appendix D). Here the author's account of military operations in Scotland could easily be mistaken for the writing of a Parliament man. Communications such as these could, of course, have included coded messages but the likelihood is that the only hidden meaning for the Jesuit recipient (Fr.Lobb) was the simple one of confirming the writer's continued freedom from arrest and imprisonment.The fact of them being written, and survival to the present day, may well indicate that there was for some months, if not years, a relaxation of the extreme 'terror' which had previously afflicted all Catholic Recusants.

However, there is good reason to suppose that the spies and priest catchers were no less vigilant between 1646 and 1649 than previously. Indeed they had become so practised in the art that, particularly in London, their nefarious trade was almost a profession.

[(20)] *Ibid.*

[(21)] *Ibid., p.563*

Pursuivants like Mayo, Luke and Wadsworth, who will be heard of again in Chapter VII, had found that the bounty paid by the magistrates for handing over a priest for trial, although as much as £50, was only paid once. A much more lucrative business was that of extortion whereby Catholics, particularly those who were wealthy, could be persuaded to pay monies over and over again to avoid arrest and imprisonment. Fixed terms were negotiated with the priest hunters, and paid on a quarterly basis, [22] to avoid the house searches and other indignities inflicted by these gangs of informers who were armed with warrants issued by Sheriffs and Justices of the Peace.

It was better for Recusants to submit to blackmail than allow goods to be stolen in the name of the law and also avoid, "outrages, abuses, and misdemeanours committed: goods, plate and jewels, in no way connected with the altar (used for Mass) taken on the plea that they were the goods of Jesuits." [23] By conniving at this system, which today would be termed a 'protection racket', the Papists of London safeguarded their property and were able to practise their religion in comparative ease.

In addition to the arrangements outlined above, the new republican government, established at the time of the execution of Charles I, January 1649, brought in a policy which they described as 'liberty of conscience'. As already mentioned, an Independent faction had already gained the ascendancy in the Parliamentary army and was opposed to the hard-line Calvinistic puritanism that had held sway previously even to the extent of declaring that no-one should be punished on the sole account of religion. More moderation was shown towards Catholic priests and none, in fact, were put to death judicially between August 1646 and May 1651, though some died in prison. The Papist community began to breathe more freely and were probably less discreet when celebrating Mass in private chapels or attending religious observances in the embassies of the governments of Spain, France, Venice etc. Some undoubtedly believed that a permanent cessation of persecution might be achieved.

"Many, however, suspected and too truly perhaps, as the succeeding calamities attest, that the acts of lenity (leniency) in favour of the recusants was not sincere, but was rather a trap whereby the more surely to discover the Catholics,who were certain to make ample use of the concessions." [24]

We have already noted the letters of Fr.Peter Wright, penned in 1647, as probable evidence of the slightly easier times and surely the preservation of so many of his sermons (Appendix B) is another indication of some relaxation of the strict penal laws. It is unfortunate that we do not know the exact dates when these discourses were written or delivered but presume them to originate between 1647 and 1650. Equally the story behind the rescue of the manuscripts, their transport across the Channel and final home coming to Stonyhurst College is unknown.

[22] *F.Foster, Letter to Madrid (1651).*
[23] *P.Caraman, Henry Morse, p.116.*
[24] *H.Foley, Records, Vol.ii. p.519.*

From these homilies, however, we can deduce much about the conditions existing in London during the period a few months prior to Fr.Peter's capture (Chapter VII). An examination of the two sermons printed in the appendices at the back of this volume will reveal that each would take at least an hour to present in oratorical style. All 62 are of a similar length and show that the Catholic congregations were not expecting to be interrupted by priest hunters while attending Mass.

The preacher does not gloss over the problems which afflicted his hearers as he exhorts them not to attend Protestant acts of worship or hear Protestant sermons. His reasoning in this was not so much that the presence of Catholics at heretical gatherings was sinful in itself but that in England, though not in France or Germany, Papists were subject to laws which sought to compel them to attend the services of the state church, the tenets of which were Protestant and unorthodox. The strong rhetorical language is worth repeating as he writes, "Though perchance to hear their sermons or to be present at their sermons or other service may be no sin or to some persons not dangerous, yet to hear them, or to seem as if we heard them, or to be present at them, or in any sort to countenance them, *because we are commanded to do so*, is so gross a denial of our Faith that our Saviour doth deservedly deny them who condescend to any such impious and unlawful action." [25] Since an ordinance of the English (Commonwealth) government, of 1650, repealed penalties on those not attending their parish churches, [26] it would appear that the sermon, just quoted, must have been written before that date.

We do not know where these homilies were spoken but there is no reason to suppose that the Winchester's house in Holborn was the only venue. Fr.Peter refers to Hyde Park and Spring Gardens in sermon number 20 and was obviously well acquainted with other parts of London. The sermons too are so full of biblical and classical references, as well as quotations from the writings of the Fathers of the Church, that he must have had the advantage of using an extensive library and had time to peruse it thoroughly. Clearly, it is unlikely that Catholics would have dared to preserve a large collection of valuable books in their London homes at such a dangerous time. Possibly he could have found the necessary texts separately in the possession of different noblemen but the most likely source, of his very detailed information, would have been the houses of the French and Spanish ambassadors.

For a number of years Papists had recourse to foreign embassies for the purpose of attending Mass, without interference from government agents, and also to receive spiritual encouragement through the Sacraments. Diplomatic immunity meant that foreign chaplains as well as consular representatives were able to travel freely to and from Europe. They could bring in the kind of books that would be useful to the English missionary priests as well as messages for the beleaguered

[25] *P.Wright, Sermon 53, 'On Confessing the Faith'.*
[26] *G.Davies, Early Stuarts, p.211.*

Recusants. Letters, and sometimes even priests, might be smuggled out of the country. The ambassadors and their wives were always anxious to help secure the release of fellow Catholics held in prison or sentenced to death. Evidence was occasionally provided to prove that a man detained for his religion had been born abroad and was not technically an English citizen. When this proved impossible, as in the case of Fr.Henry Morse in 1645, these most senior diplomats would visit the prison and be present at the execution.

In 1650, the French King through his ambassador recognised, or at lease acknowledged, the new republican administration in London as the 'de facto' government . Once again Catholic Recusants were full of hope, expecting to derive some benefit from the new regime, supposing there would be a further lessening of the fears, suspicions and hatred so long directed towards those who still owed allegiance to the Vicar of Christ and successor of St. Peter. Many anticipated that attendance at the embassy chapels would now be safe and free from the attentions of snoopers and informers.

It was not to be; for on Christmas Day an armed mob, accompanied by soldiers, attacked and ransacked the residence of the French ambassador. The spies had done their work well and knew the exact hour for the celebration of Mass and that a great crowd of English Catholics would be present. The very size of the crowd enabled the priest to disrobe and escape but a large number of men and women, both young and old, were arrested and imprisoned. Even the ambassador together with other French nobles and officials were incarcerated for some hours and after a few days ordered to leave the country. [27]

Twelve days later, on the Feast of the Epiphany, the house of the former Spanish ambassador Count Egmond (Egremont), was similarly assaulted. Sacred furniture, pictures and crucifixes were carried off and paraded through the streets along with the frightened Catholics who had so suddenly been set upon and dragged away from their devotions. This was a return to the previous era of persecution and the only clue to explain the sudden 'volte face' is to be found in the news that Charles II had been crowned King in Scotland on the first of January. A perceived threat to the infant republic could have been enough to ignite the latent embers of intolerance and hostility towards the Papists.

The pursuivants continued to receive their usual peace offerings of money bribes but egged on by the jealous soldiers, who had also obtained warrants for searching houses, they went on exploring parties through the city of London and its suburbs. "They tracked the priests at every step; they watched the houses of Catholics for every comer and goer, especially at early morning and evening, the times when, as they knew, the priests were accustomed to issue forth upon their ministerial functions." [28]

[27] *H.Foley, Records, Vol.ii, p.514 & F.Foster*, Letter 30th May, 1651 (* Foster was the Jesuit Provincial).*

[28] *Ibid.*

In a very few weeks the searchers had netted a total of eight priests including Fr.Thomas Middleton (alias Dade) the provincial of the Dominican order in England. On the Feast of Candlemas (second of February) 1651, Fr.Peter Wright, S.J., was one of those arrested in the sudden purge. Surprisingly, perhaps, this seemed to be the culmination of priest-catching activities during the Winter of 1650-51.

We have no knowledge of Fr.Peter's exact schedule of priestly visitations in the period prior to his capture. Perhaps he said Mass and preached in the embassy chapels as well as in the houses of his patron. Many priests made it their business to visit the prisons to hear confessions and say Mass for the Catholics held there. This sort of thing went on under the noses of the gaolers and turnkeys who were easily bought off if they became suspicious - although it was not unknown for a priest to be recognised and arrested on one of these errands of mercy. Our Jesuit is not mentioned in this respect but that does not mean he was not involved. He certainly received a multitude of well wishers when it was his turn to be detained.

Some puzzling questions are raised about the reasons why our particular priest was arrested at this time. Was it simply that the number of Papists attending Mass at the Winchester's home was now so large it attracted the attention of the authorities? Why was it that only the priest was captured, contrary to the conduct of the pursuivants at Count Egremont's house only a few weeks previously? Were Fr.Peter Wright's sermons drawing larger than normal crowds? Were they being talked about and was the government determined to deal with this Jesuit before he persuaded more of the common people to convert to Rome? Were the presbyterian/ independent ministers jealous of his preaching ability or was it simply that the apostate, Thomas Gage, was resolved to be revenged on his late brother's chaplain? Did the priest hunters suddenly demand more money?

The next chapter will reveal much about our martyr's steadfast courage and obvious sanctity but unfortunately cannot explain all the various motives of those who sought to destroy him. It is now time to describe the circumstances and trace the events of the weeks leading to the tragic yet glorious conclusion.

Upon thursday last the Grand Councel of the Agitators at Putney
voted to have no king, but General Cromwel understanding
what the Scotish Commissioners message was both to the king
and to the two houses, made an ernest speech unto them to the
contrary, telling them how dangerous such a vote would be to the
whole Army; for sayd he, we have hanging over our heads a black
cloude from the North, that we shal not be able to disperse; for
should we persist in that opinion, not only the whole kingdome
of Scotland with al their Presbyterian brethren here, but al
the kings party would come against us to our inevitable
ruyne. This made a stop of the busines though many of the
Agitators stormed thereat. In the printed paper enclosed
you wil finde the Scotish speech and demands, which speech
hath also troubled both the houses, they not knowing what
answeare to returne thereunto. Neither is the trouble lesse
in the Army amongst themselves for Cromwel Ireton and the
principle Officers are ernest to come to a speedy conclusion
with the king. Rainsborow and the Agitators are of a

Sample of Fr. Peter Wright's handwriting.

Chapter VII

Arrest - Imprisonment - Trial - Martyrdom - Speech from the scaffold.

It was mid-morning, the second of February 1651, [*] when 'captain' James Waddesworth, [1] Robert de Luke and Thomas Mayo (well-known pursuivants) clattered up the back stairs of the Marquis of Winchester's home in Holborn (or perhaps Covent Garden). [2] They hoped to catch Fr.Peter Wright in the act of celebrating Mass and were accompanied by a large number of professional priest catchers and bounty hunters. Since early morning the gang had been secreted in the neighbourhood waiting for the opportunity to strike. At last the back door of the property was opened by a servant returning from an errand. Perhaps this was an arranged signal but, in any event, the chance was taken to rush into the property.

Most probably the precise location of the chapel was known to the invaders because they made directly towards the upper part of the house. Hearing the commotion, the Marquis himself barred the way and demanded to know the meaning for the noisy intrusion into his private domain. For some time he was successful in detaining the raucous mob until, no doubt waving their warrant papers and pushing him roughly aside, the throng burst into the room where Mass was about to be celebrated.

The cruets were already filled with wine and water while in an anteroom a priest's cassock and breviary, in which was a picture of St.Francis Xavier, lay discarded. An informer at the later trial testified, "that he found in the said house the chapel with cushions here and there lying about, with cruets prepared . . . ; and lastly that he had seized the priestly vestments from the hands of one of the servants who was running off with them." [3] The priest was not to be found, having apparently vanished!

The delaying tactics of the Marquis of Winchester had given ample warning of the raiders and Fr.Peter could have secreted himself within a hide - it seems one was readily available - where he might have avoided capture. However, the chapel and priest's robing room or sacristy were, as was usual in Recusant houses, on an upper floor of the building with windows giving access to the roof. One of the lights was found to be open and the pursuivants correctly guessed that the Jesuit had escaped among the leads and chimneys.

A youth was sent out to investigate and the presumed priest quickly discovered and brought down to his room. It is possible that he had used the device of hiding on the roof to create sufficient

[*] 1650 by the unreformed calendar in use in England, (the year not ending until March 24th).

[1] G.Anstruther, Hundred Homeless Years, p.188 (Cf.Wadsworth in Ch,V).

[2] The apostate, Thomas Gage, stated that it was Covent Garden which might mean that Winchester possessed more than one property or be a mistake on Gage's part. (Cf.Anstruther, Ibid,, p.189).

[3] H.Foley, Records, Vol. ii, p.524.

diversion to allow other Catholics in the congregation to flee from the house. Certainly none were reported as having been taken in the surprise raid. There is also the probability that the Jesuit did not want to be caught on the premises for fear of incriminating his hosts and their family.

The prize capture, of the suspected Jesuit priest, was immediately taken down to the living quarters of the fifth Marquis of Winchester, John Paulet and his wife Margaret, where it was hoped sufficient evidence might be obtained to confirm the suspicions of the gloating crew of pursuivants and bounty hunters. However, the only confirmation of Fr.Peter's real character to be revealed was in the respect and honour paid to him by the aristocratic owners of the house. This flimsy corroboration of priesthood was later used as a proof when the martyr was indicted and put on trial.

The day of the capture, being the second of February, was, and still is, an important one in both Roman Catholic and Anglican calendars. The Feast of the Purification of the Blessed Virgin Mary (now known in the Roman Church as The Presentation of the Lord) was incorporated in Cranmer's Book of Common Prayer; although only in the Roman Church is the liturgy of the day preceded by a procession of lighted candles, giving rise to the name Candlemas(s). The Holy Day also had another significance as it marked the official end of the Christmas season. In 1650/51 the situation was somewhat peculiar in that the English Puritan Parliament had decreed against the feasts of the Church, and abolished Christmas and its season, with fixed penalties for those caught celebrating in any way. This may, in part, explain why so many raids were carried out in a short period, but another reason could be that the crafty priest-catchers (some of whom were renegade Catholics) took the opportunity to strike when and where there was a good chance of finding a large number of Papists worshipping at Mass.

The story of the arrest contains some unexplained facts in that if it was 'Candlemas(s)' no candles were reported as being found and there is no mention of a congregation other than the Winchesters and their servants. Could it be that although Waddesworth and his gang thought that a number of prominent Catholics would be present, because of the feast, they were in error? The Purification had been celebrated ten days earlier because the Catholics were adhering to the new style Gregorian calendar for liturgical purposes. This is only a supposition and cannot be substantiated.

There are good reasons to believe that the impromptu posse, that paraded its captive through the streets, was offered money as a ransom to secure his freedom. It was almost standard practice to try to effect the release of a Papist prisoner, be he priest or layman, by proffering gold. In this case we believe the pursuivants at first made as if to accept the bribe but then immediately increased their demands. Either they expected to receive more from the Privy Council or more likely a mysterious person, who hated the very name Catholic, had put up a higher sum for the capture of the Jesuit priest. [(4)]

By mid-day the captors, who were themselves sure they had apprehended the wanted Jesuit dragged their prisoner before the Court of Lord Chief Justice Rolles. According to custom they

[(4)] *Ibid., p.516.*

Fr. Peter Wright avoiding
capture on the roof

Fr. Peter Wright hearing
confessions in prison

shouted out that they had arrested a traitor and a priest - the two words being synonymous in seventeenth century English Protestant parlance. However, his Lordship would not straight away accept the proofs put forward, which were very slight, and committed Fr.Peter to the nearby Newgate prison on the charge of being a suspected priest.

Newgate prison had originally been part of the gatehouse of one of the city of London's main medieval exits. It was close to the Old Bailey criminal courts and by the seventeenth century had been much extended to house a variety of prisoners including priests awaiting trial and men condemned to execution. In those days, and for many years afterwards, the gaolers made their living from providing food and accommodation for payment. The higher the price the better the conditions and some rich men were able to live very well behind bars.

Since Fr. Peter had been arrested in a nobleman's dwelling, he was placed among the better sort of prisoners in the lower court of the gaol. It was assumed that his friends would pay the exorbitant rates but the Jesuit refused such 'luxurious' living and demanded to be moved to the upper court where he knew other priests were being held. So it was that he joined the small band of captured clerics, some secular, others regular, who accepted the newcomer into what was fast becoming a religious club. Henry Foley wrote of his character at this harrowing time, "He was, indeed gifted with a candour and simplicity of heart truly Christian without colour of deceit of any kind." [5] The only snag was that, because of a shortage of beds, he had to share a couch, as well as a cell, with Fr. (Charles) Cheney, an elderly secular priest.

The situation must have been irksome for these men of God but both seem to have profited spiritually from the experience, praying together and hearing each others confessions. The reason that we know so much about our Jesuit's demeanour and state of mind, while a prisoner in Newgate, is because of a long letter which Fr.Cheney (described in seventeenth century style as the Reverend Mr.Cheney) wrote to the Jesuit Father Provincial. In this epistle the venerable gentleman congratulated himself on his good fortune in being able to enjoy the company of a man having such a "courteous manner united by Divine grace to an upright and truly noble soul." [6] He goes on to explain how the other prisoners also observed and were strengthened by Fr.Peter's "wonderful courage and cheerfulness of soul," allied to "a certain innocent freedom void of any cloak of pretence." [7] In spite of the difficulties of prison life and the likelihood of a trial, with a probable terminal outcome, the Northamptonshire born man was from the first always calm and cheerful.

During these years, Old Bailey sessions were held every month and in the weeks before Easter Fr.Cheney, together with another secular priest, Fr.Baker (possibly an alias), were summoned to

[5] *Ibid., p.517.*
[6] *Ibid., pp.534-535.*
[7] *Ibid.*

the bar accused of treason because they were Catholic priests. The evidence against them was provided by the same notorious team of informers who had assailed the Marquis of Winchester's abode, namely Wadsworth, Luke and Mayo. In respect of Fr.Baker, it was stated that some twenty years previously he had been seen saying Mass at an altar, though no proof of ordination was forthcoming. Fr.Cheney readily admitted his priesthood but pointed out that he had been born in the Spanish Netherlands and was therefore outside the jurisdiction of an English court.

The jury found both men not guilty amidst general rejoicing and some outbursts of anger against the informers. The authorities had been thwarted in their attempts to have two Papist priests executed for treason. Nevertheless, on the following day, the pair were fined two hundred marks [*] each for having celebrated Mass in England and then returned to prison. The verdicts were seen by many Catholics as a hopeful sign and some expected that Fr.Peter would soon be set free. Unfortunately the republican legal representatives, being disappointed in this law suit, were more determined than ever to make the case against the Jesuit strong enough to secure a conviction.

Meanwhile Holy Week and Paschal time had arrived with the ceremonies honoured by the London Papists in traditional manner. Holy Thursday saw more worshippers than ever flock to the foreign embassy chapels. Newgate prison was itself a devotional venue and must have resembled a pilgrimage centre as a large number of the faithful became daily visitors. Prisons in the mid-seventeenth century were much more open than those of today and it appears the priests were able to celebrate Masses on a regular basis and give Holy Communion to the Catholic callers, providing the gaolers were amenable to the usual bribes. Henry Foley, doubtless here quoting from Fr.Edward Leedes, wrote, "Many especially of his former penitents, flocked to Father Peter, both to confess to him as previously and to be strengthened and confirmed by his conversation and example, always returning home more joyful and consoled." [8]

Immediately after Easter our Jesuit's friends began negotiating again for his release by offering a substantial sum as a ransom. The affair was conducted on a daily basis and there were hopes, more than once, of a successful conclusion. But, as before, the price was raised and obstacles put in the way. Eventually, Fr.Peter, hearing of the attempts was justly angry at the mercenary conduct of his captors and wrote to the Father Procurator, "that he was unwilling that he should treat any further with such merchants - let them do their own work; that this life was not so precious to him but that he would willingly lay it down in death to gain immortality." [9]

Even after the cessation of the ransom bids, most of the Jesuit religious as well as many lay Catholics believed that the leaders of the new republican government in England would not allow a man to die for the sake of conscience or religion. In this they were mistaken for a few days

[*] *mark = thirteen shillings and four pence - thus two hundred marks would total £133 - 6s - 8d.*

[8] *Ibid., p.519.*

[9] *Ibid.*

before the commencement of the May sessions, at the Old Bailey, news came that special messengers had been sent to Deal in Kent, by order of Rolles, the Lord Chief Justice, to summon to London Thomas Gage, the apostate former Dominican priest. The purpose behind the peremptory invitation was to ask Gage to identify and give evidence against Fr.Peter Wright. It is possible that he had made a previous deposition but of this we have no knowledge. The malevolent ex-friar was also expected to provide grounds for conviction when his one time superior, Fr.Thomas Middleton (alias Dade), was brought before the court.

By this date, Gage had become an Anglican/Presbyterian clergyman. We have mentioned him before (Ch.V) and he was infamously known for a scandalous recantation sermon which he preached at St.Paul's Cathedral on the twenty-eighth of August 1642. [10] He had been a Dominican priest for a number of years but had avowed to shake off 'the magpie habit' [*] early in 1640 and become a Protestant, though for at least a year he was still trusted by Catholics, while acting as a spy for the government. In December 1642, together with 'captain' Waddesworth he testified against the Jesuit, Fr.Thomas Holland, declaring that they had been at school together at St.Omers and that he knew him to be a priest. Inevitably the outcome was a guilty verdict and condemnation to be hung, drawn and quartered. The same pattern continued in 1643 when a Franciscan priest, Fr.Francis Bell, was executed following the renegade's evidence. [11]

This was only a beginning for on the seventh of September 1644, Fr.Ralph Corby, another Jesuit, was similarly despatched on testimony provided by Gage. The president of the Douai seminary later wrote that the apostate ex-friar was responsible for the deaths of many. When Fr.Henry Morse, the Jesuit fellow army chaplain of Fr.Peter, was condemned to die on the seventeenth of January 1645, [12] Gage's corroborative proofs were not required but there is no doubt that he was ready to provide information if necessary.

These tragic betrayals were the more poignant because Thomas Gage was not only the brother of Fr.Peter's friend, the late Colonel Sir Henry Gage, but also had two other brothers alive who were priests of the Roman Church, George, a secular and William, a Jesuit. Their parents, John and Margaret (App.G), had been well known Recusants of the county of Sussex/Surrey who were both sentenced to death for harbouring a priest in 1591, but then reprieved after forfeiting their Haling estates to the crown. [13] When Margaret died, John married again and had three further sons two of whom, John and Francis, also became Catholic priests.

Fr.George Gage had himself been arrested as early as 1628 and placed in the prison known as the Clink. From here he was rescued by the good offices of Queen Henrietta and given a place in

[10] *G.Anstruther, Hundred Homeless Years, pp. 177,178.*

[*] *'magpie habit' - the black and white religious costume peculiar to the Order of Preachers or Dominicans.*

[11] *B.Basset, English Jesuits, p.220.*

[12] *P.Caraman, Henry Morse, p.173.*

[13] *G.Anstruther, Seminary Priests, Vo1.2, p.119.*

her household. Later we find him living at the Portuguese ambassador's residence, in London, but was again captured and sent to Newgate. By September 1650, he was bailed, for three months, apparently given a commission by the government to negotiate with the Spanish authorities to secure the release of some merchants held in Lisbon. On returning to this country, Fr.George failed to surrender to his bail and so in May 1651, learning that his turncoat brother was in town, threatening further mischief, he paid him a visit and tried desperately to get him to abandon the idea of giving evidence.

There was considerable personal risk for Fr.George, in this action, as his own name had already appeared on the indictment that included Fr.Thomas Dade and Fr.Peter Wright. After exhorting and entreating his brother, in his own name and that of other friends, not to commit so heinous a crime as to give testimony against the men of God, he received an assurance that the apostate would not injure either of them.(14) Was this a false promise? It would seem so, yet perhaps Thomas Gage was not his own master. Two years previously he had been summoned before the Council of State presumably asked to supply information about Papist priests. He had recently been interviewed by both the Lord Chief Justice and the Lord President of the Council. (15)

The trial was due to commence at Justice Hall in the Old Bailey on the fourteenth of May 1651, before Henry Rolles, Chief Justice of the Upper Bench, (as it was called under the Commonwealth) Philip Jermyn and Richard Aske, justices of the same bench, Thomas Andrews, Lord Mayor of London, William Steels, the Recorder, and others. (16) But before proceedings commenced Thomas Gage was taken to Newgate and confronted with the prisoners for the purpose of identifying them. We have Fr.Peter Wright's own description of what took place from a letter he wrote to the Jesuit Father Provincial, Fr.Francis Foster, which that worthy copied verbatim and sent to Spain on the thirtieth of May (N.S.). (17)

The letter reads as follows (with seventeenth century spelling uncorrected):-

" Syre

This morning Ld.Chief Justice Rols sent one of his secretaries with Tom Gage and de Luke to know whether Tom Gage knew me. Gage at my entrance into ye roome where they weare came to me and saluted me by name. I would not acknowledge that I knew him; he told ye company that he knew me very well; that I was his brother's confessarius, that he was with me and another father of ye Societie called Lathome in ye Spanish army neere Salle divers days together; and he sayd, that afterwards I was with his brother in Oxford, and was with him when he was wounded at

(14) G.Anstruther, Hundred Homeless Years, p.187 (Quotes from Foley).
(15) F.Foster, Letter to College in Madrid.
(16) G.Anstruther, Hundred Homeless Years, p.187.
(17) F.Foster, Letter to College in Madrid.

Abington, and gave him extream unction when he dyed. and then he began to apologize for what he had sayd, alleadging two reasons for it. the first that the state had commanded it, to whom he was bound in conscience to correspond, ye 2[d] his owne conscience, and for this gentlemen, sayd he, I will tell you a story. King James, sayd he, putt fa. Garnet justly to death, because, though he perchance was no actor in ye powder treason, yett that he had not dissuaded actors, being theire Confessarius, from that plott, I will apply it now sayd he; I will not say that you had any intention to kill me, yett you being my brother's confessarius, and you knowing that he had an intention to kill me, and that he employed one Vincent Burton about it, did not dissuade him; wherefore I have cause to doe what I doe. And then he added that I had divers great friends in ye towne, and that he was in danger of his life, especially since that great Lady with whom I lived, caused one Jones her keeper in St.Giles to be stabbed: you may easily imagine upon this I gave him an answer fitting himselfe. I bid him doe his worste, what that will be I know not, and I thank God am very indifferent, and am resolved not to give ye Poursuivants one farthing, and to stand to all hazards. Wherefore I humbly beseech youres and ye prayers of all oures, and oure friends in ye towne.

Sir I am really
youre humble obedient servant
Pet.Wright

May 13th 1651 "

From the contents of this letter two things become very clear; the first that Thomas Gage was very much afraid for his life and indeed was suffering from some kind of persecution mania even going so far as to suggest that his late brother, Henry, had wanted him dead; and the second point to notice is that Fr.Peter had no fear at all.

When the actual trial began, the following day, Fr. Thomas Dade was found *not guilty* of the treasonable charge of being a priest of the Catholic Church ordained abroad. This was because the evidence given by Thomas Gage merely confirmed the fact that he was the Superior of the Dominicans in England and not necessarily ordained. He cited the case of St.Francis of Assisi who was Superior of his order but did not become a priest. The prisoner was returned to Newgate and shortly afterwards released.

The case of Fr.Peter Wright was very different and again we have his own account, written from prison on the seventeenth of May, which describes what took place. [18] [*] The pursuivants, De Luke,

[18] *Ibid.*

[*] *Thomas Gage later wrote a malicious and biased narrative entitled, "A Duel between a Jesuit and a Dominican, begun at Paris, gallantly fought at Madrid and victoriously ended at London on Friday 16 May 1651." Despite the vitriol, this confirms Fr. Peter Wright's account in essentials.*

Wadsworth and Mayo all gave evidence of the arrest and the Judge asked the Jesuit for his reactions but he asked to be excused until all the accusations had been made. It is worth noting here that in the seventeenth century no counsel for the defence was permitted in trials for treason.

The next witness was Thomas Gage who, after declaiming his knowledge of Fr.Peter's priestly activities in Flanders, near Salle and at Ghent, "strongly affirmed, this is ye man, this is that fa.Wright; for though his haire be growne more gray, yett, I know him by his eyes, his voyce, and his face, I know him to be a Priest and a Jesuit." Then the apostate continued in the vein of the day before; even telling the Bench that he was in danger of his life and asking for protection.

In this second letter written to the Jesuit Provincial, Fr.Peter admitted that he was in a quandary as to whether to acknowledge that he was a priest, "least it might be objected that I was cause of my own death." Instead, addressing the Judge he said, "My Lord I doe from ye very bottom of my heart thank Allm (Almighty) God that he hath permitted me to be brought hither, not (to use the words of S.Peter) as a thiefe or adulterer, or malefactor, but purely for my Religion, for ye Catholique Religion that hath been, is, and will be renowned through ye whole world; and this is all I have to say." Then turning to the Jury he told them to proceed according to the evidence and do what in their consciences they thought fit.

The Chief Justice, at this point, butted in saying, "You are to know you suffer not for your Religion; but for your goeing beyond that and taking orders, and comming into England and seducing ye people, etc." (This was before the Jury had retired to consider their verdict.) Our Jesuit bravely replied to the Judge, "That Nero, Diocletian and Domitian, and ye primitive Persecutors might have objected that to ye Apostles, Preists and Primitive Martyrs." The Chief Justice retorted, "ye case was different, they preached ye Ghospell we ye contrary." But Fr.Peter had the last word, replying, "that was ye question - all sects and heresyes were admitted in this kingdom but only (not) the Catholic Religion."

It is clear from these interchanges that the courtroom scenes could not be equated with modern British high court procedures although perhaps resembling some Hollywood film dramas. Indeed there was something farcical about what next ensued; Thomas Gage had been holding Fr.Peter's Breviary [*] all the time the altercation with the Chief Justice had been continuing, now he had to interrupt. Waving a little picture of St.Francis Xavier he read out a latin prayer that was handwritten in the book and followed this up with some derogatory remarks about Jesuit practices. This gave the Jesuit the opportunity to speak out once again and particularly to defend his friend and former patron, Colonel Sir Henry Gage against the slurs and calumnies made by his, now infamous brother, Thomas. He reminded the Judge that Sir Henry, "was not only esteemed of the party, for which he fought, but also by his ennemyes."

[*] *'Breviary' = Catholic book of daily prayers, obligatory for priests.*

The Judge remarked that Sir Henry was undoubtedly a Papist, but at the same time (it appears) spoke strongly against Thomas Gage for his slanderous attack on his brother's reputation. Even then the renegade was determined to harangue the prisoner and began a dispute about praying to the Saints. At this juncture Fr.Peter, to use his own words, "highly slighted ye man." So vehement was the condemnation that Gage once more demanded to have a guard to defend himself "especially since the man on trial was friendly with great and powerful men in the town." Fr.Peter replied with a saying of King Solomon, "*fugit impius nemine persequente*, this wicked man flyes and fears when nobody pursues him." [19] Shortly afterwards the jury were ordered to retire to consider their verdict; the prisoner being sent to wait in an adjoining room.

Many people in this court ante-room, jurymen, officers, citizens and other prisoners, congratulated the Jesuit on his defence and in particular for his denunciation of the key witness, Thomas Gage. Some recalled Gage's recantation sermon and how ridiculous that had seemed to them, especially a story about a mouse running off with the Sacred Host when he was saying Mass.

Despite the obvious sympathy of many in the court, however, the jury only took fifteen minutes to bring in the verdict - guilty of being a priest! [20] Fr.Peter's response was an audible, "Now God Almighty his holy name be eternally blessed."

Some of the friends of this well-loved priest immediately consulted with lawyers and drew up a petition to the Judges of the trial begging them to consider that the convict would perish by force of those very penal laws which they had themselves declared to be tyrannical and out of date. [21] It was not possible to present this petition until the next morning when sentence was due to be pronounced. In the event, the only effect of this gesture was to give the Recorder the opportunity to recount all the Acts of Parliament by which priests were liable to be condemned to die. The most significant of these Acts was that of 1585 which made it High Treason for a priest to be within the confines of the English state (27 Elizabeth, C.2).

The sentence was pronounced by the Lord Chief Justice using the chilling and familiar formula; "You shall be taken back to the prison from whence you were brought, thence you shall be drawn to the place of execution, and there hanged by the neck until thou art half dead; your head shall then be cut off, and the rest of your members divided into four parts shall be fixed up at the four usual points of the city, and may God have mercy upon you!" [22] It was Saturday, the seventeenth of May 1651, and later that same day Fr.Peter Wright concluded the second letter to his Provincial with these words,

[19] *Extracts from Fr.Peter's letter to Jesuit Provincial, 17th May, 1651.*

[20] *Ibid. (H.Foley, Records, p.528 states that the jury retired for forty minutes.)*

[21] *H.Foley, Records, Vol.ii, p.528.*

[22] *H.Foley, Records, Vol.ii, p.529. (When Fr.Henry Morse was condemned in 1645 the formula included the words, "and your privy parts cut off, and your entrails taken out and burnt in your sight." Cf.P.Caraman, Priest of the Plague, Henry Morse S.J., p.174).*

"The sentence is just, and I thanke God, I find exceeding comfort in it, and no alteration to my selfe, but great thirst to die." [23]

Tragically, it would seem to us, neither the Parliament or Council of State were sitting at this time - it was, in fact, the Saturday before Pentecost (Whitsuntide). Although the Spanish Ambassador sent his secretary and steward to try to secure a reprieve, or at least a stay of execution, from the Recorder, Lord Chief Justice and Lord President of the Council, none would move without the permission of Council or Parliament. It was well known that these bodies would not meet until after the day set for the execution which was to be Monday, the nineteenth of May 1651 (O.S.).

Fr.Francis Foster wrote, in wonderment, about the events just described, that the only way to explain the sole condemnation of Fr.Peter, of all the priests in prison, was to ascribe it to God's providence. "To me indeed, it seems, after a careful review of all the facts, that this our most blessed Father was chosen and set apart for this palm, by the special favour and decrees of God." Why indeed should this Jesuit be the first of only two priest martyrs during the period of the new republic (1649-1660)? The Provincial concluded; "this soul was pleasing to God - *Placitum fecisse Deo animum illius* - who willed to bestow the reward of glory upon His soldier for his well-earned virtues." [24] The Provincial's seventeenth century view may be difficult for our modern mind to comprehend but we can see Fr.Peter's saintliness through the way he was given strength to face his horrendous ordeal.

On returning to prison the condemned man once more made a general confession of his sins to his cellmate, Fr.Cheney, and tried to compose himself quietly for what was to come. There was, however, to be no quietness of solitude for the brave soldier of Christ in the less than two days which remained. From morning until late at night a multitude of Catholics of all ranks, and not a few Protestants, came to the prison to receive a blessing or to confess their sins. These visitors and penitents must have been very tiring for the Jesuit but all remarked on how happy and contented he seemed to be, as he conversed with them courteously and with an affable manner dispelled all their gloom.

Fr.Cheney in his letter to the Jesuit Provincial reported that Fr.Peter slept soundly, without any disturbance, during his last two nights. On the Monday morning he was awake before five o'clock and after a final general confession prepared to celebrate Mass with his prison companion serving. Some priests, Fr.Ralph Corby was one, [25] had difficulties and sad distractions when saying their last Mass but it does not appear that our Jesuit was anything but his usual cheerfully pious self. Next, after eating a normal breakfast, an artist appeared [26] (was this Mr.Giffard? See below [*]), with a letter of introduction, and Fr. Peter was persuaded, with some reluctance, to allow a likeness to be drawn; though repeatedly warning the company that he was about to be called away.

[23] *Conclusion of Fr.Peter's letter to Fr.Francis Foster, Jesuit Provincial.*

[24] *Extract from a letter to Rome, 29th May 1651 (N.S.).*

[25] *B.Bassett, English Jesuits, p.217.*

[26] *H.Foley, Records, Vol.(ii), P.537 No name given.*

[*] *Mr.Giffard was a Catholic, also in Newgate. He painted miniature portraits of several of the martyred priests including Henry Morse and Francis Bell. These are now displayed at Lanherne Convent, Cornwall. (See Ch.VIII,).*

At nine o'clock the sheriff's officer knocked at the iron bars and summoned Fr.Peter to the room where other condemned prisoners were assembled, "I come, sweet Jesus, I come," was the response as the Jesuit, accompanied by Fr.Cheney proceeded to follow the guards. The rest of the convicts, who looked to be in great distress, were very surprised by the priest's cheerful manner as he reminded them that the day would not only end their lives but, he prayed, would open the gate to a happy eternity. He was not allowed to say much more before being conducted to another place where a Protestant minister of religion was waiting to preach to him. But this man, instead of trying to convert the Catholic, was content to praise his firmness and constancy.

After thirty more minutes of quiet and reverent conversation with his friend, Fr.Cheney, Fr.Peter was summoned down to be placed on the hurdle. The officers could hardly keep up with him as he joyfully approached the ignominious article of transport. Telling his cellmate that on this bed he would lie alone, he sat on the hurdle, made an act of contrition, and was given absolution. The two holy men embraced, exchanged the kiss of peace, and were parted from each other. [27]

Shortly afterwards, the procession, already described in the introduction to this history, began to move off towards Tyburn. The straw packing on which the Jesuit sat, almost upright, was unusual but not unknown for Fr.Henry Morse had been partially supported in 1645. [28] This gesture was a sure sign of sympathetic consideration from the Sheriff of London's officers. Through Holborn and along Oxford Street, (the route can still be followed today), a distance of just over two miles, was awash with great crowds of spectators, lining the streets and filling the windows and roofs of the houses.

All the onlookers were amazed at the cheerful dignity of Fr.Peter and his Provincial remarked, [29] "The whole way from ye prison to ye gallows, Catholiques happened to be so disposed, that almost everywhere he (Fr.Peter) saw some of his penitents, or acquayntance, and many of these gott to ye very hurdle to speake with him some to kisse his garments, others to pluck some reliques (which devotion they had much practised whilst he was in prison), others to putt some Alms in his hands, that blessed by him, they might presently be distributed to ye poore, - others to beg for themselves, and their familys, his holy prayers, all to crave his benediction, which some did even on their knees, And all these there devotions weare permitted them with an unheard civility from ye officers, who never putt any off, - one devout person came and met him at least twelve tymes."

Thus, this supposedly solemn parade resembled a triumphal march, though there was some pain for the watchers when the holy priest looked up to give a blessing to his former benefactors, the Marquis of Winchester and his Lady; the formal cross, made with deep meaningful expression, was hampered by the fact of his hands being tied together. The courageous man's cheerful countenance

[27] *Ibid. pp.538,539 (Extracts from letter written by Fr.Cheney).*

[28] *P.Caraman, Henry Morse, p.181.*

[29] *F.Foster, Letter to Madrid, 30th May 1651 (N.S.).*

was a great comfort to all the Catholics present but, perhaps, most remarkable was the complete absence of any abuse of words or brickbats from the Protestants in the crowd.

At last, reaching the scaffold, the immensity of the assembled multitude, which included one hundred and fifty or more horsemen as well as many coaches, could well have posed a threat to the Sheriff's men. No wonder then that the proceedings were guarded by soldiers who had accompanied the cortège along the way. Most of the other members of the Society of Jesus, in London, had disguised themselves to be on hand to offer spiritual comfort and absolution to their confrère. Everywhere Fr.Peter looked, he met the sympathetic eyes of the priests he knew. As we have already learned, Fr.Latham, an old friend, from military chaplain days at Ghent, was on hand to assist the convict from his hurdle. Fr.Peter, himself, tried to comfort the other prisoners, but prevented from doing so by the Puritan minister attending, was then placed in a cart by himself, for about an hour, with hands raised to heaven and a rope round his neck.

As was usual when a Catholic priest was about to be put to death, the minister once more approached and told Fr.Peter that if he would conform to the Protestant religion, there was still time for pardon. The priest's reply was a firm; "Get thee behind me Satan. I will dye in this Religion and for it, though I had never so many lives to loose." [30] After this there was no more conversation.

The time for death had now arrived and Fr.Peter was allowed to speak to the crowd. A speech from the scaffold was a long held tradition and very few priests failed to take advantage of the privilege. The version given in Henry Foley's Records is as follows, though he is inclined to embroider:-

"Most noble Sirs and dear fellow-citizens, - This is a short passage to eternity. The time is short, as you see, for me; I have not much to say, nor do I desire to detain you long. Accept, therefore, the outlines of a speech. I am brought hither, convicted of no other crime but that of being a Catholic priest. I confess I am a Catholic; I confess I am a priest; I confess I am a Religious of the Society of Jesus, or, as you call it, a Jesuit. This is the cause for which I die; for this alone have I been condemned to death, nor is any other charge alleged against me than the performance of the functions of my calling in propagating the Catholic faith, which is spread throughout the whole world, taught through all ages from Christ's time, and will be taught for all ages to come till the end of time itself. These duties have constituted my greatest happiness during my whole life, and the profit of my soul; for this cause I most willingly sacrifice my life, and would die a thousand times for the same if it were needed; for I regard it as my greatest felicity that my good God has chosen me, most unworthy, to this blessed lot, the lot of the saints. This is a grace which so unworthy a sinner could scarcely have wished for, much less hoped for. And now I beg of the goodness of my God, with all the fervour I am able, and most humbly entreat Him that He would vouchsafe to enlighten you, who are

[30] *Ibid.*

Protestants, with the rays of His divine truth, to receive and embrace the true faith. As for you Catholics, my fellow soldiers and comrades, as many of you as are here, I earnestly beseech you to join with me, and for me, in prayer till my last moment, and when I shall come to heaven I will do as much for you. I give you my last benediction (at the same time making the usual sign of the cross). I forgive all men; and now farewell till we all meet in heaven in a happy eternity." [31]

As the sun was hot, a friend handed up a towel so that the condemned priest could wipe the sweat from his brow before offering a last prayer. Then raising his hand, the cart was drawn away, while those around gave a final blessing. Contrary to the usual custom of being hanged in a nightcap or other covering, Fr.Peter, at his own request, had his face exposed.

There was no distortion of the features but he appeared to be smiling and retained his usual colour. This was such a novel sight that everyone was in awe and Lord Pembroke, who was present, said later that he had seen many men die, but none like a Christian before. A common soldier when asked what his crime was answered that the gentleman had more courage than crime. [32] "It might be said," observed Father Foster, "that the innocent priest of Christ did not die by any violent separation of soul and body but rather sweetly fell asleep in our Lord!"

No attempt was made to mutilate the body until all life was extinguished. The Sheriff of London then demanded, in a loud voice, but with evident humanity, if any relations or friends of the 'noble gentleman' were present. Great numbers came forward and were allowed to take away all the sacred relics for honourable burial. Obviously there was to be no exhibition of the quarters on the gates of London and Catholics rejoiced at a great mercy and privilege. The Provincial was able to write to his superiors in Rome that he had in his possession, "the mortal remains of our most blessed brother in Christ, Father Peter Wright, more precious than all jewels and treasures. His venerable head," he reported, "is still most pleasing to look at and retains his own sweet smile." [33]

Count Egmont, the former Spanish Ambassador, had previously been present at the execution of eleven priests at Tyburn and had conveyed their relics to the continent. He was again in London, as we have noted, and ordered his servants to search the area around the Tyburn gallows where they found the charred and burnt heart of the martyr. (See Introduction)

Father Leedes (alias Courtnay, App.A.), whose biography of Blessed Peter Wright was the main source of Henry Foley's notes, [34] wrote, "His (Fr.Peter's) exit was our triumph, the glory of which was enhanced by various circumstances, it occurred in the early springtide, with a brilliant sun, tempered by a mild south-east wind; it was on the second feria of Whitsun week; lastly, the execution

[31] *H.Foley, Records, Vol.ii, p.546 (F.Foster gives a shorter version in his letter to Madrid).*

[32] *F.Foster, Letter to Madrid.*

[33] *F.Foster, Letter to Rome (Quoted by Foley).*

[34] *H.Foley, Records, Vol.ii, p.550.*

of other criminals of rank, and the great number of the condemned, truly excited the whole city. Hence an innumerable multitude of spectators had collected in the streets and fields, God so disposing it by a singular providence, that all eyes being attracted to His servant, they should be so many witnesses of Catholic fortitude, and should depart with a general astonishment at such a display of prudence, constancy and piety. Not a voice was heard deriding the priest, although the name is so odious to Englishmen, no one was heard who did not highly applaud him. For days after his death, he was the common topic of conversation, always accompanied with amplest praises. His memory is still fresh and will flourish for years to come."

Blessed Peter Wright's contemporaries were obviously convinced of his bravery and worthiness - even the 'broadsheets' of the time (the forerunners of today's newspapers) praised the courage of a priest who had been executed in defence of his religion. The members of the Society of Jesus had seen one of their number pass to his eternal reward with such an abundance of grace that the very brutality of the executioners was mitigated as they respectfully allowed all the hallowed parts to be taken away with honour. The conclusion of this narrative details the way in which Blessed Peter's memory was kept alive until his eventual Beatification in 1929.

The Martyrdom at Tyburn

Chapter VIII

Aftermath - Burial - Relics and their authenticity - Beatification.

In a footnote to the introduction of this chronicle, we find reference to a London weekly gazette report of May 1651, which praised the Jesuit martyr for the outstanding qualities of bravery and resolution he demonstrated at his execution. Even a member of Parliament, with no particular love for those who acknowledged the Pope as their spiritual head, was overheard to say, "The Papists, according to their custom, are acting their absurdities in worshipping the dead priest, but we have acted much more absurdly in condemning such a man to death." (1) To what extent ordinary public opinion was affected by the spectacle is hard to estimate; although, eventually, the time would come when the judicial murder and mutilation of Catholic priests for the supposed. 'treason' of administering the sacraments of the Church would be abolished. In the case of Blessed Peter Wright, and his 'cause célèbre', discussion continued for years. His memory was kept alive within the non-Catholic community, as well as among those in 'Peter's barque' (*), and he merits an entry in the Dictionary of National Biography which is not awarded to every English martyr.

A Protestant writer of the time, calling himself 'Christian Moderator', in a book published soon after the execution of Blessed Peter, deplored the atrocity of the sentence and also criticised the trial. He pointed out that nothing had been proved against the accused except that he had celebrated Mass in Flanders ten years previously. This was on the evidence of one witness only who confessed to having a private grudge. He continued, "May God grant that this mode of procedure, so brutal, so plainly abhorrent to the Gospel, especially this most bloody one, so distasteful to the spectators, and so little advantageous to its authors, may at least not be injurious to our continental brethren, may not cause alienation amongst friends and kindred, and scandalize the whole world." (2)

It would be wonderful to be able to record that the miscarriage of justice, the terrifying consequences together with the courage of the accused, started a movement leading to the repeal of the laws against Catholic priests practising their vocation in England. Unfortunately, only three years later, Tyburn received another victim, the secular priest John Southworth (See Ch.IV), who was executed on the twenty eighth of June 1654. Many other Catholic priests and some laymen were condemned to be hung, drawn and quartered between 1678 and 1681 during the 'Titus Oates Conspiracy' with still more dying in prison. The very last priest, sentenced in London, to be executed in so cruel a fashion was an Irishman, Dr.Oliver Plunkett, Catholic Archbishop of Armagh; (3) (in his case the degradation of disembowelling and quartering was not carried out). (4)

(1) *H.Foley, Records, Vol.ii, p.551.*

(*) *'barque of Peter' = sobriquet for Catholics having spiritual allegiance to the Pope.*

(2) *Ibid., p.553.*

(3) *Beatified by Pope Benedict XV, May 23, 1920 and canonized by Pope Paul VI in 1975.*

(4) *Butler's 'Lives of the Saints'.*

To return to the events following our Jesuit's martyrdom: two stories probably emanating from Fr.Francis Foster, the English Jesuit Provincial in 1651, were retold by Henry Foley in his Records of the English Province of the Society of Jesus. [5] The first concerned a Catholic lady, member of the aristocracy, who had visited Blessed Peter in prison two days before his death. Here she was given a present of a small picture representing Christ's nativity and asked to keep it in memory; also to recite daily a 'Pater' (Our Father) and an 'Ave' (Hail Mary) for the donor until his ordeal should be over. On the back of the parchment was written the priest prisoner's name which when the lady looked at it on the Monday, at about the hour of the expected execution, became spattered with spots of blood. The second story was about another Catholic well-born lady whose husband was violently opposed to her religion. In this case Fr.Thomas Worsley, S.J. had obtained from Blessed Peter a written promise that he would pray for the conversion of the husband at the place of execution. When the previously irate man found out about the promise he changed completely and demanded to have a painted portrait of the martyr. Later he was received into the Catholic Church by Fr.Worsley.

With our sceptical twentieth century minds, it is easy to doubt the circumstances of the bloodstained picture. The events surrounding the conversion, however, have such a ring of truth, that one can readily accept the account without question. The circulation of these particular stories, as well as others of a more general nature, are a clear indication of the reverence and affection accorded to the martyr by the Catholics of London.

Shortly after receiving the head and members of the glorious soldier of Christ (See Ch.VII), Fr.Francis Foster had them embalmed and sent on to St.Omers for interment in the Jesuit College chapel. Perhaps the estimable Count Egremont was responsible for the transport, as he had been with other martyrs' remains. Although some authorities [6] have declared that the Spanish ambassador (no name given) took most of Blessed Peter's body to Liege, we have to admit that it is not absolutely clear whether, in 1651, any relic of the body was presented to the Jesuit Anglo-Bavarian College. According to Butler's 'Lives of the Saints' [7] the body was taken from St.Omers to Liege in 1762. On arrival in the latter place the remains were probably kept in the College sacristy.

If the uncertainty and confusion, about Blessed Peter's last resting place, seems surprising, one has only to be reminded of the religious and political upheavals of the late seventeenth and eighteenth centuries to appreciate the difficulties faced by the researcher. For example, the mid-eighteenth century removal from St.Omer was occasioned by the expulsion of the Jesuit Order from France by the government of King Louis XV. The College, where once the martyr had briefly held the position of Prefect of Studies, found a temporary home at Bruges in the Austrian Netherlands (now Belgium).

[5] *H.Foley, Records, Vol.ii. pp.553-556.*
[6] *Historical notice by Fr.Joseph Crehan, S.J., 1956.*
[7] *A.Butler, Lives of the Saints, Vol. V.*

Presumably the casket containing Peter's remains would have had a brief resting place there, but we cannot be sure. Ten years later, in 1773, the Society of Jesus was suppressed entirely by a decree of the then Pope. [8] St.Omers College did not disappear but continued under very difficult circumstances at Liege although this exciting, and at times dangerous, story cannot be told here. [9]

By 1789, at the time of the outbreak of the French Revolution, there is no doubt that several of the martyrs' remains were at Liege. Five years later, with French revolutionary armies approaching rapidly, it was deemed necessary to evacuate the Academy (the name by which the former St.Omers was now known) to England, which, by this date, was less anti-Catholic than formerly. Stonyhurst Hall, near Clitheroe in north Lancashire, had been leased to the former Jesuits by Thomas Weld a Catholic landowner from Lulworth in Dorset. Thus St.Omers was re-founded and continues as Stonyhurst College to this day.

Sadly, in the evacuation to England, many treasures were left behind, or sold, including the library, mathematical room, church plate - and some martyrs' remains. Fr.Charles Plowden, S.J., chaplain to Mr.Weld, declared that these items as well as, "Fr.Wright the martyr's body - at moderate expense and with some care might have been brought to Stonyhurst." [10] Instead the holy relics were hastily interred in an unmarked grave. Earlier, in 1781, the casket containing Blessed Peter Wright's mortal remains had been opened in the presence of several witnesses who found that the "head, heart and quarters" were "fresh and whole and exhaled a delightful odour. His countenance was that of a person sound asleep; the eyebrows and eyelashes perfect; the marks of the smallpox clearly visible ..." [11]

An expedition to the English College, Liege, in 1818, by Fr.Edward Scott, S.J., had the task of locating the lead-lined casket which had been hurriedly buried for fear of the French armies. The probable location was under the sacristy window [12] but there is, unfortunately, no record of a successful conclusion to this venture and we must conclude that Blessed Peter's remains were not found.

In 1824 the college buildings were sold to the Liege municipal authorities and eventually the site became a hospital which in the twentieth century was known as 'Hôpital des Anglais'. Although many of the seventeenth century brick buildings remained, as well as parts of the garden, there was no trace of Blessed Peter's mutilated corpse or its lead lined coffin when the last search was made in 1956. [13]

[8] *T.J.Campbell, The Jesuits, Ch.XXIII. (The Jesuits survived precariously in Poland and parts of eastern Europe but were reinstated as an Order in 1814.)*

[9] *H.Chadwick, St.Omers to Stonyhurst, Chapters 13 & 14.*

[10] *Ibid., p.386.*

[11] *Faith and Doctrine of the Roman Catholic Church, Dublin, 1813, p.63. (Quoted by Fr.J.Crehan,S.J. in 1956).*

[12] *Letter of Fr. Plowden, S.J.,(Quoted by Fr.Crehan).*

[13] *Fr.J.Crehan, S.J., Historical Notice.*

Portrait of Blessed Peter Wright and other martyrs.
Reproduction by permission of Lanherne Carmelite Convent.

Perhaps the burial site was built over and may never be discovered. If still in the gardens, an exhaustive investigation by metal detectors would be the only way to expose the final resting place of the martyr's precious relics and so be able to give them the honour they deserve.

In the records of Henry Foley, published c.1883, we find a catalogue of smaller relics of Blessed Peter. At Lanherne Convent, Cornwall, a portrait is listed (shown opposite) and another unspecified item. In the main these holy souvenirs were pieces of cloth stained with the martyr's blood and some had been identified as being at Stonyhurst College, St.Beuno's College and Durham. On enquiry, the present author was given to understand that the relics at Stonyhurst were of doubtful authenticity and the present archivist at the English Jesuit headquarters in Mount Street, London, [14] was unable to discover the whereabouts of any other reputable relics other than the one reverenced at Tyburn Convent.

Tyburn Convent, in Hyde Park Place, London, Shrine of the Sacred Heart and the Tyburn Martyrs, perpetuates the memory of 105 Catholic Martyrs of the Reformation period who died close by. Mother Mary John Baptist, Secretary General of the Sacred Heart of Jesus, of Montmartre, O.S.B. wrote that the Convent only possessed one relic of Blessed Peter Wright, a small piece of the rope that hanged him. [15] An authentication of this and a number of other martyrs' relics, received by Tyburn Convent in 1912, was provided by Abbot Columba Marmion of the Benedictine Abbey of Maredsous. Some of these pious mementoes had been given to the Benedictines by a lady, called Marie Adele Garnier [*]; and Dom Bede Camm, an expert on the English and Welsh martyrs, is presumed to have noted the sources and attestations. Nothing further is known of the provenance of the relic of Blessed Peter displayed at Tyburn.

We are more fortunate with the authentication of the relic of Blessed Peter Wright now venerated at the R.C. church of St. Paul the Apostle, Thrapston, Northamptonshire. [16] The attestation [17] reads, 'Part of the halter wherewith Father Peter Wright the Jesuit was hanged who suffered martyrdome at Tybourne May19/29 1651 given me by my worthy good friend Henry Englefyeld Esq. who found it amongst his father Anthony Englefyeld his thinges when he dyed, who attested it under his owne hand wrighting.' Then added in another hand: 'N.B. The above was written by Charles Eyston Esq. of Hendred Berks, father of the late John Eyston of ditto my brother in law. Ita est Geo,Bruning 24 May 1797.'

The history behind this remarkable document is fascinating for it reveals that the relic originally belonged to Anthony Englefield of White Knights, near Reading which is very close to the Fifth

[14] *Letter from Fr.T.McCoog, S.J., 12th October, 1995.*
[15] *Letters 23rd August, 1995 and 6th October, 1995.*
[*] *Later Beatified*
[16] *Appendix C for illustration and prayer.*
[17] *Attestation written by Charles Eyston of Hendred, Berks., a very Catholic house, (Copy in the archives of St.Paul's parish, Thrapston).*

Marquis of Winchester's [*] final resting place (Ch.VI). Anthony was born in 1637 and died in 1711 when his son Henry came into possession of the precious piece of rope. It is not surprising to find Henry Englefield (1675-1720) handing the relic on to Charles Eyston for the men were not only friends but both members of strongly Catholic Berkshire families. The Eystons of East Hendred (now in Oxfordshire) were descended from St.Thomas More and claim never to have lost the Faith. Charles, a noted antiquarian, who lived from 1667 to 1721, is chiefly remembered for a history of Glastonbury abbey and town, published in 1716. [18]

The George Bruning mentioned above was a Jesuit priest who was not only related to the Eystons but resided with the family at Hendred for a time and died in 1802. The relic, however, was not given to Fr.John Morris, S.J., at the Office of Vice Postulation [**] in Mount St,, London until 1889. It was, of course, through the good offices of the Society of Jesus in London and Rome that the relic was passed on to the Catholic parish of Thrapston and Raunds, where a small shrine was erected in 1979 (See Appendix C). The precious memento arrived in a parcel from the Office of Vice-Postulation of the Cause of the English and Welsh Martyrs, dated the fifteenth of August 1979, and signed by Patrick C.Barry with a letter which stated that 'a piece of the Bl.Peter Wright rope' is enclosed. Together in the packet was a certificate of authentication signed and sealed in Rome by Fr.Paul Molinari, the Postulator General of the Society of Jesus. It is in Latin and reproduced below. A translation follows:

POSTULATOR GENERALIS
CAUSARUM SERVORUM DEI, VENERABILIUM,
BEATORUM ET SANCTORUM
SOCIETATIS JESU

Omnibus has litteras inspecturis fidem facimus ac testamur, nos ab authenticis reliquiis extraxisse particulas ex fune quo patibulo suspensus fuit Beatus Petrus Wright, presbyter e Societate Jesu et Martyr,

quas in theca metallica rotundae figurae crystallo occlusa, filo serico rubri coloris obligata et sigillo nostro obsignata collocavimus.

In quorum fidem has litteras subscriptione ac sigillo nostro munitas dedimus.

Romae, die 11 mens. iunii an. 1979

CUST. RELIQ.

POSTULATOR GENERALIS

Paulus Molinari

[*] *The Marquis ended his days at Englefield House, Englefield, Berks. Thus the relic may have been given by him to Anthony*

[18] *D.N.B.*
[**] *Office of Vice-Postulation deals with the cause of the English Jesuit Martyrs - collecting data to promote possible bcatification and canonisation.*

Translation:-

POSTULATOR GENERAL
Causes of the Servants of God,
Venerable, Blessed, Saints, of
the Society of Jesus.

To all inspecting these documents, we declare and testify, that these fragments have been taken from the authentic relics of the halter by which Bl.Peter Wright, Priest of the Society of Jesus and Martyr, was hanged from the gallows. The which relics we have collected in a metal case, circular and with a glass cover, bound with red silk thread and marked with our seal.

In witness whereof we provide
our signature and seal to this document,
Rome, 11th June 1979

Guardian of the	Postulator General
Relics, N.	Paul Molinari, S.J.

Before leaving the extraordinary story of this holy relic, it is necessary to explain the circumstances leading to the 1889 deposition in London. Apparently it was Canon William Collis of Shefford, Bedfordshire who handed the precious object to the Jesuits. This priest had been appointed, in 1869, by the Bishop of Northampton, to found a Diocesan Orphanage at Shefford but, as there was no money, he had to beg from any wealthy Catholic families he could find. One of the most generous benefactors was Mr.John Eyston of the family of More-Eyston of East Hendred, Berks. [19] Once this connection is established, it is easy to see how the souvenir of Blessed Peter Wright came to be in the possession of Canon Collis (d.1893).

One might ask why such a special relic, with its close affinity to an English Jesuit martyr, had not previously been handed over to the Society of Jesus for safekeeping. The probable answer is that the private chapel of the Eyston family at Hendred House had provided a resting place and focus for veneration. [20] However, there can be no mystery about the reason why our martyr's relic should be given to the Jesuit authorities in the 1880s . The second half of the nineteenth century had seen the introduction of the Cause [*] of 360 English and Welsh Catholic martyrs who suffered during the

[19] *St. Francis Children's Society (Diocese of Northampton), Souvenir Report, 1869-1994,*

[20] *A.A.Touring Guide, 1975 (Hendred House has a private chapel in which Mass has been said since 1291. Relics of St.Thomas More and St.John Fisher are honoured.)*

[*] *'Cause' an individual's case offered at law (the court being the Sacred Congregation Of Rites at Rome),*

persecutions of the sixteenth and seventeenth centuries. All kinds of evidence was required to plead and prove the sanctity of the heroic men and women who gave their lives for the Faith. These the Church wished to honour with the title Blessed and where possible to accord the higher accolade of Saint.

In the case of most of the English martyrs more than one attempt had been made, even during the time of persecution, to get the Church officially to recognise their self-sacrifice and honour them accordingly. The difficulties of collecting evidence made the task impossible and was also hampered by the lack of a coordinating structure among the English Catholic clergy - Vicars Apostolic when appointed were not the same thing as Diocesan Bishops.

So it was not until after the restoration of the English Hierarchy, in 1850, that the necessary work of preparation was begun. At last, in 1874, the then Archbishop of Westminster, Cardinal Manning, acting on behalf of the whole bench of Bishops, sent 360 names to Rome for approval.[21] By decrees of the Holy See in December, 1886, 54 of the number (later, 1895, raised to 63) were recognised as having been beatified by a decree of Pope Gregory XIII, in 1583, and 253 - including Peter Wright, - were accorded the title 'Venerable Servants of God'.

The Church does not want to declare any to be blessed by God if there are doubts about their worthiness and thus the next thirty years were spent in collecting the fullest possible evidence about the lives and deaths of the 'Venerabili'. This further explains why the relic of Blessed Peter came to be in Jesuit hands in 1889 - it was first class evidence.

Eventually the 'Apostolic process', or court of enquiry, into 252 [22] of the martyrs was continued at Westminster on the fifteenth of June 1923. Cardinal Bourne presided as judge delegate representing the Holy See and evidence collecting lasted exactly three years. Doubtless the catastrophe of the First World War had held up the investigations which were extremely thorough. The 'Positio', or body of evidence concerning all the martyrs, is preserved in the Westminster Diocesan Archives. In the case of Blessed Peter Wright, the information provided includes all sixty two of his sermons carefully copied out in manuscript.

For another three years the material collected was under discussion by the Sacred Congregation of Rites in Rome. Then came 1929, the centenary year of the passing of the Emancipation Act by the Parliament of Great Britain, when Catholics were once more allowed to vote and be elected as M.P.s. On the fifteenth of December, Pope Plus XI issued a decree which beatified 136 of the martyrs including, among the number, Peter Wright, the Jesuit priest born in Northamptonshire, the subject of this book.

[21] *C.A.Newdigate, S.J., Our Martyrs, Introduction.*
[22] *Ibid., Oliver Plunket (former Archbishop of Armagh) had been beatified by Pope Benedict XV in 1920 which explains how the number was reduced by one.*

In 1935 the Pope accorded Sir Thomas More and Cardinal John Fisher (See Ch.I) each the title of Saint without any further process. Much later, in 1970, after due canonical review, Pope Paul VI canonised a further 40 martyrs, whose lives and deaths were best documented, including John Paine a secular priest born in the Anglican Diocese of Peterborough (possibly Northamptonshire) who was hung, drawn and quartered at Chelmsford in 1582.

In 1987 a further 85 martyrs were declared 'Blessed' by Pope John Paul II, but, as yet no more have been proclaimed Saints. Therefore we need to ask, 'Is there any hope for the future canonisation of Blessed Peter Wright?' "To this question the answer is that such a possibility certainly exists, provided that we can furnish scientific proof of a miracle attributed to his intercession." [23] However,the Hierarchy of Great Britain have not been in favour of new initiatives relating to the particular Cause of one individual. Over the last several decades, the policy has been to make proposals with regard to groups of martyrs which would comprehend people of all walks of life.

This, for the moment, has to be the end of the story but we can all take heart from the example of courage shown by this martyr. If we wish, we can ask his intercession for our needs and the needs of others, using any appropriate prayer or the words given in Appendix C.

Throughout this narrative the person and character of Blessed Peter has gradually emerged from the shadows. His life, even where not perfectly and fully documented, has now, at last, taken on a distinct shape as someone we can know and admire. Similarly, close association with our subject's eventful story has brought a closer understanding of the difficulties and tribulations faced by all men of God during the seventeenth century.

[23] *Fr.Paul Molinari, S.J., Postulator General, Letter 21st June, 1995.*

Portraits of Blessed Peter Wright

EPILOGUE

I am very grateful to be asked to add a few words at the end of this moving story. The author is not without experience in writing and publishing but this has been a major work and I am very happy to have been among those who have encouraged him to persevere in writing the history of Blessed Peter Wright.

The problem from the outset has been the paucity of material. Others have set out to complete a biography but have given up for that very reason, the apparent lack of detail. Our author has persevered, has honoured a devout and holy man of his own county and parish, and has been able to build a much richer and livelier picture than others thought possible.

The variety and hardship of Blessed Peter's life, both his years of maturing and then his years of work as a Jesuit - as teacher, military chaplain, priestly duties in England - prepare us gradually for the final trial and martyrdom.

This book rightly begins with a line of prayerful dedication and ends with a gentle encouragement to prayer, even, where it is felt appropriate, an invocation of Blessed Peter's own prayers. It seems right, then, to end here by recalling that moment of joyful response to divine grace on the Whitmonday morning of 1651, when the gaoler invited Peter to his execution, and Peter replied, "I come, sweet Jesus, I come."

Blessed Peter Wright, Pray for us.

J.Koenig
Formerly Parish Priest of Thrapston and Raunds

CHRONOLOGY OF BLESSED PETER WRIGHT, S.J.

(Jesuit training details based on the research of Father T.M.McCoog, S.J.)

c.	1603/04	Born at Slipton, Northamptonshire.
	1613	Presented as Recusant at Slipton with mother, brother and sister.
c.	1616-1626	Worked in lawyer's office at Thrapston.
c.	1626-1627	In Netherlands - soldier for less than one month. At Anglo-Bavarian College, Liege.
c.	1627-1629	At Flemish Jesuit College, Ghent.
	1629-1630	At Watten near St.Omers in Flanders as Jesuit novice.
	1631	Studied philosophy, Liege.
	1632	" " "
	1633	" " "
	1634	Studied theology, Liege.
?	1635	" " "
	1636	" " "
?		Ordained priest at Liege.
	1637	Third year of probation (Tertianship), Ghent.
?	1637-1638	Prefect of Morals at St.Omers.
c.	1638-44	Camp missioner or chaplain to English Regiment of Colonel Henry Gage - based at Ghent - met Thomas Gage.
	1641	22nd September (N.S.) Final profession as spiritual coadjutor, or Jesuit priest professed of the three evangelical vows.
	1641/42	At Ghent - military chaplain with Frs.Henry Morse &Edward Latham.
c.	1643/44	Returned to England with Colonel Gage - at Oxford, headquarters of King Charles I. (Residence of St. Mary).
	1644	At relief of Basing House. Met Marquis of Winchester.
*	1645(N.S.)	11th January. At Collum (Culham) Bridge, Abingdon and assisted Colonel Gage, when mortally wounded, by administering the last rites.
c.	1645-1651	Chaplain to family of Marquis of Winchester -mainly in London (House of St.Ignatius).
*	1651(N.S.)	2nd February. Arrested while preparing to say Mass.In Newgate prison.
	1651	14th(Wed.)-16th (Fri.) May (O.S.) Tried and condemned on evidence given by T.Gage at Old Bailey before Lord Henry Rolles,Chief Justice and others.
	1651	Mon. 19th May (O.S.) Hung, Drawn and Quartered at Tyburn as being a Catholic Priest who had entered the country illegally (Statute 27.Elizabeth).
	1651	September: Fr.Edward Leedes/Courtnay publishes at Antwerp 'R.P.Petri Writi, Mors'.
	1874	Cardinal Manning, Archbishop of Westminster, included Fr.Peter Wright among the 360 names sent to Rome for possible Beatification.

1886	9th December - among those declared to be 'Venerable Servants of God' by Pope Leo XIII.
1923	15th June to
1926	15th June - Apostolic process held at Westminster, under the presidency of Cardinal Bourne, to collect evidence of martyrdom.
1929	15th December - Fr.Peter Wright Beatified with 135 other heroic defenders of the Faith, by decree of Pope Pius XI and accorded the title 'Blessed'.

** Some record these years as 1644 and 1650 - having failed to realise that the old style calendar year did not end until March 24th.*

BIBLIOGRAPHY

(Place of publication given only if outside London)

1. Biographical Sources

Anstruther G., A Hundred Homeless Years, Blackfriars, 1958.
Anstruther G., Seminary Priests, Vol.2 (1603-1659), Mayhew-McCrimmon, Great Wakering, 1975.
Anstruther G., Vaux of Harrowden, Johns, Newport, Mons., 1953.
Basset B., The English Jesuits, Burns & Oates, 1967.
Bellenger D.A., English & Welsh Priests, (1558-1800), Downside Abbey, 1984.
Butler A., Lives of the Saints, Ed.B.Kelly, Virtue, 1934.

Caraman P.,Henry Morse, S,J,, Longmans Green, (Longman Group, Harrow), 1957.
Catholic Encyclopaedia, Volume XV, New York, 1912 .
Chadwick H., St.Omers to Stonyhurst, Burns & Oates, 1962.
Challoner R., Memoirs of Missionary Priests, Ed.J.H.Pollen, Burns, Oates & Washbourne, 1924 (Orig.1741).
Crehan J., Historical Notice (Vol. 60), Manresa Press, 1956, Private circ.

Dictionary of National Biography, 1922 and 1960.
D.N.B., (Concise), Oxford University Press, 1992.

Foley H., Records of the English Province S.J., Manresa Press, 1877-83.
Foster F., Annual letter to Rome, 29th May, 1651,(Jesuit Archives) Unpublished.
Foster F., Long Letter to Rector of College in Spain, 30th May, 1651, (Jesuit Archives) Unpublished, (Original in Acedemia de la Historia, Madrid).

Leedes E., (alias Courtnay) R.P.Petri Writi Mors, Antwerp, 1651 (Latin)
McCoog T.M., English & Welsh Jesuits (1555-1650), Catholic Record Society, Birmingham, 1994, 1995.
McCoog T.M., Monumenta Historica Societas Jesu, Vol. 143, Rome, 1992.
Menology of England & Wales, Burns & Oates.

Newdigate C.A., Our Martyrs, Catholic Truth Society, 1935, 1946.
Newsletter for Students of Recusant History, 1966 (Includes Notes by Dr.J.Paul).
Reynolds E.E., Roman Catholic Church in England & Wales, Clarke, Wheathampstead, 1973.

Strapetona, Journal of the Thrapston District Historical Society, 1977. (Includes article by Mrs.J.Brassington).

Tanner ? (S.J.), Soc.lesu Militans, 1675 (Latin).

Wright Peter, Sermons & Letters, Stonyhurst College, Unpublished.

2. Background and Local Sources (by author)

Anstruther G., Seminary Priests. Vol.I (1558—1603), Ushaw, 1968.
Ashley M., The English Civil War, Sutton, Stroud, 1990.
Aylmer G.E., Personal Rule of Charles I, Historical Association, 1993.

Bettey J.H., Suppression of Monasteries in the West Country,Sutton, 1989.
Beckinsale R.P., Companion into Berkshire, Spur, Bourne End, 1972.
Bossy J., The English Catholic Community, Darton, Longman Todd, 1975.
Black J.B., The Reign of Elizabeth, Oxford U.P., 1959 .
Brown W.E., Reformation in Scotland, C.T.S. Scotland, 1954.
Bruce M.L., Anne Boleyn, Harper-Collins, 1972.

Campbell T.J., The Jesuits (1534-1921), Encyclopaedia, 1921.
Caraman P.,Ignatius Loyola, Harper-Collins, 1990.
Caraman P.,Translation of J.Gerard's Autobiography (c.1620), Longmans Green, 1955.
Clarendon Lord(Hyde E.), History of the Great Rebellion, Ed.Lockyer R., Oxford U.P., 1967.

Davidson N.S., The Counter Reformation, H.A.(B.Blackwell), 1983
Davies G., The Early Stuarts, Oxford U.P., 1959.
Dawson C., The Dividing of Christendom, Sedgewick & Jackson, 1965.
Duffy E., The Stripping of the Altars, Yale U.P., 1992.

Elton G.R., Reform and Reformation, Arnold, 1977.
Elton G.R., Ed., New Cambridge Modern History, Vol.II, Reformation, Cambridge U.P., 1968.

Fanning D., St. Ignatius of Loyola, C.T.S., 1991.
Ffinch M., Cardinal Newman, Weidenfeld & Nicolson, 1991.
Finch M.E., Five Northamptonshire Families, Northamptonshire R.S., 1955.
Fines J., The Pilgrimage of Grace, - c.1990.
Foster S., Cardinal William Allen, C.T.S. 1993.
Fraser A., Mary, Queen of Scots, Weidenfeld & Nicolson, 1969.

Ganss G.E., Constitutions of Society of Jesus, St.Louis, 1970.

Gay J.D., Geography of Religion in England, Duckworth,1971.
Gerard J., Stonyhurst College Centenary Record, 1894.
Gillow J., Biographical Dictionary of English Catholics, Vol.II, Burns & Oates, 1885.
Gordon.P., The Wakes of Northamptonshire, Northants. Libraries, 1992.
Goring J. & Wake .J., Northants. Lieutenancy Papers, (1580-1614), N.R.S. 1975.
Green V.H.H., Renaissance & Reformation, Arnold, 1952.
Greenall H.L., History of Northamptonshire & Soke of Peterborough, Phillimore, Chichester, 1979.
Guilday P,. English Catholic Refugees (1558-1795), Longmans Green, 1914.

Hodgetts M., Secret Hiding Places, Veritas, Dublin, 1989.
Hughes P., Rome & Counter Reformation in England, Burns &Oates, 1941.
Jackson-Stops G., Drayton House, Private, 1978.
Jeans R. & Meades M.G., Church of St.Mary the Virgin, Chipping Norton,1987.

Kelly C., Blessed Thomas Belson, Smythe, Gerrards Cross, 1987.
Kirk J., Biographies of English Catholics. Ed.Pollen J.H. &Burton E.H., (London) 1909.

Lacey R., Robert, Earl of Essex, Weidenfeld & Nicolson, 1970.

Mackie J.D., The Earlier Tudors, Oxford U.P., 1957.
Magee B., The English Recusants, Burns & Oates, 1938.
Mathew D., Catholicism in England, Longmans Green, 1936 .

Nicholls M., Investigating Gunpowder Plot, Manchester U.P., 1991.

Ogg D., Europe in the Seventeenth Century, Black, 1943.
Ollard R., War without an Enemy, Hodder & Stoughton, 1976.

Richards D., Britain under Tudors & Stuarts, Longman, 1951.
Ridley J., Henry VIII, Constable, 1984.

Scarisbrick J.J., Reformation and the English People, Blackwell, Oxford, 1984.
Scarisbrick J.J., Jesuits and the Catholic Reformation. H.A., 1989.
Serjeantson R.M. & Longden H.I., Extracts from Northants Wills (1510-1558), Northants.R.S.
Stopford-Sackville N.V., Drayton House, Private, 1939.

Tennant P., Edgehill & beyond, Sutton, 1992.
Thomson J.A.F., Early Tudor Church and Society, Longman, 1993.
Trappes-Lomax T.B., Notes on Northampton Diocese (Centenary Souvenir), 1950.

Wake J., The Brudenells of Deene, Cassell, 1953.
Wake J. & Longden H.I., Montagu Musters Book, Vol.VII, N.R.S., 1935.
Walsingham E., Alter Britanniae Heros, Life & Death of Sir Henry Gage, (Oxford), 1645.
Waugh E., Edmund Campion, Longmans Green, 1961.
Wedgwood C.V., The King's Peace (1697-41), Harper-Collins, 1974.

Wedgwood C.V.,The Thirty Years War (J.Cape, 1938), Pimlico, 1992.
Williamson N.R.,The Cardinal in Exile, Joseph, 1969.

3. Background and Local Sources (by title)

Chambers Dictionary of World History.
Charters & Insignia of Higham Ferrers, 1961.
Encyclopedia Britannica.
Lanherne, St.Mawgan, Discalced Carmelite Convent, Guide Book.
Northamptonshire Past & Present, Vol.I, II, & V, N.R.S.
Peterborough Cathedral, Pitkin, 1975.
Souvenir of 700th Anniversary of Borough of Higham Ferrers, 1951.
Victoria County History of Northamptonshire, Vo1.3.

4. Unpublished material

Collins G., Notes on early history of Northampton Diocese.
Waszak P., Notes on B1.Henry Heath, O.F.M.

5. Main Centres of Information

Bishop's House, Northampton.
British Library, London.
Catholic Central Library, London .
Catholic Record Society, Birmingham .
Jesuit Archives, London.
Northamptonshire County Library .
Northamptonshire Record Office.
Northamptonshire Record Society.
Stonyhurst College, Lancashire.
Thrapston Historical Society.
Westminster Diocesan Archives.

APPENDIX A

Notes on Fr. Edward Leedes, S.J. (alias Courtney or Courtnay) the earliest biographer of Blessed Peter Wright.

(Sources:— Bellenger, English and Welsh Priests; Anstruther, Seminary Priests; D.N.B.)

*****

Edward Leedes, born 1598/99, was one of four sons of Sir Thomas Leedes of Wappingthorne, Steyning, Sussex who was Lord Lieutenant of that county in July 1603, at the time of the coronation of James I, when he was made a Knight of the Bath. Edward's mother was Mary, daughter of Thomas Leeds of North Milford, Kirkby Wharfe, Yorkshire and she was a devout Catholic.

An older son, Thomas, born 1594, studied at St.John's College, Oxford and matriculated on the fourth of July 1609 but in 1610 he was sent to the Jesuit College at St.Omer from where he progressed to the Venerable English College in Rome on the seventeenth of October 1615. He was ordained priest by the famous Jesuit Cardinal St.Robert Bellarmine (canonised in 1930) on the fourth of November 1618 and entered the Society of Jesus exactly one week later. Eventually he became Rector of the Venerable English College in August 1649 and was penitentiary at St.Peter's in 1653. Thomas also used the alias Courtnay and this has caused some confusion with the younger brother. He died in 1668.

The whole family was reconciled to the Catholic Church circa 1610 and in 1616 retired to Louvain in Belgium. This is confirmed by the Recusant Rolls (178/4653) which state that there was an inquisition at East Grinstead on the twenty seventh of March 1616 concerning the lands of Sir Thomas and Mary his wife.

Edward, after studying classics in the college of St.Omer entered the English College, Rome for his higher course, as a convictor or boarder, under the name of Courtney, on the ninth of October, 1618 (Foley, Records, vi 287). He joined the Societv of Jesus at St. Andrew's in Rome in 1621 and was professed of the four vows in 1634 [*] (Oliver, Jesuit Collections, p.77). In the latter year he was arrested in London and committed to the Gatehouse prison on a charge of having written against the oath of supremacy (Panzani, Memoirs; Foley, Records). He was Rector of the college at St.Omer, 1646-1649, twice Rector of the English College, Rome; Provincial of the English province of his order, 1660-1664 and then Rector of the college at Liege. He died at St.Omer on the third of October 1677. He was a witness to the martyrdom of Peter Wright and probably visited him in prison.

Although author of several scholarly works on philosophical and religious subjects, he is chiefly remembered for his biography of Peter Wright written in Latin and first published in Antwerp in 1651 under the title, 'R.P.Petri Writi, Sacerdotis Angli e Soc.Jesu, Mors, quam ob fidem passus est Londini, 29 Maii 1651.' [**] (A translation of this biography was printed in Foley's Records, Volume ii pp.506-565.)

APPENDIX B

The Sermons and Letters of Blessed Peter Wright, S.J.

At Stonyhurst College in Lancashire are preserved some [***] 62 sermons written by Fr.Peter Wright probably in the period 1647 to 1650. This Jesuit school also possesses a few letters from 1647 which are most certainly in the martyr's own hand. The sermons too seem to be contemporary and exhibit the same characteristics and style. [****]

[*] *ca.1633-1634 Leedes lectured at the Jesuit College, Liege and at the University in Logic, General Metaphysics and Controversy. (P.Caraman, Henry Morse, pp.65/66.)*

[**] *A first edition copy of this book is preserved at Stonyhurst College, Lancashire, bearing the book-plate of Lord Arundel of Wardour. The approbation of censor is dated the twentieth of September, 1651.*

[***] *The numbering is inaccurate and the last is number 64.*

[****] *Fr.F.J.Turner, S.J., Librarian, Stonyhurst College expressed no doubts about the authorship when interviewed in 1995.*

The Sermons

In regard to the sermons, there are over 500 pages of notes held in a quarto volume of which the binding is comparatively modern. Modifications in the handwriting could indicate that they have been produced over a series of years.

These homilies are for Sundays and various Holydays but none bear any particular date. Peter's seventeenth century style of English presentation is not always easy to follow and betrays something of his early legal training. All evince a profound knowledge of the Scriptures and are liberally bestrewn with Latin quotations. There are passages of great interest revealing a priest who was deeply spiritual.

We are indebted to Fr.Godfrey Anstruther, O.P. for painstakingly copying out what he regarded as either the best or the most typical of Peter's method of preaching. (*) It is worth noting that each sermon would take about one hour to deliver and modern Catholics may find it surprising to learn that their seventeenth century co-religionists expected long homilies or instructions as part of their Sunday and Holyday Masses. Obviously it was not just the Calvinists, Baptists and Lutherans who 'enjoyed' long religious exhortation at this time.

Sermons number 53, '0n Confessing the Faith' and number 4, 'De Conceptione Virginis' are reproduced in full below. Extracts from other sermons also merit study and are brought to the reader's attention.

*****

SERMON 53 'ON CONFESSING THE FAITH'

He that shall confess me before men, him will I also confess before my Father, which is in heaven. Matt.10,32.

Thales Milesius, one of the seven sages of Greece, having discovered a secret in the nature of the heavens, and imparting it to his friend Mandritos the Philosopher, Mandritos asked him what he should do to requite so great a favour; to whom Thales answered: It shall be to me, Mandritos, abounding satisfaction if when an occasion is offered to speak of the thing, you ascribe it not to yourself but acknowledge me the discoverer and finder out thereof. Our Saviour hath not only discovered unto us a secret concerning the heavens, but a secret far more precious. He hath discovered and declared unto us by the Catholic Church his will in the Sacred Scriptures, the mysteries of our holy Faith, what we are to believe, what to do to arrive to eternal happiness. But for this He exacts that we before men confess Him to be the author of this Church and religion, and stoutly declare when occasion is that we are members of the same. And that we may be encouraged to do our duty herein He promiseth if we confess Him before men, He will confess us before his Father which is in heaven.

(*) *A black notebook containing manuscript copies of six complete sermons and extracts from seventeen others is preserved in the archives of St.Paul's parish, Thrapston. All the sermons were copied out for the 'positio' for the process of beatification and are preserved in the Westminster Archdiocesan Archives.*

In this sermon I will declare unto you three points. First the obligation every Catholic hath to confess his Faith. 2ndly that no Catholic can deny his Faith. Lastly, I will speak of such persons who are deficient in this important doctrine.

Eusebius 1.6,c.31 of his Ecclesiastical History writes of certain heretics who taught that to avoid persecution or the penalties of laws inflicted upon Christians, men might say or do what they pleased, so they kept their Faith sound in their hearts. Which gross heresy is plainly confuted by St.Paul, where he saith (Rom.10,9,10): If thou confesseth with thy mouth our Lord Jesus, and in thy heart believe that God hath raised Him up from the dead, thou shalt be saved, for with the heart we believe unto justice, but with the mouth confession is made unto salvation. By which words it's manifest that it's not sufficient to believe all the mysteries of our Faith, though this be the foundation of our justice, and without which it's impossible to please God, yet when an occasion is offered we are bound to confess with our mouths, and by our external actions, whatsoever we do interiorly believe, and that we are not to permit any shame, danger, or difficulty to hinder us in performing this, if we desire to acquire eternal salvation. For these last words with the mouth confession is made unto salvation plainly show St. Paul in this place distinguisheth a two-fold confession of Faith, the one internal, the other external. By the internal is declared that every true Christian is bound either implicitly or explicitly in his heart to believe that God is omnipotent, that He created heaven and earth of nothing, that the B.Trinity consists of one individual God and three distinct persons, that the second Person did incarnate himself in the womb of the sacred Virgin, died for our redemption, and all other the very last article and point of our Faith, and believing these and yielding assent unto them, because they are proposed unto us by the Catholic Church, which make that confession of Faith which is necessary for justification, and which is mentioned in these words; with the heart we believe unto justice. By the external, although the Apostle useth the word One mouth, because the proper institution of words is to explicate the mind and doing it better than any external action, we are taught that in all times and all circumstances and all places whatsoever, if we be demanded by those that have authority, to confess ourselves Catholics, and to do nothing by word or action or gesture or by frequenting or putting ourselves into any place or condition by which a contrary opinion may be framed of us. And this is a thing so necessary that without it there is no hope to obtain salvation. By the mouth confession is made unto salvation. And therefore our B.Saviour in the words of my text saith: He that shall confess me before men, him will I also confess before my Father which is in heaven, declaring by these words how highly he doth esteem and love those who, notwithstanding any persecution whatsoever openly confess Him, that is his truth and doctrine taught in the Catholic Church. For as when Saul (Acts 9) persecuted the Church our Saviour said Saul persecuted Him, so when we confess his Church, He takes it as a confession of Him, for which He will acknowledge all such constant confessors before his heavenly Father for his children. O what a comfort, what an unspeakable joy will it be to the souls of those confessors, who shall hear our Saviour to his heavenly Father say: these were those who notwithstanding the grievous laws made against Catholics, nevertheless in all occasions acknowledged themselves Catholics. These were those who, albeit they knew that loss of goods, loss of liberty, loss of life was incurred by professing my doctrine yet did always profess the same. These were those who did exalt and came rejoicing from the tribunals of this world when they were affronted or suffered injuries for the maintenance of my religion. But on the contrary in the very next verse following my text he saith: He that shall deny me before men, I will also deny him before my Father which is in heaven, that is, in that dreadful day of judgement He shall say unto them, You were those which preferred the pleasures of this world before my eternal promise, the threats of men before my judgement, temporal and poor benefits before the unspeakable joys which I prepared for my servants. Wherefore, Go ye cursed into everlasting fire, go to receive your part and portion with the damned in everlasting flames. And no marvel, for he which shall deny his Catholic Faith by words or any external action, either believes it not all, but denies it also in his heart, and then he is an infidel, or at leastwise an heretic, and if he believes it aright in his heart and yet by his external words and carriage gives the world to understand the contrary, he tells a mortal and deadly untruth contrary to the honour of God, contrary to the dignity of his religion, contrary to the profit of his neighbour, contrary to the unity of the Catholic Church. For how can it be but there must be many rents and schisms in that Church where men believe interiorly one thing and profess exteriorly the contrary? How can our neighbour be instructed in our Faith, when, by anything they can observe in us, they are ignorant what our Faith is? How can it be but the dignity of the Church must be much obscured when the subjects thereof dare not acknowledge themselves to be subjects? Or how can God's honour be dilated and spread in the hearts of men, if men through fear omit to speak or spread the same? Whereupon, St. Augustine (Ser.l81 *de tempore*) saith: Faith is to be conserved with our hearts and to be delivered by words, and upon those words of the psalm 115 *Credidi propter quod locutus sum,* he saith: They do not believe perfectly who refuse to speak what they believe.

I will now therefore discuss a question, whether Catholics in England do not deny their Faith, and consequently commit a most grievous sin, who shall frequent heretical churches, hear their sermons, be present at their service, at their Christenings, marriages, burials etc. The laws of England, or penalties imposed upon Nonconformists, that is Catholics, not going to their service are most severe and rigorous, for in the reign of Queen Elizabeth, anno 1559 there was a law made to pay twelve pence a Sunday for everyone that came not to their Church. In the year 1582 it was by Act of Parliament decreed that all of both sexes which were above the age of sixteen and refused to come to Protestants' prayers, their sermons and their churches, should pay twenty pound a month, and those who are not able to pay the same to be clapped in prison. Nay other laws there are for taking two thirds of their estate, all which laws and divers others against Catholics remain yet in force. Wherefore this being considered, some have not stuck to teach that to avoid so great penalties Catholics were not bound to abstain from going to their churches or their service, especially sith that in Germany and in France Catholics sometimes either out of curiosity, or to grace the funerals or marriages of their heretical friends, or by hearing their doctrine to be better able to refute it. Notwithstanding this doctrine is most false in England and damnable to all those who practise the same, as hath been defined by three several apostolical Breves, the first sent 1606 by Pope Paul the 5th to the Catholics of England, the 2nd the year following by the said Paul the 5th to the said Catholics to confirm the former, and the last by Urban the eight, sending three several Breves dated May 3rd 1626, the one to the King of France, the 2nd to the Bishop of Chalcedon, and third to the Catholics of England, in all which he doth by most weighty and grave words confirm that excellent doctrine which Paul V had delivered in the first Brief, whose words are these:

Truly We believe that those who hitherto have with such constancy and fortitude suffered such bitter persecutions and almost infinite miseries will never permit themselves to be defiled by communicating with those who are deserters of the divine law. Nevertheless, moved with the zeal of our pastoral office, and by the fatherly care which We daily have for the salvation of your souls, are constrained to admonish and beseech you, that by no means you go to the churches of heretics, or hear their sermons, or communicate with them in their rites, lest you incur the wrath of God. For it's not lawful to do this without detriment to the divine honour and your salvation.

By which words it's clear that it's not only a sin to frequent such places because the Pope doth prohibit it, for his words are not so much a prohibition as a declaration that all such acts are in themselves and in their own nature sinful and damnable, and therefore he doth admonish us and intreat us not to go to such places, being that it was a thing unlawful, that we should incur God's displeasure, thereby hinder his service and our own salvation: so that the Pope so expressly having declared this, no man that hath care of his salvation will dare to practise, or doubt that any man that shall practise it is in a damnable state. Which declaration of the Pope is grounded in the holy Scriptures and ancient Fathers. St.Paul (Rom.16,17) desires us to observe them that make dissensions and scandals contrary to the doctrine which we have learned, and avoid them. In his third to Titus he bids us to shun them, and St.John (2 Ep,) wills us not to say Amen unto them, for, saith he, he which saith Amen unto them communicates with them in their evil works. Now if we are forbidden by the Apostles all communication with heretics, much more are we forbidden to communicate with them in their service, which no Catholic can deny are sinful and evil actions. St.Cyprian in his book *de lapsis*, speaking of heretics saith: depart from the contagion of these men and avoid their speeches, flying them as a canker or plague, and St.Augustine: An Emperor or King commands that I serve him: well this is good: but he commands me to serve him in a place where they sacrifice to false gods, or in an heretical church: this I cannot do, for a greater power than a king's forbids me. Wherefore he must pardon me, for though he threatens prison if I refuse, yet God threatens hell if I refuse not. (Ser.6, *de verbis Domini*).

This natural reason doth excellently elucidate for although a man goes to the church unwilling and merely to comply with the laws and to avoid punishment, and believes not anything that is there said, yet by his exterior carriage he makes profession of their heresies and partakes with them in their ceremonies, for there is no more required by the law to distinguish a Catholic from a Protestant than the coming or not coming to their service. If they come they are termed Conformists, and as other Protestants are free from all punishment; if not they are held Recusants and punished as people that stand fast to the Catholic Faith. Wherefore when we are commanded by their laws to go to their church or to communicate with them in their service, we are demanded virtually what religion we are of, for the chief end of enacting those laws was to find out Catholics, that they might persecute and punish them for their religion, and as we are bound, as I showed in the beginning, not through any fear to deny our Faith, but being lawfully demanded to confess the same, so these laws being enacted by those that had power to demand of us what religion we were, when they call upon us to go to church we are bound to refuse it, and by our refusal to declare we are true Catholics, which if we do not we shall never obtain that happy blessing of our Saviour: He which confesseth me before men. I will confess him before my Father which is in heaven, but on the contrary, that heavy threat: he that denyeth me before men, I will deny him before my Father which is in heaven.

It's true, although a man is not bound always to confess his Faith, but in some cases it's not only lawful but laudable for him to conceal it, yet he can never deny it or carry himself so, either by words or actions, as if he seemed to deny it. And although when a Catholic is asked by a private man, or one that hath nothing to do, of what religion he is, he may put him off with a "What's that to you?" or some such like answer, yet when he is demanded by public authority he is obliged to confess what he is, for then is the greatest occasion given of honouring God and the true Catholic religion. And in this business of going to church of which we now speak, it's more than manifest he is asked by public authority as well of his own religion and Faith as whether he doth approve or disapprove the Protestant heresy, for he is enforced by great penalties as twelve pence the Sunday, twenty pounds the month, two-thirds of his estate, imprisonment etc, to go to those places and to such service as his presence there is esteemed by them for a sign that he declares himself to be of their heretical sect, for when St.Chrysostom (Hom.25 in Matt) had said that God created the heart of man that we should interiorly believe his truth, and the mouth that we might by our words declare the same, he presently adds: we are bound not only to confess God with our mouths, but by our five senses, and if one sense should fail it was no perfect confession. And then he proves it by this excellent discourse:

If any one should say unto you, I desire not you should eat of the meat sacrificed unto idols, but only look upon the idols and behold how beautiful they are, if thou lookest upon them, being provoked thou denyest Christ by thy eyes. Not that it's an evil thing to look upon an idol, but the evil consists in that thou dost look upon them being invited, and if thou then lookest not upon them thou confesseth Christ with thy eyes. Wherefore it is written (Ps.118): Turn my eyes that they behold not vanity. And if he saith: I desire not that thou shouldest behold the idol but only hear how that Gentile blasphemes Christ and extols his own Gods, if then thou listenest unto him, with thy ears thou denyest Christ. And if he saith: I will not that thou hearest Christ blasphemed, yet stand whilst incense is offered and smell how sweet it is, if you remain to smell thereunto, by your smelling you deny Christ.

And the like he saith of other senses, and I also of all those Catholics that frequent heretical churches, for although it be in itself a thing indifferent and no sin to go into an heretical church, yet to go thither by force of their statutes, which by their penalties constrain men to go thither, is a denial of our Saviour and consequently a damnable sin. Though perchance to hear their sermons or to be present at their sermons or other service may be no sin or to some persons not dangerous, yet to hear them, or to seem as if we heard them, or to be present at them, or in any sort to countenance them, because we are commanded to do so, is so gross a denial of our Faith that our Saviour doth deservedly deny them who condescend to any such impious and unlawful action.

Neither let anyone tell me for excuse that both French and German Catholics have sometimes practised this, and such rigid censures have not been imposed upon them. For there is a main difference between their conditions and the condition of our Catholics in England. There is no law constraining them to go to church: our English Catholics, as I have showed, are compelled by laws thereunto. They may depart when they please: our Catholics not so. They may publicly show their dislike and reprehend their errors: our Catholics must rest quiet and hold their peace, for should they speak or show dislike they would be punished for it. It's made by Act of Parliament no distinctive sign with them: our Parliaments have made it here, calling them Papists or Recusants who obey not. So that all these circumstances being adjoined to their going to church, it's an intrinsical evil, a most grievous sin, so horrid an offence that no power can dispense with the same, and therefore it's not only a sin because the Pope declares it so, but because it is in itself and in it's own nature so. Therefore his Holiness, as a careful Pastor of his flock doth admonish all his children here in England and intreat them not to go to such heretical service lest they incur the high displeasure and indignation of Almighty God.

St.Paul in his Epistle to Titus complains that there are many who confess they know God, but by their works deny Him. We will with more cause complain that in these our days there are too many who profess themselves Christians, yet dare flatly contradict what Christ teacheth and affirms in his holy Gospel. Here might I take a just occasion to express in their due colours those worst of men who notwithstanding our Saviour's words concerning His Church. Who heareth you, heareth Me, do, out of I know not what giddy humour, follow their private and puritanical spirit, who when He shall expressly say, This is my Body, do with Calvin by false and heretical glosses pervert the sense, saying it's only but a figure thereof: who when He shall grant by His Apostles and their successors absolute power to forgive sins, shall cry out with the Jews, blasphemv, and strangely mistaking the force of this donation say, None can forgive sins but God. But I pass them over as men whose Faith is worse than that of the wicked thief. His was at least conditional. If thou be Christ, come down from the Cross. If our Saviour had descended from the cross he said he would believe, but these wretches, miserable as they are, descend or not descend, they seem resolved to persist in their obstinacy. I pity them and pray for their conversion. I will speak of those who seem the sons of Nicodemus, those who either are actually Catholics or would willingly be so. Those who actually are Catholics pretend that if they do not now and then show as if they would comply with their laws in frequenting their churches, they shall lose their temporal goods, be uncapable of preferments, liable to pecuniary mulcts, subject to corporal punishments, incur their prince's displeasure etc. Those who are schismatics give out they would willingly be reconciled but it must for a time be deferred, their estates must be settled, and a fit opportunity (which oftentimes is never found) be expected.

Is this to show themselves Christians? This to profess that Faith exacted by our Saviour? Alas, alas, it is to show or profess a Faith, but such a Faith that makes all good men, and those who tender their salvation, to grieve at their misery, and with that blessed Patriarch of Venice Lau Justimonius, ashamed of their abject resolution to break forth into this complaint:

God God, can it be that the law of an earthly prince should make a deeper impression in men's hearts than the law of the eternal God? Can it be that transitory trash or fading dignities should be higher esteemed than angelical and everlasting honour? Can it be that a little temporal pleasure should be embraced and heaven neglected, because some short pains are to be undergone for the obtaining thereof? A shame to say this: a shame even to think it.

Tis true the loss of terrene riches strike deadly to these Nicodemites' hearts, and the fear of imprisonment, much more the fear of death, affrights their pusillanimous minds from all worthy actions, but "A shame to say this: a shame even to think it." Is it not a shame to think that men of understanding men endowed with reason, should choose rather to eat husks with swine than to feed upon their father's prepared dainties; to live upon garlic in Egypt than to seek for a land flowing with milk and honey; to prefer Satan before the Saviour of the world, and rather to be the devil's than God's prisoners? And yet this is their miserable case, as may be clearly shown. But as a good medicine is far more profitable to sick persons than an explication of their disease, so a good remedy will be more advantageous to these kinds of men than to unfold unto them their misery. What remedy, therefore, or what means may we apply to reduce their lost souls? Should I press those terrible threats used by our Saviour in the Gospel, that if they confess Him not in this world He will utterly discard them in the world to come? That if they fill not their lamps with the oil of such Christian confessions, they may cry with the foolish virgins: Lord, Lord, open to us! when no other answer shall be got but a 'I know you not'. Depart ye cursed into everlasting fire. This language although most true would be too harsh to their tender ears. I will therefore use St.Paul's more gentle and mild manner of speech. The time of tribulation is but short, and the reward most plentiful. Wherefore saith St.Augustine, You will say perchance it's a hard task to bear patiently persecution, but consider what is promised. Christ promiseth that all that confess Him before men, He will confess them before His Father, which is in heaven. And is it possible that one should judge that hard or esteem that a persecution which is endured for the confession of Christ, since for it they are to have so high a reward as to be acknowledged by Him before his heavenly Father? Happy sure is that sufferance that shall promise such glory: happy such torments that shall cause our Saviour to say (Apoc.6): These are those who are come out of great tribulation and have washed their robes and made them white in the blood of the Lamb. Therefore they are before the throne of God and shall serve Him day and night in his temple. They shall no more hunger or thirst, neither shall the sun fall upon them or any heat, because the Lamb which is in the midst of the throne shall rule over them, and conduct them to the fountain of living waters, and God shall wipe away all tears from their eyes.

AMEN.

Devotion to Our Lady is so much part of the Catholic Faith and at the same time a matter of controversy at the time of the Reformation, so that it seems right to include also the following sermon of Blessed Peter Wright.

*****

De Conceptione Virginis

Benedixisti Domine terram tuam. Psa1.84,2.

Moses as we read Exod.3:5, perceiving by Mount Horeb a bush all in flames and not to burn said he would go and see what that great vision was, but Alm. God did not only prohibit him to approach but commanded him to put off his shoes saying, the ground on which he stood was holy. *Ne appropries huc, solve calceamenta de pedibus tuis, locum in quo stas terra sancta est.* The solemnity of this day causes me to frame a discourse of that virgin earth which never was watered with terrene showers, of that earth in which *flores apparuerunt*, all sorts of most beautiful flowers did appear, being never hindered by the least weed or other noxious herb, of that earth that was *hortus conclusus,* a garden originally so well fenced that no Northern wind could ever get entrance to blast its fruits, or other ill air to hurt its perpetual freshness and verdure; of that earth from whence arose truth. *Veritas de terra orta est,* and which by the special overshadowing of the Holy Ghost opened itself and produced a Saviour, *aperiatur terra et germinet salvatorem*; of that earth which our Lord hath in a particular manner chosen and sanctified for his own self, for so the royal prophet saith in the words of my text. *Benedixisti domine terram tuam*, as if he had said Lord thou hast in a special manner blessed this earth and sanctified it for thy own use, conferring upon it great benedictions; and well may they be termed great, they being so great that according to St.Tho. 1 p.q.25 a.6, and other divines his omnipotence could not bestow greater. Wherefore if Moses was commanded to show such respect because the ground upon which he stood was made holy, what respect, what homage, what honour, what reverence are we to show when we approach by our thoughts to take a view of this Virgin plot, this celestial paradise out of which sprang the tree of life, Jesus our sacred Redeemer. We are all certainly bound *solvere calceamenta de pedibus nostris*, to lay aside all terrene thoughts, to elevate them on high, to believe that our Lord conserved this *terram benedictam* from all stains either of actual or original blemish, and that whatsoever was found therein was sublime, singular, excellent, celestial and altogether befitting that fruit which it produced, all which I will prove by arguments and authorities of several Doctors and Fathers of the Catholic Church, and to the end I may more methodically proceed I will reduce this sermon to three heads. First I will show the reason why Our Lord blessed this earth. *Benedixisti domine terram tuam*. 2ndly how and in what manner he blessed it. Lastly the benedictions that accrue unto us by the same.

The learned Suarez, with other school divines, teaches, although after the general day of Judgment the heavens and earth shall remain intrinsically the same, yet withal they say that both heaven and earth shall be wonderfully perfected by new accidental qualities. The heavens, say they, shall become more splendid and glorious and the earth *erit perlucido instar Christalli*, shall be as bright and clear as crystal itself. The reason hereof they give with St.Chrystom. hom.ad.pop. where he saith *Cum puer coronatur in regem nutrix participat de alumni bonis, ita mundus qui electos coronandus aluit, etiam in partem gloriae veniet*.As when a child comes to be crowned King his nurse is made in some sort sharer with him in his greatness, so shall the earth which hath maintained and nourished the elect come to be participant with them in some part of their great glory. Others prove and from hence with great facility deduce the great glory of the industrious and constant labourers in the vineyard of Alm.God, who do not only remotely concur to the pruning of this vineyard that is to the converting or conserving the elect, but do daily, as Zaverius did, feed with evangelical milk thousands of children, and are the immediate causes that whole kingdom(s) and nations are kept and brought back from the death of sin and idolatry unto the saving grace of their Lord and Saviour. The Holy Ghost saith of such men as these, *fulgebunt in perpetuas eternitates*. Which if this be so, if these be such rare favours granted to those who work in *vinea Domini* and labour to gain souls, and if the earth shall be enriched with such admirable privileges for cooperating even so remotely with the servants of God, and conferring oftentimes as many, yea more favours upon sinners than the greatest saints, what favours, what privileges, what unspeakable blessings may we imagine Alm. God bestowed upon this sacred earth, upon this all-immaculate Virgin. For she was she of whom our holy mother the Catholic Church sings *Cunctos hereses sola interemisti in universo mundo*; she was she that did produce the sun of Justice whose radiant beams gave such light to the world that they did disperse the clouds of infidelity. She was she that trod upon the prince of darkness and broke in pieces his head which is the author of all heresy. She is she that doth continually help, strengthen and encourage her servants to suppress and beat down all erroneous and false opinions; in a word, she was she *quae germinavit salvatorem*, who did not only conceive within her most pure and chaste bowels the Saviour of the world, but having nine months nourished him there did bring him forth and suckle and cherish him and use all the tender arts of love and affection which a most indulgent mother could show to so dear a babe, or a most humble handmaid to her Lord and Creator. Our Lord, *ab initio viarum suarum*, from eternity itself knew all these arts, knew how she would receive the angel's salutation, that she would receive them with these most revering and lowly words *Ecce ancilla Domini*. What therefore shall we think our Saviour did render her *Qui reddit unicuique secundum opera eius?* Shall I say he made her a garden of pleasure beset with all sort of flowers and variety of virtues. If I say this, St.Jerome serm: de Assump. saith the same in these words, *Hortus deliciarum in qui consita sunt universa florum genera, ac ornamenta virtutum*. Shall I say she was a plot of ground abounding and encircled with all the treasures of grace? If I say it, St.Damien will be my authority who in his sermon also of the assumption avers that she was *Locus voluptatis quem Deus omnibus gratiae divitiis cumulavit.* Shall I say our Saviour did so bless her that he made her a paradise. I will with Rupertus boldly say, 1,4: in Cant., he made her a Paradise which did in a superlative, yea, in an infinite degree exceed the other, for in that Paradise he only placed an earthly Adam. In this he placed himself, takes man's nature upon him, which was the same with the Father and Holy Ghost. *Pater, Verbum et Spiritus Sanctus, hi tres unum sunt.* Shall I say she was a mountain, yea, such a mountain which by reason of the sublimity of merits extended herself beyond all the choirs of angels to the throne of the deity, for the Conception of the eternal Word? I may say so, and say it most truly, having for the same so great an author as is St.Greg., who writing upon the first book of Kings and first Chap: and taking an occasion to gloss upon these words of the Prophet Isaias,c.2. *Mons domus Dei in tertio Montium,* hath these words. *An non mons sublimis Maria, quae ut ad conceptionem Aeterni Verbi pertingeret, meritorum vericem supra omnes angelorum choros usque ad solium deitatis erexit.* All these authors prove right well that our Lord *Benedixit terram suam*, did bless this his earth, but there is never an one of them methinks which proves to be the full cause or reason wherefore he blessed it, which was the thing I promised chiefly in this point to show.

A learned modern (Salacar c.8,v.26 in Prov.) compares her to the centre of the earth, in which comparison is included the cause of this her beatitude. For the centre is nothing else but *Quoddam punctum*, or *infirma totius terrae parte*, a certain point or the lowest part of the earth, and who more humble and low in her own eyes than the B.Virgin. *Nullus homo, ab humo dictus, Virgine humilior extiterit, unde fit ut nulla terra pars inferior sit quam Maria.* Zalazar cit., that is, there was never any more humble than the B.Virgin, and from hence it is that she may be truly said the lowest part of the earth, *infirma pars terrae.* It was decreed in the Conclave of the B.Trinity that our Saviour, the Second Person of the said B.Trinity, should descend for the redemption of mankind into the lower parts of the earth, which himself doth intimate by his psalmist, Ps.138, in these words: *substantia mea in inferioribus terrae*, which St.Paul also doth insinuate Ephes.4, saying, *Quod autem ascendit guid est nisi auia descendit in inferioribus partibus terrae.* By which words, saith St.Anselm, is not only endorsed his descent into hell, but of his first descension into the Virgin's womb, and Anastasius Sinaitd 1:2 Exameron, saith, *fecit salutem in medio terrae, utpote quae habitavit in medio terreni uteri Virginis Mariae*: he wrought this salvation in the middle of the earth, because he took his habitation in the terrene womb of the B.Virgin. He was in a manner constrained to come and incarnate himself here, for so saith St.Bonaventure in his psalter: *Quia domina humillissima fuisti. Verbum incarnatum ex te carnem sumere coegisti.* 0 Lady saith (sic) because thou wert the most humble of all women, thou didst constrain the Incarnate Word to come and take flesh from thee. So that hereby we see the cause wherefore our (B.Lady crossed out) Lord doth thus bless this his earth, and adorn and enrich it with so many rare favours and privileges whereof I have already spoken. It was because her humility having enforced him to come thither, he resolved to make it an habitation fit for his divine Majesty, and to make her shine with that purity, that all the purity of saints, angels, archangels, cherubims, yea put them all together, was not to be compared thereto. *Decens erat*, saith St.Anselm 1, de Conceptu Virginali,c.18, *ut ea puritate qua maior sub Deo intelligi nequit, virgo illa niteret.*

Thus we see wherefore our B.Lady was exalted to such an infinite height of glory and blessedness: it was *Quia humillissima fuit*, and so herself confesseth in that divine Canticle of hers, recorded Luc.l:49. *Quia respexit humilitatem ancillae tuae.* Wherefore, to speak something by way of application. Thus doth God deal with all those who are truly humble and confess their own unworthiness. He exalts and prefers them to great dignities. As long as King Saul was little in his own eyes, God made him General over Israel, but once growing proud and forgetting God, God forgot him and left himover to a reprobate sense. When David out of humility and reverence danced before the Ark, and albeit was a King played with his harp in the midst of the multitude, he was exceeding gracious in the eyes of his Creator, but swelled up with pride and out of a haughty mind numbering the people he felt God's favour changed, and His hand heavy upon him. *Magna mysteria fratres*, saith St.Augustine in Psa1.33. *Deus super omnia est: erigis te et illum non tangis humilias te, et ipse ad te descendit*. Consider dear brethren the great mystery we have here. God is on high and above all things: how therefore shall we come unto him? Must we elevate ourselves or lift ourselves up? No, saith he, then we shall never come near him. What must we do, then? We must keep, ourselves below in the consideration of our own vility and nothing, and then, *0 magnum mysterium*, he will descend down unto us, for as the Ps.139 *Excelsus dominus et humilia respicit et alta a longe cognoscit*. Our Lord is most high and doth look upon humble things, and knows high things afar off. Which words affords (sic) us a two-fold consideration, both worthy to be reflected upon. The first, that God is most high and consequently can behold nothing above or higher than Himself, and therefore what he looks upon, at leastwise with his eyes of approbation must be humble and low, for with his eyes of reprobation he saw Lucifer who strove to be as high as Himself. *Ascendam super altitudinem nubium et solus ero altissimo*. Isa.14:14. The second, that God knows *Alta*, this is proud men, and soaring with their thoughts on high *a longe*, afar off. For as the sun, moon and stars, who are bodies in themselves most great, yea, far greater than the earth itself, yet appear little in our eyes because they are seen by us *a longe*, afar off, so the proud albeit they be giants or mighty men in this world, yet appear in the eyes of God but little. *Quia a longe respexit illos*, because they are seen by him afar off, yea oftentimes he doth not behold them afar off, but as the B.Virgin saith in the Canticle before mentioned, *deponit potentes*. He doth utterly depose and bring to nothing those great and proud men. Who more great and proud in his own conceit than Pharaoh, who albeit Alm.God had expressly commanded him to let the people of Israel to depart, yet he resisted as much as possibly he could, saying, *persequor et comprehendam, evaginabo gladium meum; interficiet eos manus mea*. I will persecute and apprehend them: I will draw my sword; my hand shall kill them. Thus he vaunts God's commands. He should let them go, and he cries, *persequor et comprehendam*. I will kill and slay and make them know I am king of Egypt. But alas, what was the end of this vaunting? The prophet Moses Exod,l5 tells us. *Flavit Spiritus tuus et operuit eos mare*. God did but only breathe with his spirit and Pharaoh and all his hosts were drowned. Sabra also was a mighty man. He was as the Prophet Isaias:c.22:15, *Praepositus templi*, the Provost or chief ruler of the temple of Jerusalem, and thought himself no mean man in the kingdom, but for this his ambition, conceit of himself, and for his ill carriage. God sends the Prophet Isaias unto him to tell him: *Dominus asportari te faciet sicut asportatus Gallus Gallinaccus, coronans coronabit te tribulatione*. Our Lord will cause thee to be carried away, as is a cock carried, crowning he will thee with tribulation. He will cast thee as a ball into a broad and large country, and there thou shalt die. This is that which Sabra got for his pride. God is still the same God. If there be found now any Pharaoh who persecutes God's people and hinders them from exercising his true religion, or any Sabra who to obtain his ambitious ends concurs to the same: if they repent not, must expect the same punishment, for *Deus resistit superbos, humilibus autem dat gratiam*. I come to the second point, *Benedixisti etc*.

Whilst our first parent Adam remained in the state of innocency in which he was created by the hand of Alm.God, Oh, there he was happy. Well might we say of him, *Vere benedicta erat tua vita*. Truly that state of his was most fortunate and blessed, for then he had his soul beautified with grace or inherent justice, his understanding endowed with the perfect knowledge of all natural and supernatural mysteries: then he had his will rectified by the law of God, and the strong bias of his inclination directly carried to the work of virtue: then he had the inferior powers of his soul, the motion of his flesh, subject to reason, the stem of reason pliable to the Spirit, the Spirit always obedient to God: then he had no ignorance, no error, no perturbation of passion in his mind: then he had no inordinate concupiscence, no rebellion in his flesh, no propension to evil, no difficulty to do good. This was his happy state, this his blessed condition during the time of his innocency, and had to be therein preserved, how many acts of virtue, what continual occasions might he have found to have increased his merit and glory with Alm. God, lo he miserable as he was transgressing his Creator's command, fell into that lamentable plight which himself and all his successors have ever since rued. Then he found himself justly plagued with the disobedience of his flesh against his spirit: then he found and felt to his grief the commotion of the inferior or base parts rebelling against the superior: then he found the aversion he had from good and the proneness he had to evil: then he found the disorder of his passions, the infirmities of his mind, the disease of his body.

I will not here go about to prove how Alm.God did bless our priceless Virgin, our non-paralleled Queen in the first moment of her Conception: how He did in the first instant thereof dart into her soul a beam of grace, one of the greatest derivations of the divinity. I will not declare how all the infused virtues with Charity their sister Queen did enrich her will, neither will I show how her understanding was enlightened with almost all natural and supernatural things. These things, I say, I will pass over as things certain and properly to be discussed in the feast of her immaculate conception. That which I will say and that which I will hereout declare is, how our Lord did bless this his earth after the first instant of her nativity. *Benedixisti Domine terram tuam.* Divers writers interpreting those words of the psalmist *Fundamentum eius in montibus sanctis*, say our blessed lady entered the world enriched with more grace than did ever the greatest saint go out thereof, for *fundamentum eius in montibus sanctis*, her first ingression arrived higher than to the top of those mountains of merit, which ever any saint at his departure this life was made happy withal. *Fundamentum eius in montibus sanctis*, and not marvel for her soul, being from that instant great, if I may so say, with all those glorious habits, broke continually forth into so many correspondent and meritorious acts, an act of faith, an act of love, an act of contemplation of the greatness of God, an act of the consideration of her own nothing. Now she reflected upon God's unspeakable love in choosing from all eternity (her) to be his mother: then how unworthy she was to be his handmaid: here she gave him infinite thanks for that admirable favour; there she employed all her thoughts how she might best bestow herself to praise and laud his holy name: in fine, her heart, her mind, her power, her strength and whole soul were so abyssed in the love of her Creator and so settled in a deep contemplation of his unspeakable Majesty and goodness, that here no terrene thought, no worldly desire, no less than well ordered admirable affection could get any the least place. *Totam incantaverat eam divinus amor, ut nihil esset in ea quod mundanus violaret affectus, sed ordo continuus ebrietatis perfusi amoris*. Hierm, serm,de Assumpt. Here was no disagreeing: between appetites, no disorder in affections, no perturbation of mind, no trouble or disquiet in any action. Here *fomes peccati* lay fast bound, incentives to sin were always utterly abolished, and all first (?) motions never so much as heard of. Here might be seen that that great God *Qui fecerat concordiam sublimibus* Ephes.2,, who had made this admirable consort and harmony in all her interior parts, did make also *utraque unum*, did also make it plain and manifest in her exterior comportment, for as St. Ambr.orat. 1 de Nat,saith, *Nil torvum in oculis,nil in verbis procax, nil in actu inverecundum, non gestis fractior, non incessus solutior, non vox petulantior in quo corporis species simulachrum fuerit mentis*. Here was no frowning in the countenance, no incivility in words, no immodesty in gesture, here was no looseness in gait, no lightness in behaviour nor petulancy in voice: here both voice, gesture, action, countenance, comportment, clothing, behaviour and all were as so many certain gnomens or fingers to indigitate to the world in what an admirable order the clock of her soul did go. Her example taught virgins chastity, confessors perseverance, martyrs fortitude, the Apostles zeal, the Seraphims fervent charity. *O Maria, O terra benedicta*, how did you by these continual continued acts multiply your grace. Every moment was a doubling and redoubling degrees of grace till they amounted to an infinity of degrees of graces. We know grace to be of that excelling that the sole want thereof made a Lucifer the Prince of the Angels become an ugly deformed devil, and the enjoying but of one degree is able so to metamorphose a poor Lazarus and to imprint in him so beautiful a form as he shall be deemed worthy to be received into Abraham's bosom. O then when I think of the immensity of grace of this sacred Queen, and of the divine form, beauty and excelling with which it did adorn her, and would willingly declare them, O then I am enforced with St.Anselm to confess, lib. de Excellentia Virg.c;8., *Sensus deficit, lingua satiscit*. Adam was thought happy and a thousand times happy for enjoying the blessed state which in the beginning I described, and who doth not deem those souls happy that now and then are rapt into ecstasy, and are so absorbed in divine love that they have no apprehension of earthly things. What shall I therefore say of this incomparable Lady, who did not as Adam did for a moment of time enjoy that sacred quiet, or for some certain spaces was taken from terrene thoughts and elevated by contemplation higher than the highest heaven to the throne of his eternal Majesty, but from all instants of her life was beautified with those celestial favours and graces. *O vere erat terra benedicta*, it was made blessed in being blessed from all thorns of earthly cares and solicitudes: blessed in being blessed from any passion that could give or argue the least shadow of imperfection: blessed in being blessed by the freshness and and fragrance of the flowers of all flourishing virtues: blessed in being blessed by the fullness and plenitude of grace: blessed in being blessed in the beatifical vision and fruition of the Father, the Son and the Holy Ghost, the blessed trinity and individual unity. Thus you see how our Lord blessed this his earth. *Benedixisti terram tuam.* Now a word of the blessing we receive from thence, and so end.

The patriarchs and prophets, well knowing in what misery they should remain till the fullness of time was come in which should be born unto them a Saviour, did with continual sighs and tears thirst after that happy time. The angels well knowing how earnestly they desired their Messias and how particularly they should be comforted at his coming made all possible haste to declare unto them these tidings. *Ecce Evangelizo vobis gaudium magnum*, behold now, *hodie*, in this instant, is born your so long desired and expected Saviour. This no doubt was the happiest news that ever was declared and caused man the greatest joy and comfort. Yet with proportion, methinks, I may use the same words *Ecce evangelizo vobis gaudium magnum*, today appears that Aurora which is the end of all darkness and beginning of all light and joy, today is erected that *scala celestis* by which the King of glory will descend for the comfort of his afflicted people: today is born that Lady who makes them blessed which watch daily at her gates and observe at the entrance of her doors: today is born she that causeth joy to the angels, terror to the devils, grace to the just, remission for sins: she upon whom all creatures have their eyes, and with reason, sith that, as the mellifluous St. Bernard, ser.2: de Pent, in her and by her and from her, the Omnipotent hand of God did repair and remake whatsoever he had before made and created. Today is born she that, as the same St.Bern. saith, bids anyone not to speak of her praise or mention her, if having faithfully invoked her in time of necessity hath not found sovereign remedy at her sacred hands. *Ille, laudes tuas sileat, qui te fideliter invocatam meminit defuisse*, and no marvel she is present to those who call upon (her) for assistance, since she blesses those who have no thought thereof. Luc.7 I find a type which excellently expresseth this verity. I find there recorded a certain widow of Naim whom death had deprived of hcr only son, and going with divers of her neighbours to accompany his corpse to the grave, met in the way Our Saviour. Some came for fashion's sake and had no apprehension of the poor woman's loss; others out of desperation and all hope of recovery said nothing at all. Only the poor widow, swollen with grief did with tears heartily beg of our Saviour he would restore her son to life. Our Saviour moved to compassion willed her not to weep, and going unto the coffin restored unto her her son alive and sound. What was the reason, think you, our Saviour did then hasten this miracle? Or why did he not cause him to be carried back into his mother's house, and there in private, having first sent away all the people, give him his life. O, saith St.Amb:1.6, *In hunc locum, Ideo ne amplius mora afficeretur, mater maturitas additur*, therefore did Christ thus hasten this miracle lest the mother should be still more afflicted. This as I said is a true type of our B.Lady. She, when our friends forsake us, when we are abandoned by the world, when there is no man mindful of us nor we mindful of ourselves, when our sins are not only carrying us to a material grave, but that grave in which there is nothing but perpetual horror, darkness and confusion: then doth she haste unto our Saviour, becomes our Advocate, and doth so efficaciously plead our cause that our Saviour, enforced as it were therewith, answereth. *Noli flere*, cease from further intercession, and take unto you your lost child. Wherefore well said Landulphus Abbas 1: de vita ppi,, *Ille non timeat aeternum Vae, pro quo semel oraverit Maria*. If therefore he who scarce thinks of this sacred Queen, or did ever anything in her honour receives such unspeakable favour, what favour or what benefits may then those promise to themselves who are her *sodales*, her servants, her slaves, who seek to promote her honour, commend themselves morning and evening, and in all time of danger to her protection, fast her eves, say their beads daily, hear Mass and are continually offering up at her sacred altars prayers, praises and acts of thanksgiving. St.Anselm 1. *de excellentia Virginis*, knows not what to say to such an interrogation. He only asks, *Quid recipiunt*, and ends there. For my part I most assuredly persuade myself that I may here use those words of holy Scripture with which I will also end. *Nec oculus vidit, nec auris audivit, nec intravit cor hominis quod praeparavit Deus diligentibus se*, that neither eye hath seen nor ear hath heard, nor hath it entered into the heart of man to conceive what she hath provided for her faithful servants. She hath provided them heaven, a kingdom of eternal bliss, there with the Saints and angels ever to bless, praise, magnify and adore in his throne of Majesty her Son the all immaculate Lamb. Amen.

Extract from a sermon for the First Sunday of Advent

This first extract gives a sample of the original spelling and 'shorthand' of the Stonyhurst manuscript as transcribed by Father Godfrey Anstruther.

The theme of the 'end of the world' allows Blessed Peter to recall the present sufferings of Catholics, a recurrent theme in these sermons. There is also an example of the martyr's knowledge of the pagan classics as well as a hint of the forthright and outspoken nature of Blessed Peter at this time.

*****

" ... the kingdom of God is neer at hand. This doctrine I confesse is feareful especially to worldlings who I am cetayne wil not willingly leave thereof, for o[r] B.Savior sayth they shal wither away through feare, and out of an expectation what shal happen unto them, and that al the tribes of the earth shal weepe... that is al worldlings, people addicted to their pleasure, men of cauterized consciences and such as have their soules be smeared with syrrne, these tribes of the earth, these wretched men and only these shal have cause to feare and lament, for o[r] Savior speaking of the Just, bidds them courage, to be of good comfort, and wills them when they see these things to begin, to look back and lift up their heades because the tyme of their redemption draws neere.

" ... Cicero the Prince of heathen Orators in his Oration w[ch] he made for Milo breaks forthe into these words, ... O great is the force of a conscience both on the one and the other parte, the innocent person never feares but the nocent, and who knowethe himselfe guylty hath alwayes before his eyes his punishment...

"St Paul Heb:11:36,37,38, speaking of the miseryes of God's sayntes in this world sayth they were racked, they had trial of mockery and stripes more over also of bonds and prisons ... they were tempted, they dyed in the slaughter of the sword... w[ch] things worldlings seing laughed them to scorne, and accounted their lives a madness, the like hapneth even in these dayes of ours, if they see one leave the vanityes of the world, to take upon him a religious life, to enclose himselfe in a monastery or for the love of God to be banished his native Country, to loose his goods, to suffer ymprisonment, to endure those inconvenyiences w[ch] Catholiques do and must endure in England ... But lift up yo[r] heads and reioyce, for in that day they shal change their opinions and say ... we were the mad men for thinking such mens lives a madness."

Extract from a sermon 'De Judicio', On Judgement

Preachers in Peter's day evidently did not mince their words, as the following extract confirms. As our martyr recalls the seven vices we might note that in the church of St.Peter at Raunds, some four miles from Slipton, one can again see an example of that common medieval church-painting of the 'seven vices'. Though white-washed in Peter's day and not revealed again until 1874 some memories may have lingered. Is there also a hint of personal history in some of the detail of this sermon?

*****

"That day ... he shall come in the clouds and every eye shall see him. ... The proud shall bewail because they shall remember that this judge's exhortations always were ... Learn of me not to be proud but to be meek and humble of heart. The ambitious shall bewail for they shall call to mind that he who is to pass sentence against them did so detest honours that when he was to be chosen king he fled into the mountains alone. Gluttons and drunkards shall bewail for they shall meet with him who did not please his palate with delicious meats or wines but even in his greatest misery: suffered himself to be refreshed with gall and vinegar. The lascivious shall bewail because their Judge is not only Purity itself but hath enacted it as a law that no whoremonger, adulterer or lascivious person shall enter into the kingdom. Dainty and nice dames shall bewail, for they shall then know that no frizzled hair will please, no painted faces be granted but that they must then render an exact account of all the idle employment of these and suchlike strange vanities. ...

" ... there are yet other losses which will also wonderfully increase their grief, as is the eternal deprivation of the most amicable company and sight of the B.Virgin ... and all the elect of God ... Will they nill they, they shall remember the beauty and splendour of the beautified body; they shall remember the mutual salutations and embraces and loving colloquies which parents had with their children and children with their parents, and one friend or acquaintance with another.

" ... they use these words ... what hath pride profited us what advantage have we gotten by the vanities of riches? All our former pleasures are past as a shadow, as a post that rides at full speed, as a bird flying in the air whose trace is not to be found, as an arrow which speedily passeth through the air, which air presently: reunites itself. So have our days run by without bearing any marks of virtue. We have spent in malice or idleness all the time which was liberally bestowed upon us to work our salvation."

Extract from a sermon (64) De Jubileo, On Jubilee

The Spirit of the Lord is upon me ... to proclaim the acceptable year of the Lord, Is.61,1,2.

Since the rebellion of Martin Luther was occasioned by the notorious sale of Indulgences, it is not surprising to read in this sermon a lengthy defence and explanation of Indulgences. Our extract concerns repentance, mindful of Peter's own early life, and his example from military procedure recalls his own involvement with armies.

*****

" ... (So that) God may carry over us an even hand, and his clemency may be mingled with some severity, his Justice and mercy meet together, although he always of mercy pardoneth the iniquity of repentant sinners, yet he often bindeth them over to some temporal chastisement to satisfy thereby the rigour of his Justice, and this is the cause that sometimes God pardons the offence, and yet punisheth the offender with some temporal punishment, either in this world or in purgatory. Yet it may happen, though it be a thing rare, that a man's sorrow may be so great and his contrition so admirable for his sins that he shall not only obtain pardon for them and for their eternal punishment, but for their temporal punishment also, as appears by the example of St.Peter, St.Mary Magdalen, the Publican, the thief upon the cross, the adulterous woman and divers others.

" ... no man can merit or demerit for another... For example, if a Captain goes upon a piece of service to which he had no obligation, but merely to supply the place of a friend; if such a captain performs that place with courage and resolution, and doth bravely dare and put to flight his enemies, the praise of that action must be ascribed to him. He hath merited it, this is deserved it, and it cannot be given to the other captain who was not there, neither in his advice or person. Nevertheless that captain who performed the service may satisfy the obligation the other had to go upon that exploit, for sometimes it happens that if the service be done, it imports not by whom it's performed. ...(SO) the holy Church out of its general treasure or any good man out of his particular charity, may apply his satisfactory works for the satisfying that temporal penalty which is due to the sins of others."

Extract from Sermon 51 (For All Souls)

The sixteenth century destruction and dissolution of the monasteries stirred the heart of Blessed Peter as we see in this extract.

*****

"Such a multitude of deaneries, Canonries, Monasteries, Nunneries, Churches, Chapels and other oratories as we see in England erected to have prayers and sacrifices offered for their souls. To this end was erected All Souls College in Oxford and beareth that name and enjoyeth all the lands and livings belonging thereunto. To this end the Monastery of Battle in Sussex was built by William the Conqueror to pray for such as were there deceased. To this end William Rufus his son in his Charter there extant ratifieth and confirmeth his father's grant, to benefit as he specifieth his said father and mother Matilda's soul. To this end the Nunnery of Godstow not far from Oxford was built by the rich widow Ida, was repaired and endowed with a yearly revenue by King John, that those holy Virgins, according to Camden's report, might relieve with their suffrages the souls of Rosamund (Hen.II's mistress) and Henry II. To this end infinite others have been raised throughout the realm, whose sumptuous buildings or decayed ruins yet remaining, lie prostrate at our feet, stretch forth their arms, and call upon us in behalf of their founders not to be careless and unmindful of them, nor forget with the Egyptian cupbearer the great favours they have done us."

Extract from Sermon 31. On Holy Communion

Blessed Peter preached on many topics, including 'On Swearing' (Sermon 63 ... ,as if all greatness and magnaminity and courage consisted in the breath of an unbridled, uncivil and savage mouth') and another sermon (Sermon 29) where he compares people deferring their conversion to unused statues or house furnishings gathering dust. His reference (Sermon 34) to 'new Gospellers' has a familiar ring about it, though the accusations of violence are thankfully of the past.

Blessed Peter often quotes the great Fathers of the Church - Augustine, Ambrose, Gregory Nazianzen, as examples - as well as modern writers, but the following extract quoting (St.) Francis de Sales (died 1622) reminds us of that saint's immediate popularity as well as of our own changing approach to receiving Holy Communion.

*****

"You shall have Catholics, those who believe whatsoever I have already said, yet they will hardly be drawn once in a twelvemonth to frequent this sacred supper. If they do it quarterly, they conceive their ghostly father is beholding to them. How do these men injure themselves: of what an unspeakable benefit do they deprive their souls! St.Augustine doth allow that people should communicate every day, if there be no particular reason to the contrary, and the holy bishop Sales in his book which he styles an introduction to a spiritual life seems something of that opinion. But as I should not easily grant this, so I do much approve of their devotion who do every fortnight, at leastwise every month refresh their souls with the dainties prepared at this heavenly table, and I cannot see how those can vindicate themselves from a censure of an high neglect towards their souls that shall for a longer time than a month defer it, if conveniency will admit thereof."

Extract from Sermon 20

The following passage concerning the afflictions of Catholics in the seventeenth century needs no comment.

*****

"This is a thing that is not only a trouble but a great temptation to many Catholics in England, to see their goods taken away, and others of a contrary religion to enjoy quietly their own, never to be out of danger of sherrifs, bailiffs, pursuivants, insomuch they scarce rest a night in security, when in the meantime their neighbours feast under their own vines, and in all jollity eat the fat things of the earth: not to be able to provide for their children or to give them portions, albeit they be born to large fortunes, when on the other side they shall behold the children of others to be tricked and trimmed up, and for their great estates to be courted and caressed of all.
Yea, themselves and whole families to be ready to starve at these men's gates, who heretofore were their servants, or at lease far inferior to them. But take courage, dear Catholics, take courage. Your afflictions and sorrow shall be turned into great joy. For the time will shortly come that both you and they by deposing this earthly tabernacle of yours must render to death its due, and then you with Lazarus shall be carried into Abraham's bosom, and they with Dives buried in hell."

Extract from Sermon 21

It is well-known that religious opponents of this period were not afraid to be derogatory. A sense of irony appears in at least one of Blessed Peter's letters, as also in the following passage about the apparent success of the chief reformer, Martin Luther.

*****

"I know the heretics of our times much boast that Luther forsooth hath enlightened many with his Gospel, as in Germany, England, France, Scotland and other parts of Europe, but this, as Sir Thomas More, that glorious martyr well observes is as great a wonder as that a stone being flung up into the air should fall down again, or as great a miracle as that of the famous harlot Calista who bragged she allured more by her beauty to keep her company than Socrates could draw unto him by his learned lectures."

Extract from Sermon 15

Surely we hear the ex-soldier speaking in the next passage.

*****

"If one who had nicely and effeminately been bred up in Court should come among soldiers and see them at the first alarm or touch of drum not regard wind or weather, frost or snow, storm or hail, but should through thick and thin march to the place appointed, such a courtier as this would think these soldiers out of their wits, but others who know they are tied by the laws of martial discipline to do this deem such soldiers true soldiers and worthy all honour and respect."

Extract from Sermon 19

This further military reminiscence reminds us of one who, after all, found the soldier's life 'a malicious life'.

*****

"As for soldiers, a grave author sayeth very well *Militia est malitia*, a military life is a malicious life, and what by the ill example of others and what by a presumed liberty there is no place wherein there is more danger of sinning."

Extract from Sermon 27

Peter's remonstrance against idle talk instead of thinking of Our Lord's loving Passion mentions 'Hyde Park' in London where one day people would sit in the trees to see our martyr's execution.

*****

"But our discourses are of the vanities of this world, what clothes are in fashion, what's the garb among gallants, what's done at Hyde Park or Spring Gardens, or oftentimes of things which are worse; our discourses are fraught with detraction, with envy and malice against our neighbour; how we may circumvent him by deceitful bargains, and the like, and this is the reason that our Saviour forsakes us, is not in the middle of us or goeth along with us through this vale of tears."

Extract from Sermon 26: On Thomas a Becket

A fitting conclusion to these extracts from Peter Wright's sermons is surely this prayer to the great martyr - saint, Thomas a Becket whose tomb and place of pilgrimage was sacked by Henry VIII.

*****

"O thrice happy Saint ... look with a propitious eye upon our afflicted England. Heresy alas hath stolen into our Lord's possessions and the holy of holies is defiled by wickedness. All our altars are demolished and cast down, and our Jerusalem remains in a manner desolate. Your intercessions we know are powerful and can help to redress our present calamities. Be therefore, O victorious Martyr, in your good will benign to Sion that the walls of our terrene Jerusalem being again repaired we may therein in sanctity serve our God and afterwards enter into the celestial Jerusalem, there with you and all your saints praise Him for all eternity. Amen."

THE LETTERS

The letters reproduced in Foley's notes [*] are all addressed to Mr.Joseph Simons, which was almost certainly an alias for Fr.Emmanuel Lobb S.J., via a Mr.John Clayton of Antwerp. All are dated 1647 and span the period from the second of April to the fifth of December. They show that Peter, who was living in the household of the Marquis of Winchester [**] in London, was aware of many details of the political situation relating to the original imprisonment of King Charles I at Holdenby House and his later escape from Hampton Court.

Although most of the information passed on is in the nature of general comment on the political scene, the last letter, reproduced below, refers to a Protestant religious group known as the 'Dippers' who believed in re-baptising people by total immersion. The fact of a poor man being drowned is reported, with a touch of irony, as carelessness but the underlying tone is one of scandalised horror at the way these new Protestant sects were behaving.

A peculiar quirk in the letter writing is the use of the first person plural (we, us, our) when describing events in Scotland and Ireland. One would not have expected Peter to identify with the Parliamentary government - but then he was primarily an Englishman. He would also be aware that his letters might be intercepted by government agents.

The Letter December 5th (1647)

Sir, The Dippers in our country increase much; they are now for dousing over head and ears, and allege two places of Scripture for it: John iii,23 - "And John also was baptizing in Ennon beside Salem, because there was much water there." Whereupon they infer that he chose that place to douse them in because there was much water. The other text is Romans vi,4 "For we are buried together with Him by baptism unto death" which kind of death, say they, is best performed by drowning. The practice of this doctrine had lately a sad effect in Lincoln. The passage is most certain. The Dippers having persuaded a poor man to be re-baptized, brought him to the river below the bridge; and whether it was that his hair was too short, or the stream too strong, the careless Dipper let the poor creature go and drowned him. One Dr.Kayner, a famous Presbyterian, and others of his companions, have instituted this form of baptism - "I baptize thee **into** the Father," etc. Their meaning is into the covenant of the Father, etc., for of this they make a long harangue before the baptism.

Yesterday, as the Committee of Goldsmiths' Hall was treating the business of Papists' compositions, one Allen, an alderman, came and opposed, reprehending the Committee for meddling in a business they had nothing to do withal, for, saith he, all Papists' lands were given in the beginning of the Parliament, by the Parliament to the City for the security of the moneys they then lent them. Yet the Committee hath

[*] *Foley, Vol.II, pp.559-565.*
[**] *D.N.B., The Marquis of Winchester was committed to the Tower from 18th October 1645 on a charge of high treason but was allowed to live outside the prison from time to time. The charge of treason was dropped on 14th March 1649.*

sent a certificate thereof to the Council of State. What opposition Allen or any other will make there, or in the Parliament, time must tell. The Scots have lately received arms and ammunition from Holland, and their grand council is removed from Sterling to St.Johnston's. The Kirk was against this removal, but they were enforced to submit, the cavaliering party being there strong. We have taken a castle or two near Edinburgh, and our mayne goeth there gallantly on. They begin to shoot at us from the Castle, but they kill more of the Edinburgh folk than they do of us. We have had an insurrection in Norfolk by the Presbyterians, which we hope we have appeased; yet some letters say that Rosseter and King are still up in the Isle of Ely. Last night our State had ill news from Ireland; that which we expressed of Clanricards' beating was not considerable, and since that they have killed seven of our best troops of horse, not giving quarter to any one of them. Adieu.

Yours,

P.

December 5th.

APPENDIX C

Brief history and description of the shrine dedicated to Blessed Peter Wright in the Lady Chapel at the church of St.Paul the Apostle, Thrapston.

By 1979, Fr.Charles Crawford, then parish priest at the church of St.Paul the Apostle, Thrapston, Northamptonshire had made two important discoveries. The first was that Blessed Peter Wright, S.J. was deemed to have been born in the village of Slipton within the parish boundaries; and the second was that the martyr had worked for a solicitor in the town of Thrapston itself. The next step was to contact the Jesuit authorities in London, at the office of Vice-Postulation in Mount Street, who, on being consulted, reported that they possessed a small part of the halter with which the martyr had been hanged. Providing the Postulator General, in Rome, was agreeable, they would permit the relic to be displayed and reverenced in a suitable reliquary at Thrapston.

When all the necessary formalities had been completed, the small piece of rope was, on the fifteenth of August, despatched to rural Northamptonshire with an official authentication signed by Fr.Paul Molinari, S.J., the Postulator General (See Ch.VIII, Conclusion). Fr.Crawford next obtained a reliquary with a suitable stand and on this fixed an enlarged portrait of Blessed Peter. The original of this likeness was found in the 'biography' written by Fr.Leedes/Courtnay, S.J., in 1651.

Finally a suitable prayer was composed and approved by the Ordinary of the Diocese of Northampton, Bishop Charles Grant. In due course the prayer was properly inscribed and mounted in a frame to be placed beside the reliquary for the Faithful to venerate. The shrine thus constituted was given an honoured place within the Lady Chapel.

The full text of the prayer:

Blessed Peter Wright, S.J.
Martyred at Tyburn 19th May, 1651. (O.S.)
Beatified 15th December, 1929.

Blessed Peter Wright
you gave glory to God
and brought honour to this parish of Thrapston
by your martyrdom at Tyburn,
but also by your birth at Slipton, and gradually
discovering there the truth of the Catholic Faith;
by working in Thrapston in a lawyer's office;
then, after your Army service,
finding your true and final calling
in the Society of Jesus,
as priest, chaplain, counsellor, missioner,
confessor, both abroad, in the Low Countries,
and here, in England;
you served in the households of the great and
the poor, with the wealthy and the needy;
with those who were at liberty as well as those
who were in prison:
WE PRAY NOW FOR THIS SPECIAL INTENTION (name it)
AND ASK YOUR INTERCESSION,
that God will give us the grace we need
to do his will,
to make his Church known and loved,
to have peace and happiness in our home,
to find our talents fulfilled in the work we do,
to share the Faith with those with whom we live,
& to have the strength to persevere in our holy religion,
and we promise to make known - for God's
glorification, not our own! - any graces we
receive by your intercession,
so that everyone may be led, through the
example of your life, to share what you possess,
for their eternal salvation,
and, finally, we ask these humble prayers, by
presenting them to our Blessed Lady, to take
for you to her Divine Son,
who lives and reigns, in the unity of the Holy Spirit,
to the glory of our heavenly Father.
For ever and ever. Amen.

(Approved by Bishop Charles Grant, drawn up by Father Charles Crawford - now hanging in the Lady chapel of Thrapston church, by the relic of B1.Peter Wright.)

Catholic Church of St. Paul the Apostle, Thrapston

Shrine and relic of Blessed Peter Wright, Thrapston

APPENDIX D

Some Northamptonshire born priests (1558-1763)

(Information from:- English & Welsh Priests 1558-1800, Ed.Dom.Aidan Bellenger, & The Seminary Priests, Godfrey Anstruther, Vols.I & II etc.)

Abbreviations

(BP)	Bishop
(BL)	Blessed
(ST)	Saint
B.Pl.	Date & Place of Birth,
T.	Trained (at)
P./Ord.	Date of Religious Profession or Priestly Ordination
D.	Date of Death,
Sec.	Secular Priest
Fran .	Franciscan
Ben.	Benedictine
Jes.	Jesuit

Martyred **Bold**
Died in Prison *Italics*

Name	Type	B.Pl.	T.	P./Ord.	D.	Alias
BOWKER,Alexander[1]	Sec.	?Slipton	Douai	1608	1618	Butler/Boucher
BRAMSTON,James Yorke (BP)	Sec.	1763 Oundle	Lisbon	1799	1836	Bramley
BUTLER, Alban [2]	Sec.	1709 Appletree,nr.Aston-le-Walls	Douai	1734	1773	Cross
BUXTON,George	Sec.	1686	Rome	1713	1759	Thomas/Hanmer
CARPENTER, Richard Francis[3]	Sec.	1606 Passenham	Rome	1635	1670	Vincent/Dacre
DARCY, Arthur	Sec.	1605 Gt.Addington	Rome	1630	?	Angelino
EVERARD, John	Jes.	1584 Deene	?Douai	?	1649	Smith
FARMER (or Fermor)John	Sec.	? Easton Neston	Douai	1605	1660	?
FISHER, George	Sec.	1580 Earls Barton	Rome	1606	1645	Ashton/Muscote
FISHER, Thomas	Sec.	1578 Earls Barton	Douai	1603	1667	Ashton
FONTAINE, Wm(Placid) de la	Ben.	? St.Greg	Douai	1731	1780	?

Name	Type	B.P1.	T.	P./Ord.	D.	Alias
GARTER, John	Ben.	? Brigstock/St.Edmund	Paris	1643	1650	?
HANSE, Everard (BL)	**Sec.**	**? Harrowden**	**Rheims**	**1581**	**1581**	**Ducket**
Hanse, William	Sec.	? Harrowden	Rheims	1579	?	Drayton
HEATH, Henry (Paul) (BL)	**Fran.**	**1599 Peterborough/(St,Bonaventure's)**	**Douai**	**1625**	**1643**	**?**
HOLLAND, Henry	Sec.	1550 Daventry	Rheims	1580	1625	?
JENNINGS, Michael	Sec.	?1597	Rome	1628	1667	?
KELLISON, Matthew	Sec.	1561 Harrowden	Rome	1587	1641	Pemberton/Strong
LEWIS, John	Jes.	1721 Earls Barton	?	?1747	1788	Leppard
LOVETT, George	Jes.	1576	?	1611	1640	Robinson
MANBY, Thomas	Jes.	1588 Broughton	Rome	1611	1620	Rogers
MULSHO, John	Jes.	1584 Finedon	Douai	1608	1661	Day
NEWPORT, Charles	Sec.	?Ashby St. Ledgers	Douai	1601	?	Harris
NEWPORT, Richard(BL)	**Sec.**	**1572 Ashby St. Ledgers**	**Rome**	**1599**	**1612**	**Smith/James**
OSBORNE, Edward[4]	Sec.	1555 Kelmarsh	Rheims	1581	1600	?
PAGE, Richard	Sec.	?	Douai	1610	1653	Morris/Harriott
PAINE, John(ST)	**Sec.**	**? Peterborough**	**Douai**	**1576**	**1582**	**?**
POULTON, Andrew	Jes.	1654 Desborough	?	1685	1710	?
POULTON, Charles	*Jes.*	*1616 Desborough*	*?*	*1637*	*1690*	*Roberts/Palmer/ Sanderson*
POULTON, Ferdinand	Jes.	1605 Desborough	?	1625	1666	Palmer
POULTON, George	Jes.	1689 Desborough	?	1732	1739	?
POULTON, Giles	Jes.	1600 Desborough	?	1622	1666	Palmer
POULTON, Giles	Jes.	1694 Desborough	Rome	1719	1752	Palmer
POULTON, Henry	Jes.	1583 Desborough	Valladolid	1612	?1643	Pollard
POULTON, Henry	Jes.	1679 Desborough	?	1700	1712	Palmer
POULTON, John	Jes.	1610 Desborough	Rome	1636	1656	Palmer/Conyers
POULTON, John (Joseph)	Fran.	1682 Desborough / St.Bonaventure	Douai	1707	1748	?
POULTON, Thomas	Jes.	1668 Desborough	?	1694	1725	?
POULTON, Thomas	Jes.	1697 Desborough	?	1724	1749	?
POULTON, William	Jes.	? Desborough	?	?	1596	?
POULTON, William	Sec.	1616 Irthlingborough	Rome	1655	1672	Spencer/Sackeverell/ Sackville
POYNTZ, Francis (James)	Ben.	1661	Paris	1688	1718	?
PRATT, Henry (Felix)	Ben.	? Wellingborough	Douai	1606	1634	Thomson/Walker
PRESTON, William	Jes.	1637 Slipton	Rome	1661	1702	Vincent/Baines

Name	Type	B.Pl.	T.	P./Ord.	D.	Alias
ROBERTS, John	Sec.	1560 Kelmarsh	Rome	1587	?	
SWEETMAN, John or, Swetnam or, Swetman	Jes.	1579 Gt.Harrowden	Valladolid	1606	1622	Nicholson
TIMCOCK, Anthony	Ben.	1581Walgrave	Valladolid	1609	1668	Walgrave/Culpeper/ Waldegrave
TRESHAM,Francis	Fran.	1592	Douai St.Gregory's	1643	1660	
WILKINSON, Henry	Jes.	1594	?	1617	1673	
WILLIAMSON, William	Jes.	1577 Denford	Rome	1611	1626	Smalley/Small
WOODWARD, Thomas	Sec.	?	Douai	1624	1662	Barber/Kelly
WAKE, Richard[5]	Sec.	1607 Antwerp	Rome	1634		
WRIGHT, Peter (BL)	**Jes.**	**1603 Slipton**	**Liege**	**1629/36**	**1651**	**Beale**

Additional

(County unknown but of Peterborough Diocese)

Name	Type	B.P1.	T.	P./Ord.	D.	Alias
DEAKIN(S), John	Sec.	?	Rheims	1587	1618	?
HARRISON, John	*Sec.*	*?*	*Rheims*	*1585*	*1586*	*?*
NORMICOT(E), William	Sec.	?	Rheims	1579	?	?
NEWMAN, Andrew	Sec.	?	Douai	1606	?	?
SADLER, Walter (Dom Vincent)	Ben.	?	Rheims	1592	1621	?

*****

KNIGHTLEY, Andrew — Sec. — 1660
- 12th child of Edward Knightley of Offchurch, Warwickshire. Andrew Knightley's grandfather was Sir Valentine Knightley of Fawsley, Northants - a very strong Puritan.

[1] Alexander BOWKER is believed to have apostasised and been executed for coining. Circumstances obscure and peculiar. But cf. P.Caraman, Henry Morse, p,14; states Bowker was reconciled in prison and died very well.

[2] Alban BUTLER author of renowned 'Lives of the Saints' still being published.

[3] Richard Carpenter apostasised but reconciled before death.

[4] Edward Osborne apostasised but repented.

[5] His father was of the Wake family of Hartwell and Courteenhall - a merchant who migrated to Antwerp c.1605 and reared a very Catholic family. Three daughters became nuns and one, Mary Margaret was Prioress of the English Carmelites at Antwerp (1665-1678) - a portrait is preserved at Lanherne Convent, Cornwall. (Cf. P.Gordon, Wakes of Northamptonshire, Ch.7).

APPENDIX E

(Lists of Recusants in Lowick and Slipton; extracted from Recusant Rolls by Fr.G.Anstruther,O.P. and deposited in N.R.O., 1967; recorded in Northamptonshire Subsidy Rolls (1609-1629) - Isham/Longden M.S.S. Vol.xxxviii, 31, 125 and in Peterborough Diocesan archives, where painstaking research might yet reveal more names/dates.)

** LOWICK RECUSANTS (1607-1657)

(Many of these are recorded for several differentyears, but to simplify the list, usually only one year is given. Recusants might also be presented several times in any one year if the authorities were being diligent.)

Bankes, Ann		1657
Banks, Daniel and Elizabeth his wife		1657
Bannister, Thomas and Mary his wife		1610
Barker, Susanna		1610
Bollin, Alice		1607
Bolney,Elizabeth		1610/1612
(Burchall, Henry and Elizabeth his wife	)	1612) Also in
(Chamberlayne, alias Laughton (labourer)	)	1607) Slipton
Child, John and Alice his wife		1624 1628
Childs, Ann and Mary		1657
Dawlin, Andrew		1607
Fishman, Martha		1616
Foscott, Elizabeth		1607
Gibbons, Mary		1621
Gibbons, Robert		1621
Grundy, Anne		1607
Hall, Francis and Mary his wife	(1582)	1605 1614
Ibbott, Elizabeth		1607
Ibbott, Agnes (wife of Ewin carpenter)		1607
King, Anne		1626
Matlock, Katharina		1607
MORDAUNT, THE LORD (HENRY)		1612? Does this referto John?
Parker, Elizabeth (husband Richard was a cook and had moved from Rushton)		1626 1628
Pitts, John (labourer)		1607
Plowright, Robert (yeoman)		1626 1631

Procter, Richard and Elizabeth his wife	1621
Robinson, Ursula	1607
Rowlett, Margaret	1631
Sillman, Martha	1610
Smith, William, Ann his wife and a servant	1657
Stile, John	1621
Stoughton, John	1610 (In the Tower 1588)
Stoughton Anne (wife of John - a widow in 1624)	1607
Tarrey, Clement (joiner) and Susan his wife	1612 (many other refs,1628)
Tarry, Susan and Clement (son)	1657

(Clement Tarry indicted for going with ferrets and nets to catch connys in Lord Peterborough's warren at Drayton)

(Tippin, Robert (joiner) with wife	1656 1657
(Tyrpin, Alice (wife of Robert)	1626
Underwood, William, Martha his wife and Mary (1610)	1607
Wakelin, Richard and Elizabeth	1607
Widd, Elizabeth and daughter Mary A,Smith	1657

(Not every Recusant is listed above,as evidence the spy's report in Chapter III)

* The Northamptonshire Subsidy Rolls for 1628 record the following being fined viii[d] for, not receyving the holie Communion by the Space of one whole yeare past':

LUFFWICK (LOWICK)

Clemt Tarrey and Susan his wife
Elizabeth Parker
John Childe, gent, and his wife
Anne typple (or Tyrpin)

SLIPTON RECUSANTS (1605-1657)

Bannister, Thomas and his wife (moved from Lowick)	1618
Beale, Margery (wife of Thomas)?(Margaret)	1624 1628 1631
Bealle, Alexander and his wife	1628
Blaxeley, Henry and his wife	1628 1631 (yeoman)
Bowker, Alexander and Anne his wife	1605/1606/1607/08/09/10/1631
Bowker, Alexander (junior)	1610
Bowker, Francis 1607 1610 and Elizabeth his wife	1616,
and Joan his wife	1624
Bowker, Elizabeth (spinster)	1612

Name	Year(s)	
Bowker, Katherine	1610	
Bowker, Anne (spinster)	1624	
Burchall, Edward and Alice his wife	1615	) Also
Chamberlayne, Henry alias Edward, and Alice his wife		) in
	1615	) Lowick
Ibbit, Ann	1610	
Killingworth, William	1624 1628	
Lyon, Robert	1631	
Lyon, Robert with Catherine his wife and Mary their daughter	1657	
Measures, Beatrice (widow)	1657	
Michill, Mary	1608/09/1610	
Preston, William gent, (SEE BELOW)	1628	
Preston, William, Elizabeth his wife and Olde Robert' (servant)	1656	
Swetnam, Hester (servant to Preston above)	1657	
**WRIGHT, ROBERT AND MARGARET HIS WIFE	1606/07/08/09/12	
WRIGHT, MARGARET (widow)	1613 1617 1628	
WRIGHT, PETER (yeoman)	1613	
WRIGHT, JOHN	1613	
WRIGHT, MARGARET (spinster)	1618	

(Just to confuse the researcher a Margaret Wright married a Thomas Beayle at Rothwell on the fourteenth of September, 1621 according to Mormon Ge. Records at N.R.S.)

* The Northamptonshire Subsidy Rolls for 1628 record the following being fined viii^{d} for, 'not recyving the holie Communion by the Space of one whole years past':-

SLIPTON

Alexander Bowker and his wife
Margaret Bealle
Margaret Wright
Henry Blakesley and his wife
Willm. Killingworth

SUDBROWE (SUDBOROUGH) (neighbouring parish)

William Preston and Elizabeth his wife (also Edward Preston)
Susan Preston
Olde Robert
Ann Underwood

(It would appear that William Preston was a farmer/landowner with lands in Sudborough as well as Slipton - See reference to his son William born 1637 and later a Jesuit priest. (Appendix D.)

* The Northamptonshire Subsidy Rolls reveal a large number of other parishes where Catholics were prepared to suffer the consequences of failing to take communion in the Anglican church in the years 1609 to 1629. For example: Irthlingborough, Allwinckle (sic), Desborough, Weldon, Wellingborough, Mears Ashby, Earls Barton, Pilton, Orlingbury, Walgrave, Great Harrowden, Great Addington, Tansor, Glapthorne, Benefield.

* * The name WRIGHT also occurs frequently in the Anglican registers for the parish of LOWICK which begin in 1542, with one of the baptisms a Thomas Wryte, but the only ROBERT WRIGHT recorded was baptised in 1591 - too late to be the father of Peter. From the Mormon Genealogical Tables for Northamptonshire other ROBERT WRIGHTS were found at Castor, 1554; 1567; East Haddon, 1578 and Raunds, 1598 but none of these was known to be Recusant.

The parish registers of Lowick are, however, quite revealing in what they do not show. From 1559 to 1578 very few baptisms are recorded compared to the years before and after. Very few Recusant names appear in the late sixteenth and early seventeenth centuries although in 1584 Mary, daughter of Arthur Darcye, gent. was baptised and in 1584/5 Elizabeth, daughter of Alexander Bowker. These are the only Recusant family names appearing before 1600 apart from the Mordaunt family (Lords of the Manor) with the following: Frances, 1591, Margaret, 1591, John, 1598/9, Anne, 1599/1600.

No other Recusants have their children registered in the book until 1621 when Elizabeth, daughter of John Child (see list) was baptised. Then in 1623, Henry, son of John, Lord Mordaunt, was baptised, the first of seven children, but by this time the family's Catholicism was on the wane following his lordship's marriage to Elizabeth Howard, a noted Puritan. (This same Henry b.1623 was to return to Catholicism in 1687 - D,N.B.) Only one other baptism of a Recusant family child is recorded up to 1660 and that was Mary, daughter of Robert and Mary Floret (alias Plowright) in 1643. This last entry proves that not only priests used aliases to avoid the penalties incurred for practising the Catholic faith.

The register for marriages begins in 1557 but contains even fewer Recusant names; 1584, Daniel Gayge married Mrs. Elizabeth Mordaunt, presumably a widow, (there were at this time Gage families at Rushton and Raunds who were related to the Gages of Sussex - see Chapters V and VI); 1599, John Biningham (?) married the Venerable Lady Katherine Mordaunt; 1629, John Keyes married Margaret Poole, (was this John the son of Robert Keyes executed for complicity in the Gunpowder Plot in 1606?).

The register for burials contains only three Recusant names; 1602, Mary Mordaunt daughter of Lord Henry Mordaunt; 1620, Ursula Robinsonne; 1638, Robert Plowright.

This lack of correlation between the Recusant lists for Lowick and the Anglican parish registers leads to the conclusion that there were, in effect, two separate communities dwelling there during the last years of the sixteenth century and the first half of the seventeenth. The larger body was Anglican/Protestant but a very substantial minority was Catholic and the members of this other fraternity not only refused to worship using Anglican rites but continued to have their children baptised, themselves married and their parents buried according to Catholic tradition.

APPENDIX F

Jesuits in Northamptonshire (1580-1651)

(Information from T.B.Trappes-Lomax Diocesan Centenary Souvenir, 1950 and various other sources such as G.Anstruther's 'Seminary Priests'.)

It is possible to identify 15 major strongholds of the Catholic Faith, during this period, where Jesuits probably visited and sometimes stayed as chaplains. Some of these houses are still standing and in a few instances the same family has possession, although no longer Catholic. The list is as follows:-

Deene, Harrowden, Rushton, Ashby St.Ledgers, Denton, Desborough, Drayton, Easton Neston, Little Oakley, Upper Heyford, Brampton Ash, Dingley, Kirby and probably Teeton and Welford.

To these one could add other Recusant houses mentioned in the Montague Musters Book.(*) This list dates from January 1612/13 when all Catholics of any substance were ordered to surrender their arms. The spelling is the original:-

(East Division),
The Lord Vaux his houses at Harroden and Arthelborow.
The Lord Mordantes house at Draighton.
The houses of Sir Thomas Brudnell, his houses at Rushton and Deene.
The Ladye Meryall Tresham her house at Liveden.
Sir Thomas Griffins house at Brabroke.
Sir William apRises houses at Brampton, Dingley.
Mr.Roger Charnokes house at Wellingborough.
Christopher Lewis Gent' his house at Earls Barton.
John Newports house at Ecton gent'.
Robert Syers Gent' at Isham.
Frances Polton of Arthlingborough gent'.
Edward Preston of Sudborow.
Alexander Bowker of Slipton.
Arthur Darcye of Addington magna esqr.
John Stoughton of Lowicke gent'.
Edw. Kirke of the same.
Mr.Kinsman of Loddington.
The house of George and John Polton of Desborow.
Ferdinando Bawde and his house at Thorpe Underwood and Walgrave.
The hospitall at Rowell.

(*) *Wake J. and Longden H.I., Montague Musters Book, N.R.S., Vol. II, pp. 224-226.*

Mr.Andrew Mallory of Stoke parke.
Mr.Barnard Garter of Brigstock.
Mr.Pryce of Tansor.
Mr.Henry Fitzwillyams of Glapthorn.
Mr.Barker of Ashton.
Thomas Lawe of Benyfeild gent'.
Thomas Vavisor of Rushton gent'.

(Weste Devision)
Sir George Sherley his house at Astwell and the Lodge under the government of Henry Sherley esqr.
Mr.Albon Butler at Ashton in the walls and the Lodge.
Mr.Edmund Braye of Whitlebury.
John White of the same.
Mris Tomasin Powell of Brackley mort'.
Thomas Charnocke of Grunden gent.
John Flamsted of Denton.
Willyam Andrew of the same.
Mr.Willyam Saunders of Welford.
Mr.Laurence Eaten of Brokhall.
John Britten of Teeten gent.
The house of Mr.Morgan of Heyford.
Frances Saunders of Stoke Parke.

(At the end of this list we find appended instructions for carrying out the search including the sentence: 'Fourthly it is agreed if there be any Resistans to breake into the houses and to Comytte them that Resiste to prison.'

There follows a number of names of persons who are to assist in this work which quite strangely includes several who were probable Recusants and one, 'Willyam Saunders', who is actually shown as such.)

It is impossible to know the names of all the Jesuit priests who worked in this county but what can be deduced is shown below:

PLACE	FAMILY	JESUITS ASSOCIATED WITH DATES (Most aliases omitted).
Deene	Brudendell	John Percy (alias Fisher or Fairfax) April 1606 (6 nights) and on other occasions.John Radford (or Thomas alias Tanfield) various visits 1589-1621.(Fr. Radford reconciled Thomas Manby b.1588 - See Appendix D) John Everard born here 1584.

Notes: Lord Brudendell reported as consorting only with Jesuits, 1647. Close connections with Catholic Digby Family of Stoke Dry, Luffenham etc. Rutland.

Harrowden	Vaux	Edmund Campion 1580/81 - Lord Vaux penalised for harbouring. Robert Parsons 1580/81? Richard Cowling resident chaplain 1597/98. John Gerard resident 1598/1605 - made it his headquarters. John Percy (1599-1605?) (1606-1611) resident chaplain. Nicholas Hart - chaplain - captured herewith Percy in 1611. Robert Southwell - harboured at Lord Vaux's house at Hackney and probably here before 1595. Nicholas Owen - laybrother, made the hiding holes. Henry Garnet) stayed 15th Sept. 1605 Oswald Tesimond) and probably at other times. Thomas Laithwaite captured here 1605 -became a Jesuit 1607. John Singleton) Chaplains? Thomas Strange) Here Nov.1605. Richard Banks chaplain. Thomas Cornforth chaplain - captured while saying Mass for Mrs.Elizabeth Vaux in Newgate Prison August 1612 and escaped. Anthony Hopkins here c.1603. Hugh Sheldon- laybrother here 1598. John Swetnam - educated here 1590s. John Mulsho - educated here 1590s. Henry Killinghall - educated here 1590s. John Lilly - laybrother - helped Gerard escape from Tower -here 1600. Roger Lee - convert of Gerard - here 1600. Edward Bentley reported as consorting with Lord Vaux 1629. Thomas Poulton - one time steward to Lord Vaux. Thomas Hodson (alias Smith) - one time tutor to children of Lord Vaux before becoming a Catholic, Entered S.J. 1601.died Lancs,1646.
Rushton	Tresham & Brudenell	Edmund Campion - 1581 - Sir Thomas Tresham imprisoned in his London house at Hoxton for harbouring. William Weston) lived at Hoxton John Cornelius) 1586-1587.

		Robert Persons ? - 1580/81. Edward Oldcorne reported at Rushton 1586-1589. Henry Garnet here 1605. John Gerard ? probably.
Ashby St. Ledgers	Catesby	Oswald Tesimond (alias Greenway) possibly chaplain here c.1597-1605. Edmund Campion ? 1580/81.
Denton	Flamsted/Andrews	None by name.
Desborough	Poulton	John Percy reported heading for Desborough 1606. Five sons of the house recorded; during this period (see Appendix D). Charles 1637; Ferdinand 1625; Giles 1622; Henry 1612; and John 1636. (None of these known to have worked in Northants.)
Drayton	Mordaunt	No chaplains known by name but several inferred in Leedes/ Courtnay's 'Life and Death of Peter Wright'. Robert Beaumont (possibly an alias for Robert Jenison) might have been chaplain in 1625. See below: 'Report in Life of Archbishop JamesUssher, published in 1686 states that be was invited to Drayton,November 1625, to discuss religion with Lord and Lady Mordaunt and a priest called Beaumont.' (Ussher was Anglican (Protestant) Archbishop of Armagh but frequently in England.) 'Result of discussions was that Lord Mordaunt stopped practising as a Catholic and went on to die a Protestant in 1642.'
Dingley	apRise/ Griffin	Edmund Campion. 1580/81. Robert Persons ? 158O/81.
Easton Neston	Fermor	None known. Son a priest, not S.J.
Kirby	Mallory	John Percy 1606 3 nights. John Gerard 1598/99. Nicholas Owen) Laybrothers Hugh Sheldon) 1599.
Little Oakley	Bentley (Also in Derbyshire)	Priest continually in the house 1594-1595. Richard Cowling chaplain 1601-1602. Three sons of family priests: Edward ? 1609; Henry 1609; John ? 1611.

APPENDIX G.

The Gage Family (Simplified Lineage) c,1400 - 1815
Shows descent of COLONEL SIR HENRY GAGE and also
connections with Northamptonshire

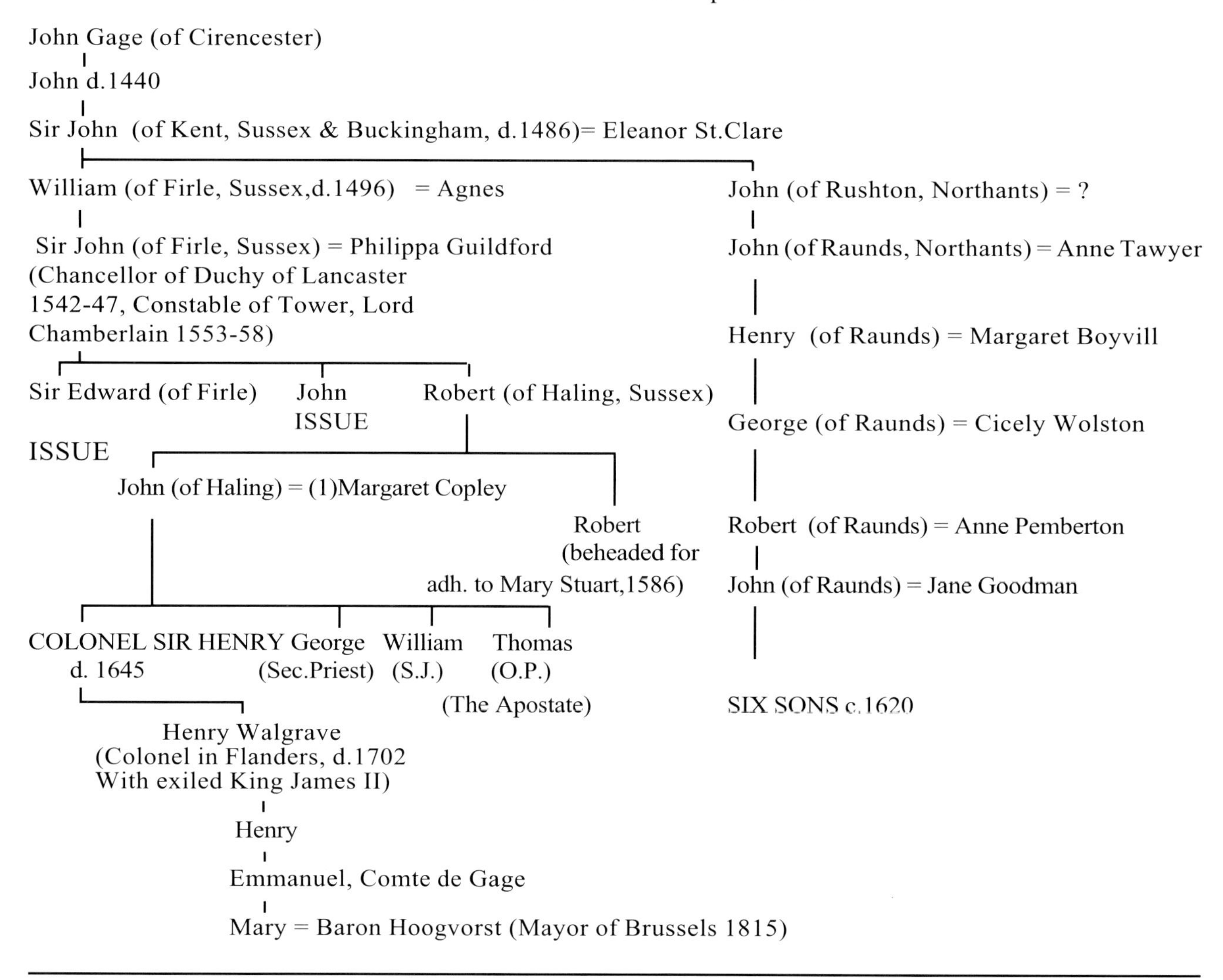

THE GAGE FAMILY RAMIFIED THROUGHOUT SOUTHERN ENGLAND, IRELAND AND EUROPE.

EPITAPH TO SIR HENRY GAGE

From Kirk's Biographies of English Catholics, London, 1909, p.92:-

"Sir Henry Gage's death took place Jan.ll, 1644/1645.[*] He was interred in Christ Church Cathedral, Oxford, at the public expense, being attended to his grave by all the court, the army, and members of the University. A monument was erected in the same church at the public charge, bearing the following inscription to his memory,

His Situs est Militum Chiliarcha
Henricus Gage, Eques Auratus, filius ac
Haeres Johannis Gage de Haling in Agro
Surriensi Armigeri, Pronepos Johannis Gage,
Honoratissimi Ordinis Periscelidis Equitis,

In Belgio meruit supra Annos XX in omni proelio et obsidione Berghae ad Zomam, Bredae, ac praecipue S.Audomari. Ex Belgio ad M.Britt. Regem missus attulit armorum, VII.M. Missus cum imperio, Bostalii Aedes expugnavit. Mox Basingianis praesidiariis commeatu interclusis, strenue (re jam desperata) suppetias tulit. Castrum Bamburiense cum Northamptoniae comite liberavit. Hinc Equestri dignitate ornatus Hostes denuo Basinga fugavit. Iamque Gubernator Oxon. creatus, cum ad Culhami pontem in hostes jam tertio milites audacter duceret, plumbea trajectus glande occubuit die XI.Jan., 1644,[*],Aet47. Funus Solemni luctu prosecuti Principes, proceres, milites, Academici, Cives, omnes Dolorem testati ex desiderio Viri Ingenio, Linguarum peritia, Gloria Militari, pietate, fide et amore in principem et patriam eminentissimi.

Hanc Memoriae Epitomen posuit illi
Pietas moerens lugensque fratris, Georgii Gage. "

Translation

P.M.S.

Here lies Colonel Henry Gage, Knight,
son and heir of John Gage of Haling
in the County of Surrey, Esquire,
great-grandson of John Gage, Knight
of the most honourable Order of the Garter.

In Belgium he served more than 20 years in every battle and siege of Berg op Zoom, Breda and in particular St.Omer. From Belgium being sent to His Majesty the King of Britain, he took up arms on his behalf, being put in charge of 7,000 men, and took by assault Boarstall House. Soon after he vigorously brought help to the garrison of Basing House, whose supplies had been cut off and who were in desperate straits. He freed Banbury Castle together with the earl of Northampton.

[*] 1644 O.S. = 1645 by the new style calendar.

From there, being honoured with the dignity of Knight, he once again forced the enemy to flee from Basing House. And having now been created Governor of Oxford, when he was already for the third time leading his soldiers against the enemy at Culham Bridge, he was shot by a lead bullet and fell on the 11th day of January 1644,(*), aged47. Princes, nobility, soldiers, members of the University, citizens, attended his funeral with sober mourning, all bearing witness to their grief at the loss of a man most eminent in talent, in skill of languages, in militarv prowess, in piety, in loyalty and love for his King and country.

The grief-stricken devotion of his brother,
George Gage, has caused this summary of his
life to be placed in his memory.

(*) 1644 O.S. = 1645 N.S.

Index of Acts of Parliament as mentioned in the text

(*) *This Act (27 Elizabeth, c.2) was the one under which Blessed Peter Wright was condemned.*

Index of Names from Chapters I to VIII

(References include footnotes and are not exclusive)

Abbreviations:-

(Bl.) - Blessed.
(St.) - Saint.
M.P. - Member of Parliament.
O.F.M. - Franciscan.
O.P. - Dominican.
O.S.B. - Benedictine.
Sec. - Secular Priest.
S.J. - Jesuit Priest or Brother.

Index of Places, Counties, Countries and Rivers , mentioned in Chapters I-VIII

(References include footnotes and are not exclusive)

(Places in Northamptonshire are listed under that heading)